Story, Myth, and Celebration in
Old French Narrative Poetry 1050-1200

D. Karl Uitti

Story, Myth, and Celebration in

Old French
Narrative Poetry

1050-1200

Princeton University Press
Princeton, New Jersey

Publication of this book has been aided by the Princeton
University Research Fund and by the Whitney Darrow
Publication Reserve Fund of Princeton University Press.

This book has been composed in Linotype Times Roman.

Printed in the United States of America
by Princeton University Press, Princeton, New Jersey

for
Ken, Kris, and Michelle,
in gratitude for the chance they have taken

Preface

THE following pages stem from a number of confrontations. To mention only the most recent, let me cite my own first attempts to cope with Old French narrative literature in stimulating graduate seminars led by Professors R. N. Walpole and the late P. B. Fay at the University of California (Berkeley), then the very special coming to grips with texts one undergoes when teaching them, either in the original language or in modernized versions, to interested undergraduates. A preceptorial on the *Roland* or on *Lancelot* can be an awesome thing! Finally, and perhaps most important of all, I mention the confrontation with the poems that results from presenting them, as a kind of canon, to graduate students—students who first must learn the language and its literary tonality before working with the texts creatively, and then who, in some instances, go on to advanced studies and dissertations. Each of these experiences, or confrontations, has found its way into my study, but the latter has meant a special effort—the formulating of categories within which I might communicate my experience of the texts to a common, shared reading of them: the seminar.

I do not address myself here, therefore, primarily to scholar-specialists in OF literature. Most of the facts adduced —if not the interpretations—are known; no startling revisions of dates or of attribution are proposed, no new manuscript readings. Nor do I mean to "cover" any period(s) of the OF narrative. I deal very selectively with two independent poems (*Alexis*, the Oxford *Roland*) and, somewhat more generally, with the *œuvre* of Chrétien de Troyes. (An appendix contains some preliminary remarks on Jehan Bodel's *Saisnes*.) In the period extending from, roughly, 1050 to 1200, then, more is "left out" than is "brought in." My commentary ought not to be construed as a "survey" or as a reference book, though, to a certain degree, the scholarly apparatus—relatively greater in the case of the *Alexis* section than in that devoted to

Chrétien de Troyes—is determined by the nature of the texts studied and my assumptions concerning the reader's likely familiarity with them.

By the same token the technical level on which most of this book is written as well as its historical bias no doubt preclude its appealing to a broadly conceived general public. For this reason I have decided to leave all quotations in the original language, giving glosses or translations only when absolutely indispensable. I hope, then, that my work will prove of some use to the undergraduate or, more probably, to the graduate student in literature who is experiencing an initial contact with OF narrative poetry. With this in mind I have endeavored to set up contexts—some purely formal, others rather more historical—designed to provide touchstones for an appreciation of this literature. I stress the late eleventh and twelfth centuries for reasons expressed very well by Father C. Spicq: "Le XIIᵉ siècle forme la grande coupure dans l'immense millénaire médiéval. C'est le siècle-clef, le pivot de l'évolution en tous domaines, depuis la littérature jusqu'aux formes sociales." (*Esquisse d'une histoire de l'exégèse latine* . . . [Paris, 1944], 61n.)

The period in question establishes the ground rules and possibilities open to OF narrative; at least some acquaintance with the works I discuss is essential to study of subsequent periods. Finally, I believe that the poems examined here have great intrinsic merit—a merit, let me add, that an entire scholarly tradition has willingly recognized. However, the value of these poems has not always been understood in terms of the extraordinary dignity accorded literature and literary discourse during the twelfth century. To be sure, Faral, Curtius, and others have analyzed that age's "literariness," but seldom have these critics—to whom, I hasten to note, our collective scholarly debt is immense—paid sufficient attention to the fashion in which individual works were put together. I have tried to relate, explicitly and implicitly, the notions of literary dignity and given poetic structures.

In recording my thanks to some of those who have helped

me to complete my study, I mention first of all the students in Romance Languages and Literatures 510 (Spring 1971); without their questions, interpretations, indeed without their collaboration, I should never have finished. To my wife as well as to my colleagues, P. F. Dembowski (University of Chicago), A. Díaz Quiñones (Universidad de Puerto Rico), and A. K. Forcione (Princeton), I am grateful for many comments and for encouragement. I should also like to thank the Regents of the University of California as well as my friend Yakov Malkiel for permission to reproduce *in extenso* my article, "The Old French *Vie de Saint Alexis*: Paradigm, Legend, Meaning," *RPh*, xx (1966-1967), 263-295; some reference is also made here to *RPh*, xxii (1968-1969), 471-483. Thanks also go to my very dedicated assistants, Vera Basch (Princeton, '72) and Margaret Wolfe (Princeton, '71), for their cheerful and invaluable help. Finally, I note my gratitude to Princeton University, its Department of Romance Languages and Literatures, and its Research Board for leave time and for material assistance.

Princeton, April 1972   KARL D. UITTI

Contents

Story, Myth, and Celebration in
Old French Narrative Poetry 1050-1200

CHAPTER I

The "Life of Saint Alexis"

INTRODUCTION AND SUMMARY

THE Old French *Life of Saint Alexis*, though usually dated around the middle of the eleventh century, by no means constitutes the earliest example of vernacular French narrative. Many such texts surely have been lost; a goodly number of tales were probably never formally committed to writing or were set down much later. Certain texts—the *Passion of Our Lord* (often referred to as *La Passion de Clermont*) and the *Life of Saint Legier*—may be traced back to the closing years of the tenth century. The lyrico-narrative *Cantilène de sainte Eulalie*, probably the oldest surviving literary text written in Old French, belongs to the final quarter of the ninth century. Also, a number of Old Provençal narratives antedate the *Alexis*. Yet most critics agree that the OF *Alexis* is a masterpiece, some claiming that it is the first major literary work of the language. Gaston Paris' judgment is measured, but nonetheless very favorable: "Le poème . . . offre, dans sa simplicité gracieuse et sévère, de réels mérites de style et de sentiment; il ouvre dignement l'histoire de la poésie nationale."[1]

Of course it is hard to remain entirely insensible to the charm and considerable craftsmanship of the venerable Clermont *Passion*. Many of the devices later to be exploited by the *Alexis* poet are already in full evidence there.[2] Yet we may be justified in beginning our investigation of the

---

[1] G. Paris and L. Pannier, *La Vie de Saint Alexis; poème du XIᵉ siècle et renouvellements des XIIᵉ, XIIIᵉ et XIVᵉ siècles* (Paris, 1872), vi.

[2] The first-person narrator device, for example (see below pp. 58ff. and fn. 17).

3

French narrative with a study of the *Alexis*; indeed we may even agree with Gaston Paris that the *Alexis* does in fact "open . . . the history of French poetry," despite such noble antecedents as the *Passion*, because, as we shall see in due course, the poem *summarizes* a kind of narrative poetics. The *Alexis* derives from a tradition that, more than any other early OF poem, it helps to perfect and pass on, under the guise of narrative possibilities, to subsequent works. The *Alexis* thus partakes of a literary and historical process, but the intensity of its participation in this process makes of it a kind of milestone. Little would be gained here by our returning to earlier works. Conversely, had we neglected the *Alexis* much would have been lost. We should be unable to read as thoroughly either the *Song of Roland* or Chrétien's *Yvain*. And, let me say right off, the *Alexis* is a jewel: it is intellectually very rewarding to come to grips with this intricate and thoroughly beautiful text.

Before taking up the critical issues, let me recapitulate briefly the events of the poem (as given by MS *L*, the version usually preferred by editors since Gaston Paris).

In olden times, when faith and justice and love prevailed, when our "ancestors" were true Christians, the noble Roman count Eufemien and his wife prayed God for a son. Their wishes were granted; they baptized the boy Alexis. He received the best education possible. When it was time for him to marry, Eufemien betrothed him to a noble Roman maid. The marriage takes place. On the wedding night Alexis goes to his bride: he sees the girl, but thinks of his Lord, fearing that sin will cause him to lose God. He tells his wife of the frailty of mortal life. In this world, he avers, there is no "perfect love." She should take for her husband Him who has saved us with His precious blood. He then presents her with his sword-belt and a ring; he commends her to God and leaves his father's dwelling, fleeing the country. A ship awaits him in port; he pays his passage and embarks for Laodicea (Latakia). After an indefinite sojourn there, Alexis removes

4

to Edessa (*Alsis* in the poem, today called Orfa),[3] where there exists a famous "image" that the angels had made in the name of the Virgin. He distributes all his belongings to the needy, after which he becomes himself a beggar, keeping only of the alms given to him what is strictly necessary to maintain life, and giving the rest to the poor.

The narration shifts back to Rome, where Alexis' father, mother, and bride express their grief. Eufemien sends two servants to look for his son. Ironically, they find him and even give him alms, but so completely has he been transformed by his ascetic existence that they do not recognize him. They return to Rome empty-handed. Alexis' mother bitterly laments her own and Eufemien's loss; she destroys Alexis' old room with all its furnishings. Her violence contrasts with the bride's soft sadness: "From now on I shall live in the manner of turtledoves . . . I wish to stay with you." And the mother reflects this softness in giving the bride permission to remain: "Let us together bewail the sadness we feel over our beloved friend; you for your lord, I for my son."

Alexis serves his God in Edessa. Seventeen uneventful years pass; he is utterly faithful. God causes the "image" to speak. It commands the "altar servant" or custodian to call in the "man of God," for he is worthy of entering into Paradise. The custodian does not know whom to call; the "image" specifies: "The one who sits beyond the door"—Alexis. The news is out; the entire city wishes to honor Alexis, but he will have none of the celebration. In the middle of the night he slips away, once again, to Laodicea, where he boards a waiting ship. Buffeted by winds, the vessel changes course, arriving at a port near Rome. Alexis is afraid lest he be recognized and

[3] A recent editor of the OF *Alexis*, G. Rohlfs, records F. Babinger's suggestion that *Alsis* might better be associated with the old Cilician town of *Sis* (north of present-day *Adana*). *Al* would stand for the Arabic article. See Rohlf's edition, *Sankt Alexius. Altfranzösische Legendendichtung des 11. Jahrhunderts*₄. Sammlung rom. Übungstexte, xv (Tübingen, 1963), 63; cf. rev. by P. F. Dembowski, *RPh*, xix:4 (1966), 627ff.

that his parents "burden him with the honors of the world." He does not intend to be welcomed back into his family; a very moving speech, or prayer, contained in stanzas 41 and 42 expresses his feelings. Strolling through the familiar streets of Rome, Alexis meets (and recognizes) his father. For "his son's sake," he requests board and shelter in Eufemien's house, specifying a humble abode under the staircase. Eufemien answers: "For the love of God and on behalf of my dear friend, I will give you, good man, all that you have asked for—bed, shelter, bread, meat, and wine." A servant is freed provided he consents to look after the "stranger's" needs.

Alexis takes up residence in Eufemien's house, under the staircase. He sees his father frequently, as well as his mother and his bride. No one thinks to ask him where he was born nor does he volunteer any information. He observes their tears but is resigned to silence. He does not wish his mother to know about him: "He loves God more than his own flesh and blood." Alexis eats only enough to keep body and soul together; he goes often to church; he suffers the insults and demeaning conduct of the household help (who throw dirty scrub water on him), but begs God's pardon on their behalf. Seventeen years go by; Alexis has lived thirty-four years of total devotion and he knows that he is about to die. He requests ink and parchment of his servant so that he may write down his story.

In the very week that Alexis is fated to die, a voice is heard three times outside the church; it commands the people of Rome to seek out the "man of God" in their midst. The people are frightened lest the city be destroyed. Rich and poor alike ask Saint Innocent, their pope, for advice and counsel. The pope joins them to seek the holy man in Eufemien's house. (Some turn on Eufemien at this point for having hidden the fact that a holy man was at his house, but Eufemien and all his household deny any knowledge of this blessing.)

Meanwhile, as the pope, the emperors, and town elders pray, Alexis' soul departs from his body, going straight to Paradise. His servant rushes to announce the news to Eufemien, telling him that the unknown guest "was a good Christian," that in fact, he must be the "man of God." Eufemien returns home; he finds Alexis' body, the "fair handsome face" of the saint. But he cannot remove the letter from the dead man's fist. He hurries back to the pope and tells what has happened. Pope and emperors, praying all the while, make their way to Eufemien's home. The pope takes Alexis' letter, giving it to a "wise clerk" to read: Alexis' story becomes public.

Eufemien launches into a long *planctus* that expresses his grief that his son did not live the way a nobleman of his rank ought to live, "carrying the flag of the emperor." The disturbance brings on Alexis' mother, who faints upon seeing her dead son. She tears her hair and mortifies her body: "Oh son, how you have hated me!" she cries, "And how blind I have been!" Her complaint is long and bitter, full of reproach and pain. The bride's beautiful *planctus* is the last of the series: eloquent, bereaved, but somehow also serene and composed. Thus: "Had I known you were here under the staircase . . . nobody in the world could have stopped me from joining you . . ."—this after her moving recollection of her husband's "beautiful mouth, beautiful face, beautiful body" now to "rot in the earth," and preceding her decision to serve God, "the King who governs all." The contrast with Alexis' mother is striking.

At this point the pope intervenes. He explains that the occasion is one not of sadness but of joy. All Rome crowds around Alexis' body. The people pay no attention to money scattered before them in order to make them disperse; Alexis has brought them a truer happiness. The deaf, the blind, the crippled, the lepers, the mute, the paralyzed—all the sick who congregate about Alexis are cured: "Whoever approaches in tears, departs singing." The emperors carry Alexis' body to the church of Saint Boniface. For seven days the body remains there before at last being buried in a marble sepulchre that had been decorated with gold and jewels. Father, mother, and bride once more give vent to their grief; all Rome joins them

7

and "a hundred thousand tears are shed that day." But, the narrator reminds us, that "holy body" has saved Eufemien, his wife, and the faithful maid.

Saint Alexis is finally in heaven; his bride from whom he had been so "estranged" is now with him, together with God and the angels: "Their souls are united; I cannot tell you how great their joy is!" The last three stanzas of the poem explain the lesson of Saint Alexis' life; they constitute a sermon, beseeching us to remember the holy man and to pray to him so that we may enjoy peace and happiness in this world and the most lasting glory in the next.

CRITICAL PERSPECTIVES AND BACKGROUND

An understanding of the narrative processes at work in the *Life of Saint Alexis* must be built upon a systematic examination of factors, or dimensions, usually studied fragmentarily or separately. Critical interpretations of the poem's literary characteristics and meanings, textual questions, and the problems related to the poem's legendary background all stand to benefit from a joint review of what might be called their relational possibilities. Many of the issues have been touched upon in previous studies; much information is available. Thus, the OF manuscripts, their possible filiations, and the most "accurate" reconstruction of the lost eleventh-century *Urtext* have, for over a century, occupied the attention of scholars whom one might call the school of Gaston Paris.[4] To this

[4] In addition to the previously quoted work by G. Paris and L. Pannier, we ought to mention: G. Paris, *La Vie de saint Alexis*, *CFMA* (Paris, 1903), frequently reprinted; W. Foerster and E. Koschwitz, *Altfrz. Uebungsbuch₅* (Leipzig, 1915), texts of MSS *L*, *A*, and *P*, variants from *S* and *M*—the 1935 edition (rev. A. Hilka) also contains *V*. (first printed by Pio Rajna, *ArchRom*, XIII [1929], 1-86); M. Roesler, *Sankt Alexius* (Halle, 1928 [also 1941]); J.-M. Meunier, *La Vie de saint Alexis* (with modern French translation) (Paris, 1933); C. Storey, *Saint Alexis, étude de la langue du manuscrit de Hildesheim, suivie d'une édition critique du texte* (Paris, 1934); see also Storey's Blackwells French texts edition (Oxford, 1946); and most recently his

unquestionably brilliant philological tradition may be added still other scholars who, though not ostensibly concerned with the editorial problem as a whole, have nonetheless contributed interpretations and information of considerable use in revising and even in reading the OF text(s).[5] On the other hand, the structure and literary texture of the poem have been dealt with, in various ways, by diverse critics.[6] Not unnaturally, these scholars have worked with one or more of the previously established editions of the poem; only incidentally have they added any commentary of a textual nature to the philological discussion. Curtius, who examined the *Alexis* in terms of the poetics current at the time in order to refute the aesthetic anti-historicism of critics like Emil Winkler, constitutes a rare exception to this trend toward specialization and fragmentation in *Alexis* studies; while Gaston Paris, though, as we saw, certainly not insensitive to the poem's impressive beauty, never really studied its literary character.

The broader and highly complex question of the pan-Christian Alexis legend—intimately related to the OF *Alexis* scholarship—has been the concern of yet a third group of scholars.[7] Ramifications of the Alexis story have been traced

---

edition in the TLF series (Geneva: Droz, 1968); finally the above-quoted Rohlfs edition, to which I shall refer by line number in the present study.

[5] Thus, the discussion of "les renges de s'espethe," in D. Legge, *Rom*, LXXVII (1946), 88-93, and T. Fotitch, *ibid.*, LXXIX (1968), 495-507.

[6] E.g., E. Winkler, *ZRPh*, XLVII (1927), 588-597; E. R. Curtius, *ibid.*, LVI (1936), 113-137; L. Spitzer, *ArchRom*, XVI (1932), 473-500; A. G. Hatcher, *Trad*, VIII (1952), 111-158; P. R. Vincent, *StPh*, LX (1963), 525-541.

[7] In addition to the Bollandists and the various editors named earlier, one thinks of H. F. Massmann, *Sanct Alexius Leben* (Quedlinburg-Leipzig, 1843); A. Amiaud, *La Légende syriaque de saint Alexis* (Paris, 1889); M. Roesler, *Die Fassungen der Alexiuslegende mit besonderer Berücksichtigung der mittelenglischen Versionen* (Vienna-Leipzig, 1905), and the two later articles by the same scholar: "Alexius-probleme," *ZRPh*, LIII (1933), 508-518, and "Versiones españolas de la leyenda de San Alejo," *NRFH*, III (1949), 329-352. To these

back to fifth-century Byzantium (Roesler) beside Syria (Amiaud), or even earlier.[8] Later Greek renewals of this material extend to Rome and, quite mysteriously, it has been claimed, even to tenth-century Spain. From Rome the story,

---

add G. Paris and L. Pannier's inquiry into the French tradition (see fn. 1). Amiaud had claimed that the legend originated in Syria, was thence transported to Constantinople, and finally reached Rome. In her 1905 monograph Roesler questioned Amiaud's conclusions concerning the presumed lost Greek intermediary archetype. Despite the evidence of a Greek Alexis tradition offered by Joseph the Hymnographer's ninth-century "Canon," Roesler claimed that the Latin versions could easily have developed on their own and have evolved a composite *Life* with no help from any Greek intermediary. Yet her own discovery, in Venice, of an unpublished twelfth-century MS containing a version strikingly similar to the "first" Syriac Life and, according to her, even antedating that version (*ZRPh*, LIII), caused her to revise her judgment. Not only did the Byzantine tradition predate the Latin "composite" tradition; it probably outranked the Syriac "first" *Life*: "Obwohl die Hs., in der er enthalten ist, wahrscheinlich erst aus dem 12. Jh. stammt, halte ich es für fast sicher, dass das Original, von dem sie eine späte Abschrift mit zahllosen orthographischen Schnitzern ist, die ursprüngliche Fassung der Legende war, die man sich so lange vergebens zu finden bemüht hat" (508). She postulates a lost Syriac text that would have served to transmit the earlier Byzantine legend to Syria, a text rather more free of certain elaborations than one finds in Amiaud's version and that served as the latter's source: "Von Wichtigkeit ist für uns ja nur, dass ein syrischer Text vorhanden war, dem manche Erweiterungen der späteren Versionen fehlten, ein Übergangstext von der Marcianusfassung [her Venice discovery] zu den Fassungen, die den Heiligen aus dem Grabe verschwinden lassen" (517). Roesler's hypothesis is attractive (see fn. 12), but not entirely conclusive; absolute proof in these matters has not been forthcoming. (For a brief discussion of the composite legend's diffusion to Rome see fn. 13.)

[8] Herrmann has argued, interestingly, that Alexis' prototype was none other than Commodian, the "beggar of Christ." "Alexis" (the Greek equivalent of Commodian) and the Syriac "Mar Riscia" would, indeed, be the same name, since, in Syriac, [l] and [r] were easily confused and *Mar* simply means "Mr., Lord": *Alexis>Liscia* ("Qui est saint Alexis?" *L'AntClass*, XI [1942], 235-241). B. de Gaiffier (*AnalBol*, LXII [1944], 283) finds that H.'s deductions "trop subtiles et savantes . . . laisseront . . . plus d'un lecteur sceptique."

in renewed form, spread to medieval, Renaissance, and modern Europe. Reworked Greek, Romance, and later Latin versions rival in number and variety with Middle English, Middle High German, Czech, Russian, and other texts. To the extent that relationships between the OF *Life* and the legend have received attention, these have usually been formulated in a kind of genetic framework designed to shed light on the "origins" of the OF poem and its textual make-up. Such studies have unearthed many significant facts. It is clear that the OF *Life*—in both its oldest and its rejuvenated manifestations—belongs to a general European legendary tradition that must be related specifically to a Latin source dating, presumably, in its basic form, from the tenth century and rather closely resembling the "composite" prose text of the *Vita S. Alexii* published by the Bollandists (*Acta Sanctorum*, 17 July, iv: 251-3).[9] There remains some doubt

[9] In his "Thiébaut de Vernon" (*MA*, XL [1940], 30-43), Herrmann discusses G. Paris' 1872 assertion that Tedbalt might have composed the OF poem; he claims that Tedbalt actually wrote the Latin *Vita metrica* (*BHL* 293) and that it was this version, not the prose *Vita* (*BHL* 268), that constituted the source for the anonymous OF *Life*. Herrmann's conclusions seem to have convinced few scholars (B. de Gaiffier, *loc.cit.*, rightly remarks: "On peut se demander si c'est d'un texte à l'exclusion de l'autre et non de l'un et de l'autre que se serait inspiré le poète français"). Let us also mention M. Sprissler's *Das rhythmische Gedicht "Pater Deus Ingenite" (11. Jh.) und das altfranzösische Alexiuslied*, FRPh., 18 (Münster, 1966). This interesting inquiry focuses upon the text of two MSS (*A*, Cod. Admont. 664; *P*. Cod. Palat. Lat. 828), the former appearing in *Misc. Cassinese*, I (Montecassino, 1897; cf. *BHL* 296), the latter published by E. Assmann in *Festschrift Hofmeister* (Halle, 1955). S.'s monograph examines the sources of this poem and the relationship between it and the OF *Life*: "Der Rhythmus ist unter den bisher bekannten lateinischen Texten der mit den engsten Beziehungen zum altfranzösischen Alexiuslied" (100). S. argues that this text and the *C*-type MSS (*BHL* 287) of the prose *Vita* constitute the main sources of the OF poem. I discuss the merits of these claims in a separate review, *RPh*, XXIV (1970), 128-137; for our immediate purposes, the detailed mechanics of such a filiation remain largely irrelevant. S. proposes to illumine, conjecturally, certain concrete phases in the vernaculariza-

whether, as Amiaud contended, its oldest traces are to be found in the fifth- or sixth-century Syriac *Life* he published and translated into French. Yet Roesler's early Byzantine text and Amiaud's Syriac *Life* are so similar that they may conveniently be described as representing together the "earliest stage" of the legend. This early (Græco-?) Syriac version was, in any case, subsequently refashioned in Byzantium, and the story, thus revised, reached the Latin West, where it was codified and rediffused over Europe and, ironically, back to the Eastern Mediterranean.

How, then, might one usefully posit a functional relationship between the textual, the literary, and the legendary factors of the OF *Life*? To what extent may we reconcile our poem's historical—or "existential"—and literary existence, and, within a literary framework, hope to define better its extraordinary artistic importance at once in relation to its proper time and in relation to its "narrative possibilities"? Theoretical and practical problems abound. Recent discussion of the textual question, as exemplified in the polemic between H. Sckommodau and H. Lausberg, has not led to any definitive solution of that issue. Exclusive focus upon the establishment of the hypothetical *Urtext* has caused both those learned critics to introduce, somewhat arbitrarily, data from the poem's historical context in ways that render the work's status as a poem highly insecure.[10] An *Urtext*, though certainly a

---

tion of the Western Alexis tradition; we instead now focus upon the structuring of this tradition and the implications of this structuring. There is no need, then, to retreat from the statement that the Bollandist *Vita* does in fact underlie the OF poem.

[10] See, in addition to Sprissler's afore-named dissertation, H. Sckommodau, "Zum altfranzösischen Alexiuslied," *ZRPh*, LXX (1954), 161-203; "Alexius in Liturgie, Malerei und Dichtung," *ibid.*, LXXII (1956), 165-194; "Das S'. Die Datierungsfrage und das Problem der Askese," *Medium Ævum Romanicum* [*Festschrift Rheinfeider*] (Munich, 1963), 298-324; H. Lausberg, "Zur altfranzösischen Metrik," *ASNS*, CXCI (1955), 183-217; "Zum altfranzösischen Alexiuslied," *ibid.*, 285-320; "Das Proömium (Strophen 1-3) des altfranzösischen Alexiuslieds," *ibid.*, CXCII (1955), 33-58; "Zum altfranzösischen Alexiuslied," *ibid.*,

legitimate object of scholarly investigation and therefore worthy of careful study on its own terms, differs essentially in kind from the sort of object that must also legitimately interest students of literary operations, *a fortiori* when, as is the case with the *Alexis,* competently edited texts (with variants) are available along with diplomatic transcriptions of the principal manuscripts. Curtius has shown, however, that unyielding anti-historicism hardly advances the cause of literary analysis.

CXCIV (1957), 138-180; "Kann dem altfranzösischen Alexiuslied ein Bilderzyklus liegen?" *ibid.,* CXCV (1958), 141-144. Let me summarize the polemic: rejecting G. Paris' evaluation of *L,* Sckommodau claims that, on grounds of language, versification, number of stanzas, scribal traits, and thematic verisimilitude, *A* (B.N. acq. fr. 4503) should be accorded editorial preference as the base MS in the reconstitution of the "lost original" of the OF *Life.* Lausberg's equally learned intervention proves meanwhile that none of the extant MSS definitely represents the *Urtext;* for reasons of his own, he remains faithful to *L.* Conjecture nullifies conjecture. In defending their positions, both scholars shift ground radically from the MSS themselves to the history of the legend. Each equates the *Urtext* with his private vision of the legend in 11th-c. France. *A* comes closest to Sckommodau's view, while *L* supports Lausberg. Each seeks his justification, and describes his "text" (Lausberg even composes stanzas of this "authentic text"), guided by the criteria transposed from the domain of the legend. Yet their disagreement shows, compellingly, I think, that neither has managed to establish a pertinent relationship between the text and legend— not, at least, one capable of solving the problem of the lost original and its reconstruction. Nor has their shift from the text to legend and back to text provided significant help in grasping the very real relationship bracketing a literary work like the *Alexis* and its historico-legendary context. The notion of *Urtext* coupled with a purely genetic view of context has impeded progress along these crucial lines. Methodological eclecticism of this sort was once extremely useful in that it allowed scholars to think constructively about textual establishment and also to unearth data indispensable for an ulterior statement of real literary problems. So much was unknown. However, in the case of *Alexis,* surely such initial spadework has already placed most of the raw facts within our reach; hence their eclecticism, if practiced to the exclusion of other approaches, leads to a critical impasse. (Let me record at this point that H. S. Robertson's recent defense of MS *A* does not induce me to change my mind; see *SP,* LXII [1970], 419ff.)

And, as for genetically oriented studies of the Alexis legend, we must agree in principle with Tatiana Fotitch, who reiterated Roesler's early (and later partly retracted) criticism of Amiaud in her 1958 article: "It would be vain to attempt any classification or to establish genealogical trees of the Alexis legend on linguistic grounds. Manuscript tradition, Church history, theology, and folklore play here a much greater part." Yet, since, as we observed, many of the issues involved in a critical study of the OF *Alexis* have been touched upon with remarkable insight and with the most careful sifting of available data in the work of the textualists, critics, and historians so far mentioned, care should be taken to place these insights in the perspectives that stand the best chance of helping us gauge the poem's value and meaning.

Rather, then, than blurring our focus in yet another discussion of the "lost original" of the *Life of Saint Alexis* or, worse, simply ignoring the textual problem altogether, we must try to respect both the "poem" and the surviving manuscripts. The manuscript situation is too well known to bear detailed repetition here, but, for the sake of clarity, a brief review is appropriate.

The presumed mid-eleventh-century original, has, of course, been lost; since G. Paris, most editors have chosen to base their texts on the twelfth-century MS *L* (Lamspringen, now Hildesheim), the version containing 125 stanzas of five assonanced decasyllabic lines with epic caesura. The language of this manuscript is the most archaic of the surviving texts (falsely so, according to Sckommodau). MS *A* (Ashburnham, now Paris, B.N., nouv. acq. fr. 4503), also twelfth-century, offers a shorter version, ending with stanza 110 (Alexis has been buried; no mention is made of his family's salvation); *A* also lacks five or six isolated stanzas and individual lines. Yet, by and large, the texts of *L* and *A* coincide: they clearly derive in the last analysis from a common source (Sckommodau claims with some cogency that, despite inconsistencies, the true verse pattern of *A* is the five + five *décasyllabe*). MS *V* (Vatican Lat. 5334, discovered by Mons. Mercati but studied by Pio Rajna and published in *ArchRom*, XIII [1929], 1-86) contains roughly the last two hundred lines of the poem and is likewise fairly close to *L*; Rajna ascribed it to the mid-twelfth century. The thirteenth-century MS *P* (Paris, B.N., f. fr. 19,525) follows *L* quite closely: several stanzas and a number of lines are lacking. (MS *P²* Manchester, a fragment, offers the first thirty-five stanzas.) Other, to us less important, MSS include: *S* (Paris, B.N., f. fr. 12,471), thirteenth-century, assonanced (and containing the *rédaction interpolée* of G. Paris); *Ma* (Paris, B.N., f. fr. 1553), a thirteenth- or fourteenth-century MS of minor importance; *Mb* (Carlisle), a rhymed version of the same tradition as *Ma*. A subsequent *renouvellement*, the mid-fourteenth-century text in monorhymed alexandrine quatrains (*Q*), has been preserved in seven MSS (cf. G. Paris and L. Pannier, *op.cit.*, 327ff.), but these need not concern us.

The lost eleventh-century OF *Vie de saint Alexis* is most conveniently defined as belonging to a general West-European tradition of late Latin and vernacular *Lives*; it forms a part of the West-European Alexis "legend." This text, "deriving" then from a source resembling the Bollandist *Vita* and "creating," within the pan-European legend, an OF vernacular Alexis tradition to be further developed by later texts like *S*, *Ma*, *Mb*, and the *Q* corpus (for these texts, see G. Paris and L. Pannier), is most adequately represented by *L*, but, to all intents and purposes, it also figures in MSS *A*, *P*, and *V*. The three last-named do not, in our view, differ substantially from *L*; or, put another way, such differences from *L* as they do show are far less substantial than those which distinguish *LAPV*, taken *en bloc*, from the Bollandist *Vita*, on the one hand, and, on the other, from the later amplifications. *LAPV* may be seen as together forming a construct—a literary *O* or *"Urtext"*—at once related to, yet distinct from, the Latin "source" and the later vernacular versions. It is essentially to this "construct" that we refer when we speak of the "original" OF "poem" or *Life*, and it is this construct that we shall attempt to describe, interpret, and understand.

15

Again for the sake of convenience, we shall utilize G. Rohlfs' revised fourth edition (Tübingen, 1963) in our quotations, both for the Latin *Vita* (Rohlfs supplies the Bollandist text and M. Roesler's notes) and the OF "poem," though when specific reference to the individual MSS is in order, we shall refer to Rajna's edition of MS *V* and to the *L*, *A* and *P* texts as transcribed by Foerster and Koschwitz in their *Altfranzösisches Übungsbuch*₅ (Leipzig, 1915).

Having reinterpreted in this way the "ontology" of the OF *Life*, I hope not only to posit and establish an authentically critical "functional relationship" between those facets of the poem which we defined as its textual, literary, and legendary factors, but also to utilize this complex critical perspective for a pertinent comment on the poem's nature and meaning as well as, eventually, on its contribution to the history of French narrative. The scheme is stimulating because it offers, experimentally, the chance to incorporate into the literary discussion of the poem—in an avowedly problematic way—certain relevant textual and "historical" questions. In recent years it has become increasingly apparent that the highly significant relationship of "history" and "legend" and literary compositions are by definition problematical. Myth implies a kind of historical potency or productive fact. Medieval poetic texts, like the *Roland* and the Grail romances, ought, then, to be approached initially in terms of the ways these texts participate both in specific literary genres and in a historico-legendary *matière*. The fact of such participation and its special modalities are themselves objects of the scholar's legitimate concern, precisely because the poem not only derives from such *matière* but embodies it in distinctive ways, and, of course, contributes to its continuity. The important problem of poetic genesis and meaning is inevitably sacrificed when, over a period of many years, almost undivided attention is devoted to the unidimensional cause-and-effect framework of textual genesis in order to resolve purely editorial issues.

Jean Frappier has alluded to this and analogous problems in his salutary "Réflexions sur les rapports des chansons de geste et de l'histoire" (*ZRPh*, LXXIII [1957], 1-19). He quotes Jehan Bodel's late twelfth-century thematic and generic distinction between the "vains et plaisants" Breton tales—these belong to the "domaine du merveilleux et de l'illusion séduisante"—the "sage et de sens aprendant" romances of the *matere de Rome*, and the "true history" of the *chansons de geste* ("Et de ces trois materes tieng la plus voir disant"). Theme, literary kind, and degree of "truth" intermingle in this fundamentally generic distinction. Both poem and genre react upon the *matière* to which they belong. A mechanism governing the effective relation of text and historical (or legendary) context may be isolated by the scholar, provided he sifts his material with care and acumen; this mechanism, when brought to bear on the literary analysis of the text, may shed light upon the latter's workings. Once we establish a truly literary framework, it becomes clear that, in the case of the *chansons de geste* at least, the question of text and historical context need not always be phrased exclusively in terms of origins and *Urtext*: "Les rapports de l'histoire et des chansons de geste ne se confondent pas avec le problème des origines . . . ils ne se limitent pas à lui, . . . leur examen conduit à leur découvrir des aspects divers, et même opposés." In fact: "La chanson de geste a tiré parti de l'histoire contre l'histoire elle-même, si cette formule n'est pas trop paradoxale, et cela à des moments différents d'une création de longue durée. Dans un cas comme dans l'autre, c'est la notion même de poésie épique qui a joué son rôle, en vertu d'une certaine inspiration, d'une certaine idéologie, d'un certain art(1)." Furthermore, an analysis centered upon the work's poetic nature is not only legitimate in its own right, but, when handled with discrimination, should feed back useful insight into the work's textual construction and, for that matter, into its real—i.e., pertinent—historical background.

The OF *Alexis* participates in at least three isolable historical contexts: (1) the history of Alexis himself, as developed in Christian legendary tradition, (2) the history of the *Life*, as it wended its way first across the Mediterranean and then across Europe over many centuries, (3) the poem's immediate textual history in, say, eleventh- and twelfth-century France. Essential data concerning the second and third contexts have been brought to light and are readily available, as are the facts needed to examine cogently the first context. But the knowledge accumulated by Alexis scholarship must be rephrased so that we may see how, in mid-eleventh-century France, what Frappier calls the "notion même de poésie" played its role—how it "utilized" all three contexts—in elaborating the OF *Life*. Rather than stress the chronologies involved merely in order to illustrate increasingly vapid causal relationships, let us use such data to improve our grasp of the processes that shape all the material. By sharpening our sense of these processes—i.e., by examining closely the "functional relationship" between the text of the OF *Life*, its "poetic nature," and its legendary implications— we may expect to reach a keener understanding of our poem's relevance.

Essentially, it is a question of contrasting somewhat abstract patterns with the concrete data embodied in given texts situated in specific times and places; the various relevant components, thus isolated, may then be compared with one another so as to suggest the legend's sweep over time and space. "Legend" and "text" are at once "the same thing" and "different things"; though separate entities, they are mutually influential. No "legend" can exist without "texts," but it is convenient to interpret texts, in the case of the Alexis story, as specific manifestations of a broader contextual construct called the "legend" and its several (sub)traditions. On the one hand, the OF *Life* is a saint's life; it participates fully in an old genre of undisputed popularity and historical importance. On the other hand, it participates in an Alexis legend that, itself, belongs to a hagiographic tradition. One may therefore conceive of the legend as mediating between a broad hagiographic pattern and the various texts that tell, in different ways, Alexis' story. Thus, the legend, in its various versions, was transmitted from country to country and from century to century, in conformity with the basic possibilities of hagiographic composition. We must determine how these possibilities were textually interpreted in different places at different times; finally, we should use what we have discovered to ascertain the workings and meanings of the OF poem. We shall deal especially with thematic and rhetorical structure.

THE MYTHIC PARADIGM

The general lines of the hagiographic composition may be briefly sketched out. After Constantine's conversion, and particularly in Eastern Christendom, the faithful demonstrated increased interest in the holy man (or woman) who, unlike the earlier martyrs, practiced a rigorously conceived style of life and dedication to God summed up in the concept of *askesis*, the confessor saint. The ascetic confessor, through his renunciation of the world, his humility, and his constantly renewed faith, came to be known for his miracles. These miracles testified above all to the fact of his historical existence and, of course, justified his cult. In short, the saint came to participate in the mystery and model of the Incarnation. Like Jesus, the saint is a historical event to those who believe in him. In Delehaye's words he is "le personnage qui est honoré dans l'Église d'un culte public, [et qui] offre ceci de particulier que son histoire commence, pour ainsi dire, là où se termine celle des grands hommes, [et que] son existence a des prolongements indéfinis, même en ce bas monde, par les honneurs qui lui sont décernés, par des événements où ses fidèles se plaisent à reconnaître son intervention."[11]

By definition the saint enjoys a special, saintly historicity. The faithful subordinate the "real life" of the saint—what he in fact did—to his performance as a holy man, particularly what he accomplished at the moment of his death. Thus the

---

[11] H. Delehaye, *Cinq Leçons sur la méthode hagiographique* (Brussels, 1934), 7f.

19

"lives" of saints were scrutinized for early signs of their holiness and, conversely, typically saintly behavior was ascribed to saints simply because they were saints. No one hesitated to embroider upon "historical truth," as we define the term today. The faithful demonstrated an interest in the confessor saint's biography—his earthly history—equalled only by their need for, and fascination with, the ideal of saintliness. At any given time, then—and, even more significantly, over the centuries—each confessor saint retained his individuality because the faithful stressed the fact of his historical existence, but at the same time, as confessor saint, he came to share with other holy men a number of well-defined general attributes. The saint's "legend" is, essentially, a coherent body of lore constituted immediately upon his designation as saint. Any given redaction of his "life" contains a "complete legend." The legend may best be understood as a mythic construct involving "accurate" or "inaccurate" historical data as these are made conformable to the mythic paradigm of Christian saintliness as well as to the interpretative understanding of the communities for which the myths were "adapted." Meanwhile, in contrast to the legend's "immediacy," what may be slow and convoluted is the legend's diffusion; this becomes clear as one painfully retraces and compares the various versions and traditions of most legendary *corpora* over time and space. Hence it is quite misleading to speak exclusively, as so many have done, of the "evolution" of a monolithic Alexis legend from "historically (almost) accurate" Syriac versions at the beginning down through fantastic Byzantine and subsequent *rifacimenti*, since the term "evolution" conjoins the concepts of diffusion and of structure. The earliest and most sober Syriac text is in the fullest sense just as mythic as the most extravagant sixteenth-century Spanish version. However, one can and should compare the most significant texts, in order to grasp more completely the sense of the version in which one is most directly interested, even though such a comparison need not always be genetically oriented.

One must not be led astray by the apparent paradox that characterizes many saints' lives, namely the persistence, over time and space, of a well-defined hard core of anecdotes traditionally associated with a saint counterbalanced by the definite inventiveness—new episodes, new anecdotes—that also plays its role in the tradition. Fidelity to the literal tradition exists in tension with the desire to interpret and amplify that tradition. Such is always the case with mythic tradition; fidelity to the oldest versions has nothing to do with our modern concepts of historical accuracy.

The patterns of saintliness combine with what is known of the saint's biography to shape the legends that grow up around the lives of individual saints. These legends translate, in more or less thoroughly fictionalized biographical terms, the components derived from the patterns of saintliness. The components often take the form of motifs. Thus—in keeping with the tendency of hagiographic literature to stress the earliest observable signs of holiness—we note that, in this literature, extraordinary circumstances frequently attend the saint's birth. This motif is very common. St. Theodore of Sykeon was the bastard son of the beautiful (but promiscuous) Mary, who, made pregnant by a casual guest at her mother's inn, dreamed of the unborn child's future glory. This motif introduces into the hagiographic pattern variations on the Biblical story of Abraham, Sarah, and Isaac, or, even closer to Christian tradition, variations on the story of St. Elizabeth, Zachary, and their son John the Baptist, as well as, of course, Jesus himself. St. Daniel the Stylite's parents were barren until his mother made special prayers, miraculously answered when she conceived and bore him; Alexis too was God's answer to his parents' entreaties and vow—as expressed in some versions of the legend—to remain chaste should their prayers be answered. Unlike Isaac, however, the saintly child is seldom, if ever, sacrificed to God by his parents; like Alexis, he offers himself, usually in opposition to his parents' wishes. Characteristically, the saint's sojourn on earth is troubled by dramatic bouts with demonic temptation. Here the observance

21

of ascetic ideals—the saint's "exercise" and "victory"—purifies him and allows him to cure those who have been possessed by the devil. Though the Latin Bollandist *Vita* makes no mention of diabolic temptations in the case of Alexis, other traditions deemed it necessary to fill the lacuna. Late Spanish versions of the legend explain, for example, how the devil visits Alexis in exile and tempts him by claiming that his virgin bride has been repeatedly unfaithful to him in his absence. (The OF MS *L*, we recall, makes but one oblique reference to the devil: *Ses enemis ne l' poe[i]t anganer* [160]; the line is missing from MS *A*.)

A fascinating Eastern motif, probably developed from the thaumaturgical uses to which Scripture was put, stresses the powerful virtue of the saint's written word. St. Daniel the Stylite cured many afflicted by writing to them; his letters, when physically applied to the ailing, made them whole again. It has been said that St. John the Almsgiver, after his own death, restored a tablet, its original seal unbroken, to a woman penitent whose sin was so grievous she could not bring herself, while he was still alive, to confess it orally, but who had written it down in the hope that the saint would intercede for her. Upon his death the woman went to his tomb and, quoting the Bible (Wisdom 5:15), repeatedly proclaimed her belief that he had not really died. The good saint thereupon rose from the dead and returned the tablet to her; gratefully, she broke the seal to find her own writing blotted out and replaced by a statement forgiving her her sin. (Alexis' letter, discovered with his body, may well be a topical reflection of this motif.) Still better known is the convention that, in death, saints exhale sweet odors (*odor sanctitatis*); this contrasts, especially in the Eastern lives, with the filth they customarily lived in, and not only justifies the utter contempt with which the ascetic habitually views his body in life, but, somewhat paradoxically, symbolizes the purity of their souls by constituting a sign of their posthumous corporeal incorruptibility.

Many saints are chaste throughout their lifetime; the motif of chastity is, however, extremely complex. In hagiographic

literature the saint's renunciation of the world and his or her
consequent dedication to divine love are often dramatically
symbolized by a rejection of carnal love: the saint refuses to
marry or, if already married, does not live conjugally with his
or her spouse. Much is implied by such renunciation, for the
saint thus sets himself apart from other men. (And the
Church, to say the least, did not always favor such conduct;
see M. Huersche, "Alexiuslied und christliche Askese,"
ZFSL, LVIII [1934], 414-418.) Yet, since the saint in so
distinguishing himself does not for all that relinquish his
humanity—he remains subject to temptation, to illness, to
death—his exchange of earthly for divine love "humanizes"
divine love as much as it "deifies" the love human beings are
capable of. In fact the saint's death serves to illustrate the
frailty of earthly love. This polarization is highly effective and
its resolution constitutes the thematic matter treated in many
hagiographic structures. The saint, as flesh, embodies divine
love just as Christ did, but, not being the divinity Christ is,
his exemplification of divine love remains set in a purely
human—i.e., historical—framework. In terms of his human
situation, his own "historicity," the saint copes triumphantly
with the very human experience of love, an experience com-
mon to all men. Thus in many saints' lives the motif of chastity
becomes a central theme. The confessor saint must be chaste,
but his chastity, though an indisputable attribute, cannot be
depicted as a mere formality either in his life or in the story
of his life. The biographic repercussions of his chastity con-
stitute in and of themselves components of the mythic para-
digm as these are dramatically translated both into the legend
as a whole (texts, iconography, proverbs, etc.) and into indi-
vidual literary redactions. In no facet of the confessor saint's
life more than in his renunciation of earthly love do his human
situation, the facts of his history, and his holy vocation fuse so
meaningfully, so perfectly, and, indeed, so mysteriously into a
single dramatic construct. The renunciation symbolizes the
saint's acceptance and awareness of his status. It is therefore
certainly no surprise to note that, in those saints' lives in

which the saint's renunciation of earthly love is depicted with a particularly strong dramatic focus, the saint's miraculous powers consistently manifest themselves immediately after he has denied his sexual instinct: The refusal of one kind of potency engenders the other.

Alexis is a case in point. In his fine "Intactam sponsam relinquens: À propos de la *Vie de S. Alexis*" (*AnalBoll*, LXV [1947], 157-195), B. de Gaiffier examines the problem of Alexis' leaving his bride on their wedding-night. Rejecting Winkler's condemnation of the OF poem's lack of moral depth, he adopts Petit de Julleville's (1896) and L. Spitzer's interpretation of the episode: "C'est qu' [Alexis] l'aime lui-même comme il en est aimé; c'est qu'il veut . . . mériter pour elle et pour lui la réunion éternelle par la vertu d'un double sacrifice." In support of his argument, Gaiffier cites numerous saints' lives in which the protagonist chooses to avoid marriage altogether or, when married, persuades the spouse to live chastely, either together or apart. To suppose that Alexis and his bride agreed to preserve their virginity in order to dedicate themselves to a more *parfite amor* corresponds perfectly to the compositional possibilities of the *pieuse histoire*. Of course, Alexis' leaving home for the Orient before meeting the bride his parents had chosen for him is equally possible; the earliest Syriac version of the legend offers this tradition. Both versions reiterate the insistence upon chastity common in hagiographic writings; both utilize the "uncomprehending parents" motif. Yet the mysteries involved in Alexis' exchange of earthly for divine love are far more richly exploited in their human complexities by texts that, like MS *L* of the OF tradition, develop the bride's role and define her relationship to him as something rather different from his relationship to his parents. Both versions succeed in setting Alexis' saintliness in an entirely human context: His historicity—that which makes him accessible to Christians—is literarily rendered more palpable; hence his saintliness both acquires greater complexity and becomes more appealing.

The idea of chastity, then, is construed mythically and, in

this form, functions thematically in hagiographic literature. It is incorporated into the larger and more difficult notion of *caritas* and, as such, belongs to the repertoire of motifs associated with the saintly hero and his story. The saint's chastity comprises and defines his relationship to love, both earthly and divine, and thus provides a valuable key to the ritual structure that determines how and why Christians address themselves to God through the saint. Hagiographic literature celebrates this motif of chastity (along with the other typical motifs mentioned), and so invites the Christian public to participate in the celebration.

I have used advisedly the words "celebration" and "mythic." To read any work of literature demands that one participate effectively in the full gamut of its formal and rhetorical possibilities. But, in texts that show close affiliation to broad legendary constructs—hagiographic composition, popular song, folk epic, folktale—the sense of the formal patterns I have described depends heavily on the public's capacity to respond ritualistically to the historical, religious, or psychological motifs that these patterns are designed to represent. The response may be merely aesthetic: one grasps the myth and appreciates the economy with which it is worked out in a given literary work. Indeed, the mythic construct itself may be called upon to play a secondary role—iconographic or illustrative—in a work concerned with other matters. However, for the Christian audience of times past, when saints' lives were vital spiritual fare, the response or participation was, though channeled through viable literary modes, of a more profound sort. A kind of performance is at issue here. For, in conforming to the hagiographic patterns, the saint's life not only offered a biography composed of coherent, eventful signs corroborating the hero's saintliness, but also confirmed the public's own devotion and translated its understanding of reality and the mysteries of its faith. This is why the hagiographic genre knew such popularity throughout Christendom and why, indeed, its popularity was similar in scope to that enjoyed by, for example, the *chansons de geste*

25

in France and the *romancero* in Spain. For the Christian public the hagiographic work was bio-history of the deepest sort; the lives of holy men—their biographies—mirrored some of the profoundest earthly aspirations of that public from Byzantium to Western Europe. Works like the *Alexis*, taken either generally in the full sweep of the traditions associated with them or in redactions linked to particular times and places, did much to formulate their public's aspirations, and hence both engendered and maintained a sense of community among those who saw themselves as participating in the ritual. By the same token, these works allowed the individual "listener" to understand his own relationship to his community and led to a more perfect conception of his proper role within it. Thus, such works can be said to have contributed much to the creation of the community *qua* community as well as to the individual's notion of his own identity. This is why the critic and historian must not neglect to interpret the wider Alexis tradition and the specific textual redactions in terms of rhetorical functions and, of course, comparatively.

The literary implications of mythic participation go beyond the hagiographic genre itself; other legendary *corpora* behave similarly. But the hagiographic genre offers the student of literary operations virtual laboratory conditions for the study of these implications. The "laws" of the genre are themselves entirely determined by the conditions of mythic participation governing the kind of literature lives of saints are designed to be. Thus, inasmuch as participation in the telling of a saint's life was itself an act of faith, an act of witness, it not only permitted but required constant thematic and stylistic variation in the body of the story. This explains why, though the tale does vary over time and space and clerks were aware of such variation, they seldom cast serious doubt upon its veracity as history. But, conversely, such participation is also, literarily speaking, "ritual," hence the equally remarkable fidelity with which the many versions adhere to the central data, the structure, of each saint's legend. We shall have occasion to observe the literary effect of the "community" in the elaboration of Alexis' legend and, particularly, in the structuring of the OF *Life*.

THE ALEXIS LEGEND

It is our good fortune to possess numerous texts that recount, in many languages, the life of St. Alexis. Certain of these are particularly helpful in that they may be used pertinently to shed light on our OF poem. As I noted above, it is not entirely clear whether the legend originated in Syria, in Byzantium, or, perhaps, elsewhere: the earliest Syriac texts published by Amiaud resemble Roesler's hypothetical Greek archetype (*ZRPh*, LIII, 508-511) so closely that, by basing our analysis on Amiaud's translation of the primitive Syriac *Life*, we may adequately discuss the legend's structure in its first known manifestation. We may then move on to the later (presumed) Byzantine composite *Life*. (This "composite" *Life* relates not only Alexis' Syrian adventure, but also his "second" existence, his return to Rome.) Though no pretenth-century Greek manuscripts containing the entire composite Byzantine version have as yet been discovered, the later Greek texts are so similar to the early Latin *Vitæ* that, again for our purposes, we can conveniently "reconstruct" the missing link by relying essentially on the tenth-century Latin *Vita*, as published by the Bollandists. Major structural changes differentiate the composite *Life* from its Syriac (and perhaps early Byzantine) predecessor(s), hence the utility of isolating the two "stages" of the legend. Finally, we shall examine in considerable detail a different kind of relationship, that of the OF poem and its Latin "source." The distinctions here are of a stylistico-rhetorical sort. Diverse West-European versions of the *Life* will be cited as needed in order to illustrate certain points. Other manifestations of the legend—e.g., Joseph the Hymnographer's "Canon," the "second" Syriac *Life*, the Karshûni redactions, etc.—need not concern us, since our analysis will focus on the three legendary constructs most relevant to our purposes: (1) the early "first *Life*"; (2) the

Græco-Latin composite version culminating in the Bollandist *Vita*; (3) the OF poem, which we have described as forming part of a West-European tradition derived from the *Vita*.

Amiaud's reconstructed version of the "first" Syriac *Life* (late fifth, or, more probably, early sixth century, cf., Amiaud, xliiff.), based largely on MS *A* (Brit. Mus. add. 17,177), is introduced as follows: "Story of the Man of God, [native] of the City of Rome [Constantinople?], who acquired glory and the crown of sainthood at Edessa, by his works of poverty, in the time of the illustrious and holy priest Mar Raboula, bishop of the City of Edessa." We learn how a wealthy young man rejected the pleasures of the world, left his family, and dedicated himself to fasting and chastity in order to merit the New Jerusalem. His parents were from Rome; prosperous, noble, but childless, they had prayed for an heir. When the child was born, he was at once showered with riches and honors, and he was expected to indulge in the pomp and luxury befitting his station. But even in childhood he showed no concern for worldly things, and his parents were saddened, believing he was "simple and unfit for the life of this world." They procured for him gay company; his mother assembled a troop of beautiful slave-girls to entertain him—all to no avail. They even found him a wife. But just before his bride is scheduled to arrive at the marriage-feast, the young man persuades one of his servant companions to accompany him on a stroll to the port. There he asks the servant to wait until he has finished his walk. The saint stands off to pray. He begs God to open His door unto him. A boat, ready to leave for Syria, appears; the saint boards. He lands at the port of Seleucia and travels as a beggar to Edessa, where he remains, spending his days in church, his evenings begging for alms. To no one does he tell his story. The tale shifts back to Rome. The abandoned *paranymphus* finally returns to the wedding feast after learning of his master's departure on the ship. The saint's parents, deeply chagrined, resolve to search for their son. Their slaves arrive in Edessa, where one of them apprises Bishop Raboula of "the story of the Man of God"; the slaves find their master but fail to recognize him. "It is even probable that they gave him alms," recounts the anonymous writer. Much later, a virtuous church custodian (Amiaud's *portier*; Lat. *paramonarius*) observes the saint; fascinated by his strange ways, he resolves to learn his story. Finally the holy man tells him, but on condition that the custodian promise never to reveal a word to anyone. The custodian becomes the holy man's disciple. When the saint falls ill, he takes him to the foreigners' hospital, where he visits him every day. But God "protects the holy man's humility" by preventing his friend from seeing him on the day of his death. When the custodian finally reaches the hospital, he discovers that the holy man has died and has been buried. Together with the bishop, he visits the grave in the foreign cemetery; upon opening it they find only the saint's rags, his body is gone. Raboula decides to double his efforts to welcome, and care for, foreigners, since among them might be others as holy as the saintly "Roman." The tale ends by reporting that the story was written down and published by the *paramonarius* who had been the saint's friend.

The stark sobriety of the story underscores its effect of verisimilitude. Yet the typical hagiographic pattern as such is closely adhered to in this not artlessly conceived drama. Note the opening summary of what will come; the tale "illustrates" its title. The "crown" of sainthood may well refer to a halo, i.e., a physical sign of holiness applied to saints in Christian iconography as early as the sixth century (see A. Kruecke, *Der Nimbus und verwandte Attribute in der frühchristlichen Kunst* [Strasbourg, 1905]). The Syriac term used, *ethcalal*, means "crowned with foliage or a garland" but came to signify, metaphorically, "crowned with martyrdom" or "crowned as a confessor." The man of God achieves his crown (his category as saint) through his "active renunciation of worldly goods"; he becomes a kind of ikon, recognizable as such to those capable of "seeing" his crown, i.e., of appreciating his saintliness. The tale's unfolding is interesting. We are asked to believe the holy man's custodian friend, who nar-

29

rates both what he has been told and what he has seen. A rhetorical parallelism is established: the custodian is witness to the holy man as the saint is witness to God. The events of the saint's life fall into two categories: his existence in Rome and his new life in Syria. The text itself—in Amiaud's translation—makes this point: "Et le saint l'avait instruit de toute sa vie: de la première partie qui avait été le temps de la grandeur, et de la dernière qui fut celui de l'humilité" (9). His real grandeur corresponds, of course, to the second phase. Each part terminates with an event demonstrating the saint's special relationship to God: the first section ends with the almost preternatural appearance of the boat for Syria, the second with the empty grave and the resolutions Raboula takes upon making the discovery.

All the elements of the story are combined by means of dramatic antitheses. The saint's parents are barren, they pray for a son, and God grants their wish. But they misapprehend what God has given them. The wedding-day, with all it implies, is the moment the saint chooses to leave; one "new life" is rejected for another; the saint's former servants dole out to him alms; his friendship with the poor church custodian threatens the saint's humility, yet it is through this same custodian that Raboula, and Christendom, learn of him and can profit from his example. The custodian takes his sick friend to the hospital, but on the day of his death he is prevented from making his usual visit. The parents' good will is a source of misunderstanding and impotence; it is artfully contrasted with the doorkeeper's predisposition, which, though frequently (and properly) thwarted, provides, with God's help, the key to the reader's total grasp of the holy man's effort. Yet this dualistic dramatic structure is worked out in very static terms. The saint's *askesis*—his fidelity to his calling and his mortification of the flesh—is merely his way of illustrating, ikon-like, that for which he was summoned. His role is a passive one in what is, actually, the emergence of a deep religious awareness of charity on the part of the custodian and Raboula. This awareness is translated into moral terms; it spurs the custodian and his bishop to greater good works. The former exclaims upon learning of the holy man: "If this man, who was brought up in the greatest luxury, can sustain such mortification, what must we poor accomplish in order to earn our salvation!"

Much ink has been spilled in attempts to explain the conditions under which the story we have just summarized underwent revision in Byzantium, and thence was transmitted to the Latin West, as well as back to Syria. (For later Syriac versions develop the composite, or "double," *Life*, not only the "first *Life*" as just epitomized.) It seems reasonably clear that a new (or renewed) Alexis tradition was established at some time between the sixth and ninth centuries; Joseph the Hymnographer's *Canon* concerning Alexis dates from the ninth. Possibly the older Alexis tradition was already confused, as it certainly was subsequently, with the legend of St. John Calybite. Such bifurcations are hardly unusual in hagiographic literature. Be that as it may, reconstruction of the entire composite Byzantine *Life* shows a complete reworking of the matter contained in the Syriac work, a widening of the paradigmatic context by means of intensive fictionalization. We may proceed in the collation by first isolating what the reworking "added to" and "eliminated from" the data assembled above.[12]

[12] A few remarks on Roesler's hypothetical Byzantine "original" of the "first *Life*" are in order here. This conspicuously early Greek work substantiates many of our findings. It stresses above all the saint's *askesis*, what one might be tempted to tag the pure "mechanics" of saintly life. The Virgin appears before the Edessa custodian in a dream and describes the holy man to him solely in terms of his daily routine (what he eats, where he gets his water, how and where he prays, etc.). Later, when the saint identifies himself, he expressly refuses to reveal his name but rather tells who he is by reporting what he does: he delineates his ascetic daily life, e.g., how he keeps but twelve lepta a day of the alms he receives, buying bread with ten, vegetables with two, etc. These "realistic" details merely serve to exemplify the saint's ascetic conduct, his adherence to the saintly paradigm; they are mythic. Certain ingredients present in Amiaud's Syriac text are unknown to Roesler's Byzantine MS: the slave-girls,

The principal addition to the plot concerns the saint's departure from Edessa for Tarsus via Seleucia and the marvelous storm that diverts the ship home to (the Italian) Rome. This accretion is perfectly justified even in terms of the older Syriac story, since, when Raboula and the custodian opened the man of God's tomb in Edessa, it was empty. The fictionalization is entirely vindicated by what some later Byzantine "readers" might have construed as an inadequacy of the plot. The saint's "second life" includes: his arrival in Rome; his meeting with his father, whom he asks for board and lodging (without revealing his identity); his life under the staircase; his vilification by his father's servants; his death-bed writing of his life story; his death; the voices announcing to the people of Rome the presence among them of a saint; the discovery by the people (including pope and emperors) of the body; the revelation of the letter (and identity); the *planctus* of his father, mother, and bride; the miracles of healing; and the saint's sumptuous burial.

All these changes caused a number of inconsistencies to creep into the subsequent and later Karshûni redaction. In fact, the second (i.e., composite) Syriac *Life* complains that those who wrote of the saint in Rome "did so without any knowledge of his death in Edessa," leading one to suppose that the Syriac redactor, in typical hagiographic fashion, recognized the historical validity of the local version of the saint's life at Edessa as well as the authenticity of other ver-

---

for example, and, in effect, the account of the holy man's youth at home. Raboula is played down, though he does appear unnamed. The tone is rather more Roman; the sea is situated some eighteen miles from the city. (The Syriac text, conversely, could have been hinting at Constantinople.) Thus, though (to quote Roesler), "der Verlauf der Begebenheiten ist ungefähr derselbe wie im I. Teil des von A. Amiaud herausgegebenen syrischen Texts," the difference between his Syriac versions and her presumed early Byzantine text show the latter to be distinctly more abstract: the structure does little more than sketch in the barest outline of the hagiographic pattern of *askesis*. The saint's ascetic life is indissolubly associated with his enjoying God's favor and the public's veneration.

sions. The complaint furthermore eloquently recalls the importance attached to the saint's place of death by hagiographer and faithful alike.

In a deeper sense, the later Syriac *non sequiturs* are really due to the ways the (second?) Greek handling of the story emphasizes motifs and themes either unknown to, or played down by, Amiaud's primitive Syriac texts. Whereas the latter had stressed the moral implications of the saint's example—hence the importance of the custodian and Raboula in the tale's dramatic development and antithetical structure (literarily, they are the only real characters, the saint is a presence) —the later Greek legend, so far as one can discern from the surviving Latin and Greek texts, subordinates the fact of Alexis' *askesis* to the mysteries it embodies: the holy man's history illustrates and exemplifies mystic *caritas*. Furthermore, by stressing "Rome," the Greek revision insists upon a highly structured, universalist *communitas*—a far wider social framework than the Syriac Edessa. The local saint has been "universalized."

The newer Byzantine story's development is lyrico-dramatic in that it consists of specific scenes involving a number of characters in their highly personal, if symbolic, relation to the saint. Each scene depicts a facet of what saintliness means; the mystery of *caritas* deepens even as these meanings gain in clarity. The whole is set in an essentially fictional framework: the characters have names, real as well as symbolic identities. Alexis' travels from Rome to the East and back to Rome provide a narrative coherence on which the various dramatic episodes are strung, and serve moreover to isolate Alexis as a personage at the same time as they highlight the poignancy of his relevance to those with whom his earthly life has brought him into contact. Space and time are managed in a novelistic way; specified periods of time pass, geographic references are explicit, yet this fictionalization of time and space destroys chronology and stages the action in the consciousness of the reader. Time is *ævum* and locale is the Christian *communitas*; both time and space are internalized. The processes of fiction

33

affect even details. Thus, the pope and the two emperors, who are usually named, possess the attributes of historicity but, like Alexis' parents, they are mythic creations—institutions—designed to support the illusion of history that promotes the reader's participation in the hagiographic paradigm.

The simplicity of the first Syriac text reflects the simplicity of its intentions. The entire story centers upon the saint's relationship with the custodian: what precedes and what follows this friendship is filtered through the episode describing it. The reader must project himself into the custodian's situation. The reworked Byzantine version is structurally more intricate; consequently, the custodian, though not completely eliminated, is subservient even to the image of the Virgin, who, through him, causes Alexis' holiness to be known in Edessa. (Great importance, we recall, is also accorded the Virgin in Roesler's twelfth-century manuscript: she appears to the custodian in a dream; the saint's parents, however, are barely mentioned.) All that Alexis has done is miraculously justified by what the image reveals; we understand him as his parents, for example, could not.

The greater anecdotal detail of the composite Byzantine legend—when compared with the earlier Syriac version—may be due, as G. Paris and others have intimated, to its being "farther removed" from "what really happened"; the Byzantine hagiographer(s) needed to compensate for the distance by being more "concrete" and "circumstantial." Unfortunately, such an explanation, though perhaps psychologically countenanced, does not adequately account for the higher level of structural complexity one detects in the Græco-Latin tradition. Both the primitive versions and the subsequent reworkings constitute equally "pure" examples of hagiographic composition, but the latter quite obviously exploit far more thoroughly the possibilities open to the genre. G. Paris' explanation "covers over" the important fact of the composite *Lives*' being systematically more complex than the primitive version; it also conceals the meaning of this new complexity. I have alluded to a "widening of the paradigmatic context."

How is this expansion achieved, then, and what are its implications?

We have already mentioned the plot extensions and we have hinted at the process of fictionalization. We have also noted that the Syriac text emphasizes the purely moral repercussions of *caritas*, whereas the later history uses Alexis' *askesis* to illuminate and embody the deeper mysteries of *caritas*. Finally, we saw that the central rhetorical function of the Syriac custodian is partially replaced, in effect, by the new narrative structure. (The parents remain essentially, in both versions, those "who misunderstand," though in the revised tradition, they—especially the father—merit our compassion; see the treatment of this point by A. G. Hatcher and, especially, by P. R. Vincent.) What we have so far not observed directly, and therefore must now analyze, is the role of Alexis' bride in the narrative and rhetorical framework. She too "replaces" the Syriac custodian in the "wider" Græco-Latin construct; through her, the hagiographic motif of chastity—linked, we recall, to the notion of *caritas*—is worked into, and made to determine, the structural contours of the tale.

For the sake of expediency we may assume, for our purposes, that the Bollandist *Vita* reproduces with sufficient fidelity this "wider Græco-Latin framework" and that, consequently, by referring specifically to that text, we may clarify some pertinent structural relationship to be found in the later (presumed pre-tenth-century) Byzantine *Life*.[13] Furthermore,

---

[13] Numerous scholars have, as we saw, debated the genesis of the Latin Alexis tradition. The "source investigation" is complicated by many unknowns. Thus, late 10th-c. Rome manifested a special interest in Alexis, but it is dubious whether this vogue marked a renewed bestowal of favor on a saint previously known, if conceivably somewhat neglected, or the establishment of an entirely new cult. Recent research has unearthed evidence that the Alexis story circulated in Latin versions dating from the second quarter of the tenth century and preserved in San Millán de la Cogolla (now Real Academia de la Historia, Emilianense 13) and Santo Domingo de Silos (the later MS is in the Bibliothèque Nationale, lat. nouv. acq. 2178). These versions,

direct reference to the *Vita* will permit us to pose within our functional framework the question of source and its workings in the eventual constitution of the OF *Life*; most scholars agree that a Latin text, or texts, very close to the *Vita* in fact inspired the creation of our poem (cf. fn. 9).

---

though comprising the whole of the saint's "two lives," are truncated: they fail to mention Alexis by name (he is *Fimiani filius, beatissimus puer*, etc.) and they omit a number of episodes found elsewhere (see L. Vázquez de Parga's tantalizingly incomplete "¿La más antigua redacción latina de la leyenda de San Alejo?" *Revista de Bibliografía Nacional*, II [1941], 245-258, and B. de Gaiffier's rev., *AnalBol*, LXII [1944], 281ff.).

Spain, however, is not Rome, and, undeniably, Alexis' (new? restored?) popularity in the papal capital roughly matches the arrival there of the Damascene Archbishop Sergius, a refugee who was given charge of the St. Boniface church (ca. 977) by Benedict VII. Sergius and his monks were quick to take up Alexis' cause; they deemed themselves eminently qualified to serve as the guardians of his memory. Reputedly, they possessed the Madonna that had announced to the Edessa custodian Alexis' saintly status. Much has been written about Sergius' alleged role in introducing Alexis to the West. However, short of accusing him and his companions of merely feigning an interest in the saint, and of cynically—or worse, stupidly—laying claim to authority in a matter more familiar to their prospective dupes, one must conclude that (1) Sergius introduced the legend in its now official form (though possibly with variations) and, in so doing, relied on an extensive Byzantine model, or (2) he and his monks revitalized an "incomplete," fragmentary Roman legend by infusing into it Greek elements imported by them from the East, or—least plausibly—(3) Sergius and his followers found, upon their arrival in Rome, a fully constituted local Alexis cult which they proceeded to take over.

Whether one prefers (1) or (2), the existence of a complete Byzantine reworking of the legend prior to, say, 950 (and probably much older if Roesler's position in "Alexiusprobleme" is to enlist support) cannot be seriously doubted. Consequently, either two rather distinct Greek and Latin legends fused into one (with variations), under unverifiable circumstances, or the Greek contributed much to the Latin, as it came to be formulated. (One recalls, moreover, that St. Adalbert of Prague, author of a homily on Alexis entitled *In natale S. Alexii Confessoris* and preserved at Monte Cassino, stayed with Sergius' St. Boniface community in 990. Canonization procedures were initiated on Alexis' behalf in Rome in 993.)

With respect to the OF poem, the Alexis tradition reaches a decisive turning point, a watershed, in the Latin text(s). The *Vita* embraces all the pertinent features of the Alexis story as these had been developed by the Byzantine elaboration. No subsequent *rifacimento* will either add or subtract any essential hagiographic component of the tradition. Considerable stylistic variation will occur in subsequent versions, but such variation will immutably conform to the fixed structural patterns of the Græco-Latin version as these appear in the *Vita*.[14] Once we ascertain the sense of these patterns and the processes governing them, which we shall attempt to do in our analysis of the bride's role, we shall be justified in moving on to examine the nature of the stylistic modifications that impart its special character to the OF poem and, concomitantly, to describe the processes that formally relate that poem to its source.

The structural complexity of our reconstructed Græco-Latin *Life* results from, or is exemplified in, the protagonist's acceptance of his marriage. Instead of leaving Rome before the wedding takes place, Alexis goes through with the ceremony, departing only after having spoken with his bride. This fact of marriage, we remarked, centers the reader's attention upon the motif of chastity and what this motif means with respect to the tale's unfolding of Alexis' ascetic life. Alexis' love for his wife is real; if it were not genuine and profound, his history would make little sense. I have already stated my agreement with the interpretation offered by (among others) Petit de Julleville, Spitzer, and B. de Gaiffier. Furthermore, this fictionalized love should be linked to the theme of *caritas* that the later Byzantine *Life* and its congeners illustrate in a manner quite different from the *caritas* of the preceding "first life."

---

[14] By this I mean that no sister or brother of Alexis will come upon the scene, nor will Alexis found a monastery, or write a learned doctrinal treatise. Many strange tales will be told of Alexis' miraculous intercessions; these will be mere appendages—other stories concerning other people—to rank as consequences, perhaps, never as a part of his proper history.

37

Alexis, then, marries the girl selected for him by his parents. He goes to her after being told to do so by his father: "Ut autem intrauit, coepit nobilissimus iuuenis et in Christo sapientissimus instruere sponsam suam et plura ei sacramenta disserere, deinde tradidit ei annulum suum aureum et rendam, it [id] est caput baltei, quo cingebatur, inuoluta in prandeo et purpureo sudario, dixitque ei: 'Suscipe hæc et conserua, usque dum Domino placuerit, et Dominus sit inter nos' [MS *P*: et sit Dominus inter me et te]." He then departs from his father's house, telling no one of his intentions. Few words are spoken, but when one recalls the laconic sobriety of the *Vita*, the episode becomes crucially important. In giving his bride the ring, the cloth (veil?), and the *caput baltei*, or sword-belt, Alexis clearly defines his relationship to her. T. Fotitch argues that these gifts mean Alexis is compensating his bride upon terminating the marriage, that he is making a clean break: "The ring, symbol of unending love, signifies that he considers the union as broken; the veil, symbol of virginity, that he returns the bride untouched; the belt (or any other object), symbol of earthly riches, that he returns the dowry" (506). The point is interesting, but Alexis' gestures cannot be construed, as she suggests, to mean that Alexis is returning to the *status quo ante* (505f.). Indeed, if the ring be symbolic of eternal love, one might conclude that Alexis is reaffirming his love for his wife by giving it to her. The phrase "Suscipe hæc et conserua, usque dum Domino placuerit, et Dominus sit inter nos" puts us on the right track: far from cancelling, or annulling, his marriage, Alexis, in offering these presents to his wife, provides her with a course of action. He does set aside his previous, worldly marriage, but only to suggest a new, fuller, spiritual union in which her task is to remain perfectly faithful.

The marriage as such endures. The bride is to remain Alexis' wife; she is "redefined," so to speak, as part of her husband's relationship to God: "et Dominus sit inter nos," or "inter me et te." The bride is meant to understand her young husband: how completely she does so, at least at first, is difficult to assess, but her status as his wife demands that she participate in his saintliness. This she does, and throughout the *Vita* she is fidelity incarnate. Her ability to love Alexis is touching, and, I think, signifies that she does understand him, even though at the outset she cannot fully conceptualize what has happened. Whereas Alexis' mother gives vent to self-mortification and savage recrimination in her two *planctus*, the bride, though desperately grieved, obeys Alexis' implied injunction and plays out her part: "Sponsa uero ejus dixit ad socrum suam: 'Non egrediar de domo tua, sed similabo me turturi, quæ omnino alteri non copulatur, dum ejus socius captus fuerit; sic et ego faciam, quousque sciam, quid factum sit de dulcissimo conjuge meo.' " After Alexis' death (and identity) became known, his mother, "quasi leæna rumpens rete ita scissis uestibus exiens," began to scream her loss and spite. The bride's comprehension of her wifely role is neatly shown in her contrasting, though parallel, complaint; the mirror image is particularly significant: "Sponsa quoque ejus induta ueste attrita cucurrit plorans et dicens: 'Heu me, qui hodie desolata sum et apparui uidua. Jam non habeo in quem aspiciam nec in quem oculos leuem. Nunc ruptum est speculum meum et periit spes mea. Amodo coepit dolor qui finem non habet' " [or, in MS *B*: et ammodo plorabo usque ad mortem].[15] These are hardly the words of a repudiated woman, nor do they translate the pride one might be tempted to associate with a "puella ex genere imperiali," as the bride is described. Rhetorically speaking, his bride's fidelity justifies Alexis' behavior; his conduct is rendered persuasive and that of his mother condemned. Literally then, as well as dramatically, the bride acts as a kind of foil to both Alexis and his uncomprehending parents; she wins the reader's sympathy from the start, and does so without endangering the sympathetic reverence one must feel for Alexis himself; she provides the essential rhetorical key to the reader's participation in the

---

[15] This interesting reading seems to imply "until death when I shall be reunited with him"—exactly the sense imparted to the bride's role in many later versions.

very human situations that emerge from the fact of Alexis' saintliness.

If our interpretation of the bride's role is correct, we may now postulate a more complete view of her structural function in the work. We assume that Alexis, on his wedding-night, re-weds his wife, spiritually, and confides his mission to her by requesting her eternal fidelity. Thus his relationship with her has been made over into an integral part of his total relationship with God and has been essentially transformed by such spiritualization, though, as such, the marriage itself remains intact. The situation is not without certain catharistic overtones. If we are right in concluding that, since the fact of Alexis' marriage rhetorically situates his sainthood, it provides the clue to his saintliness, to his practice, through *askesis*, of *caritas*, then it must follow that the bride's status as his wife is essential to the development and meaning of the story.

Apart from the Syrian *paramonarius*, the bride is the only major character to go unnamed in the *Vita*. Alexis, his parents, the emperors, the pope, even the obscure clerk who reads the dead saint's letter (Ethius), are all endowed with names. The bride is first referred to, we recall, as "puella ex genere imperiali"; she is subsequently called simply "sponsa." Like Alexis, she is a Roman; her imperial lineage moreover specifies her as such. Indeed, upon reflection, one is overwhelmed by the Roman-ness of the story: "Fuit Romæ uir magnus . . ." are the opening words; references to specific churches, to the emperors, to the pope, to the people of Rome abound. Some of these Roman allusions are confused, and, especially when one compares the different Greek and Latin versions, one is struck by numerous inconsistencies. Invention, confusion, and mistranslation combine with obvious propaganda to make one doubt the age or authenticity of the tale's Roman quality. But whether "Rome" is Rome or Constantinople, or, historically, a combination of both, need not concern us now. What is striking is the fact of Roman-ness, that is, the text's insistence upon a well-defined community, with institutions, a church, a universalist vocation, and a many-leveled social structure: Alexis is born and schooled in Rome, marries a girl of imperial stock—her only distinctive trait—leaves, returns, and dies in Rome. His second, and principal, designation as saint takes place in a Roman church with, presumably, the whole population present, when a voice is heard, commanding: "Quærite hominem Dei ut oret pro *Roma*." And, at the end of the *Vita*, the pope, the emperors, and the entire city join in the saint's burial. When sweet odors emanate from his tomb, "*populo suo* conferre dignatus est subsidium." These are the same people who, somewhat earlier, "wept tearfully" (*lachrimabiliter flebat*) after hearing the bride's sad lament. Her personal grief—born of earthly love and loss—is finally subsumed, by the story, into Rome's joy at having had a saint in its midst. The dramatic contrast is touching, but the story itself resolves the tension. (The resolution is explicit in the OF poem, however, since MSS *L*, *P*, *A*, and *V* all show the pope intervening, after the bride's *planctus*, to explain: "Qui qui se doilet a nostr'o[e]s est il goie" [503].)

Given the bride's anonymity, or rather her identification as "ex genere imperiali" and, principally, as Alexis' wife, and given the social, or pan-Christian ("Roman"), implications of Alexis' sainthood, it seems likely that the bride is not only the dramatic device utilized by the *Vita* to clarify the sense of his saintliness, but also, significantly, the means by which, from the very beginning, his holiness is effectively linked to Rome. Her identity is dramatically personalized in her designation as Alexis' wife; Alexis' eventual involvement with Rome is meanwhile rendered more precise by her "anonymously specific" status as a representative of the structured "Roman" community. The saint, we recall, stands between God and man: the figure of the bride embodies, in a purposefully unabstract way, through her double and special connection to both Alexis and her city, the effective relationship Alexis, as saint, establishes between his God and his people. In this sense, her fidelity may be construed as a counterpart to his *askesis*; it contributes to the reader's appreciation of how the fruits of this *askesis* came to be shared by the Roman—i.e., universal—Christian community. Alexis' remaking of his marriage prepares us for the joyful regeneration of Rome that we witness at his death. The saint understands God's will and acts accordingly, but it is what he does that defines his holiness for other men. What Alexis does and how he does it intimately involves his wife—as the story unfolds before us—and it is to a large extent through his relationship to her that we are able to participate in his history on all levels of its formal complexity. The rhetorical framework becomes operative: the Roman *communitas* is built into the structure and meaning of the story, and, through the institution of marriage (if not through identification with the bride herself), each reader or "listener" is given cause to celebrate individually the saintly ritual. The bride, as device, links the individual plane to the communal one: the mythic ritual can take place.

SOURCE AND TEXT

The mythic properties of hagiographic literature are nowhere more manifest than in the tendency of that literature to use fictional means to illustrate the fundamental thematic constructs it contains. I have described the structural patterns present in the primitive Syriac as well as in the later Græco-Latin Alexis tradition, and I have indicated how they work—especially the Græco-Latin fictionalization thanks to which Alexis' historicity is rendered mythically efficacious within the possibilities of the hagiographic paradigm. If, then, the Bollandist *Vita* effectively represents a homogeneous Græco-Latin tradition made up of the thematic and rhetorical components analyzed above, this tradition may be opposed, historically, to the various European vernacular and later Latin versions that derived from the texts fundamentally similar to the *Vita*. The *Vita* may be profitably construed as a kind of zero degree against which the stylistic developments of the European vernacular texts (including our OF *Life*) may be pertinently projected and described. Genetically speaking, the *Vita*, as edited by the Bollandists, does constitute the authoritative "source" of the OF *Life* and its European counterparts. But rather than focus upon this "source" genetically—i.e., rather than seek to determine how the *Vita* "engendered" the vernacular mode to which the OF *Life* belongs—I shall, by comparison, endeavor to describe the nature of the stylistic modifications that that vernacular mode and, in particular, the OF *Life* brought to bear on its source. In short, I expect to show how the *Vita* functioned literarily as source and, though the exhaustive analysis of our poem's literary characteristics cannot be attempted here, I shall attempt to provide a solid basis for such a formal inquiry as well as for the investigation of narrative techniques.

As we noticed, then, the figure of the bride was invented by the Byzantine tradition and maintained thereafter in order to serve certain purposes imposed upon the legend by the paradigmatic patterns at work in its development. The literary possibilities open to this figure in subsequent versions of the legend, once her essential function was determined, were virtually boundless. New episodes were fashioned (amplifications); the various *rifacimenti* reflected tastes proper to the times in which they were composed; new relationships were explored, as were new aspects of the traditional relationships; and many novel devices were tried out. A West-European experimental mode came to characterize the diverse *Lives* of Alexis written in the several vernaculars (and even in Latin); this mode fully pervades the OF poem.

The process of fictionalization alluded to above was, then, continued by stylistic means. Thus, one notes that the bride undergoes increased personalization and, concomitantly, that attention is centered more and more about Alexis and his bride as a couple. Meanwhile, the figure of Alexis himself acquires increased mystical overtones. In many texts the bride receives a name; these names are typically literary: Adriatica, Sabina, even—in late medieval (post-Dante) Italian versions—the *donna angelica* incarnate, Beatrice!

Elsewhere she is unjustly accused of infidelity; she must prove her loyalty to Alexis and does so when her husband's cadaver releases to her alone the letter he wrote on his deathbed. The myth of Griseldis is, one might say, partially incorporated into the Alexis story; the bride's chastity and fidelity are never, to my knowledge, overcome in any subsequent version of the tale. Thus the saint's holiness extends to his "lady," as the "relics" that he bestows upon her would seem to have indicated. Such devotion seems, moreover, well established in medieval hagiographic literature; in her "Prologue," even Chaucer's Wyf of Bathe grudgingly remarks:

> For trusteth wel; it is impossible
> That any clerk wol speke good of wyves—
> But if it be of hooly seintes lyves—
> Be of noon oother womman never the mo (688ff.).

In numerous European versions of Alexis' *Life* (eleventh-century and later) his bride dies shortly after Alexis' burial; she rejoins her husband in death and in paradise. This amplification links her loss with Rome's joy and explicitly provides for her own joy. The *Vita* is glossed by this episode, which is, of course, a standard stylistic variation of the type under study. One recalls the end of the two Latin texts found in Munich and, in 1843, edited by Massmann (Cod. Monac. Ratisbon. civ. LXX et Scheftlar. 138).

Here is the episode referred to: About two years have elapsed since Alexis' death; his wife dies and, in compliance with her wish, is buried with him: "Aperto itaque sarcofago niue candidiora inuenta sunt ossa beati uiri. Que continuo mirabile dictu in latus se contulerunt sarcofagi ut esset locus locando beato corpori. Brachium quoque transposuit ut quasi dilecta sponsa leuam sub capite dextram se amplexantem haberet. Quod multitudo uirorum ac mulierum intuens laudauit et glorificauit deum per omnia benedictum, qui facit mirabilia solus. Amen" (Massmann, 165f.). The episode recurs in the MHG MSS *A*, *F*, and *H* edited by Massmann (66f., 138, and 155f.); in each of these texts, it provides the culminating miracle of the saint's "life." This most concrete miracle is highly effective: the wife's chastity is rewarded and, by the same token, Alexis' abandonment of his bride is totally vindicated. What is implied in the Bollandist *Vita* is here rendered explicit. The texts stress—and define—Alexis' sanctity, his power to intercede on behalf of those who, through contact with him, have rendered themselves fit for salvation. Having refused earthly conjugal love, Alexis receives his wife at her death in a marriage-bed that he, as man of God, has transformed, for her, into the miracle of grace. The bride has been more completely delineated as a person, and Alexis, meanwhile, has been shown to adhere more perfectly to the mysterious saintliness to which his vocation had called him. Love enabled him to return, after death, to claim his own; the story reaches full circle. The German poet of MS *F*, after describing this scene and Rome's great joy, draws his moral: "Nû hilf uns guoter Alexius got bitten . . . dass wir kumen dar/ mit fröuden in der engel schar."

The OF MS *L*, like the MHG tradition, is more explicit in this regard than the *Vita*. Though not nearly so detailed in its amplifications as the German texts, MS *L*, I believe, faithfully reflects the OF literary archetype. The bride remains unnamed. Yet the poem is remarkably concrete, despite its loyal adherence to the sobriety of the Latin work's plot. The story moves at a fairly rapid pace, but the sense of each episode is clearly and vividly silhouetted. (Was it this concrete—though not visualized—quality of the episodes that prompted A. G. Hatcher to describe very sensitively, though not always convincingly, the unfolding of Alexis' *askesis* and its meaning in terms of the poem's episodic structure [*Trad*, VIII (1952), 111-158]? Following Spitzer's cue, she quite rightly stresses the bride's crucial role in the poem.) The OF *Life* voices its originality with respect to its Latin source(s), but also differs from the later European tradition of which it is a part. Thus, after his father orders him to join his bride Alexis "ne volt . . . sum pedre corocier." He visits his wife, speaks to her, and leaves:

Vint en la c[h]ambre, ou er[e]t sa muiler.
Cum v(e)it le lit, esguardat la pulcele,
Dunc li remembret de sun seinor celeste,
Que plus ad ch[i]er que tut aveir terrestre:
"E! Deus!," dist il, "cum fort pec[hi]et m'apresset!
Se or ne m'en fui, mult criem que ne t'em perde."
Quant an la c[h]ambre furent tut sul remes,
Danz Alexis la prist ad apeler:
La mortel vithe li prist mult a blasmer,
De la celeste li mostret veritet.
Mais lui est tart que il s'en seit turnet.
"Oz mei! pulcele, celui tien ad espus
Ki nus raens[t] de sun sanc precius.
An ices[t] s[i]ecle nen at parfit' amor,
La vithe est fraisle, n'i ad durable honor,
Ceste lethece revert a grant tristur."
Quant sa raisun li ad tute mustrethe,
Pois li cumandet les renges de s'espethe
Ed un anel, a Deu l(i) ad comandethe.
Dunc en eissit de la c[h]ambre sum pedre;
Ensur[e] nuit s'en fuit de la contrethe (55ff.).

Compared with the above, the Latin passage (quoted earlier) resembles a preliminary sketch, yet nothing in the OF text contradicts its source. Alexis understands what he must do and explains his conduct to his bride: there is no perfect love in this life; present joy (*lethece*) turns into sadness, a reflection implying that what may be sadness now can, and will, become joy in the eternal life. The motif is stated and will remain central to the poem. The word reappears in the mother's *planctus* addressed to the nuptial chamber: "Ne ja ledece n'[i]ert an tei demenede!" (142), as well as in the bride's final lament:

"Or(e) par sui vedve, sire," dist la pulcele,
"Jamais ledece n'avrai . . ." (492f.).

46

The absence of joy is their sadness. But, in vv. 533 and 536, the term recurs, in its rich positive sense. The people of Rome cry out:

"Si grant ledece nus est apar[e]ude
D'icest saint cors n'avum soin d'altre munre. . . ."

And the narrator comments:

Unches en Rome nen out si grant ledice (536).

Finally, the absence of earthly joy becomes eternal felicity, when, through the miracle of Alexis' sainthood, his bride joins him in heaven, and the poet uses the term one last time (this passage is missing in *A* and partially missing from *P*, though *V* contains it in full):

Sainz Alexis est el ciel senz dutance,
Ensembl'ot Deu, e[n] la compaign(i)e as angeles;
E la pulcele dunt il se fist (si) estranges,
Or l'at od sei, ensemble sunt lur anemes.
Ne vus sai dirre cum lur ledece est grande! (606ff.)

The meaning of these episodes coincides with what the *Vita* has led us to expect, and the poet's careful art is clearly evident in his handling of the joy-sadness motif.[16]

The passages quoted also do much to further our understanding of the relationship between the OF text and its source. We have already described our poem's position with respect to the thematic material; it remains to be seen how the stylistic variations are technically achieved. Curtius (art. cit.), upon examining the poem's rhetorical figures and *topoi*, has shown them to be at once artfully conceived and typical of the time when it was composed; his conclusions in regard

[16] A recent German dissertation studies this motif: K. Gierden, *Das altfranzösische Alexiuslied der Handschrift* L: *Eine Interpretation unter dem Gesichtspunkt von Trauer und Freude* (Meisenham-am-Glan, 1967), 181 pp. I analyze this work in *RPh*, xxiv (1970), 128-137.

to the latter question are supported by Zumthor's study of the few other surviving literary works in Old French that antecede the *Song of Roland* (*L'Inventio dans la poésie française archaïque* [Groningen, 1952]). Yet, for our purposes here, we need merely recall that Curtius' and Zumthor's research proves the sophistication of the OF *Life*, its artistic integrity, and the validity, in principle, of applying critical approaches to it.[17]

Disregarding momentarily the thematic elaborations that characterize this *Life* with respect to its Latin source and recalling our poem's serious literary intention, one may define its technical originality as standing out especially in its use of the first-person narrator[18] and in its convincing adaptation of techniques of amplification.

The *Vita*, basically a clerical work, faithfully translates the composite Byzantine tradition. Literarily, it does not innovate. It is straight narrative; dialogue (or monologue) is used sparingly to vary somewhat—to heighten and illustrate—the narrative line. Thus, when Alexis goes to his bride we learn that "coepit nobilissimus juuenis et in Christo sapientissimus instruere sponsam suam et plura ei sacramenta disserere." He does speak and is directly quoted, but only briefly, when he tells her to receive and keep the presents he gives her. The pace is quick. The OF text, in which the narrator is retelling the story, operates quite differently: Alexis does not wish to anger his father, so he visits his bride; upon seeing the bed

[17] I record my thanks to Professor L. Friedman for reminding me of J.W.B. Zaal, "*A lei francesca*" (*Sainte Foy*, v. 20), *Étude sur les chansons de saints gallo-romanes du XIᵉ siècle* (Leiden, 1962). Though dealing specifically with the *Sainte Foy*, Zaal's approach, involving "hagiographic activity" in Gaul and the socio-religious conditions under which this activity was deployed, leads him to discuss the OF *Alexis*. His breakdown of rhetorical operations (ch. iii) is particularly valuable.

[18] As has been noted, works earlier than the *Alexis* have also relied heavily upon this device (*Passion*, *St. Legier*), but we shall examine in detail the "perfect fit" of the device within our poem's economy. (See the following section on *Narrative Economy and Ambiguity*.)

and looking at the girl, he remembers his heavenly Lord. The sexuality of earthly love is contrasted with Alexis' holy vocation, as in the *Vita*, but here the matter is presented in a double focus, that of the narrator and as though it passed through the protagonist's own eyes: it is translated into the character's gestures and words. (Later OF versions will interpolate here an even more explicit *descriptio*: e.g., the highly amplified *Roman de saint Alexis*—G. Paris' "rédaction interpolée du XIIIe siècle"—as well as the fourteenth-century monorhymed alexandrine text; the intermediary thirteenth-century "rédaction rimée" gives the idea: "Kant Alexis ot se femme veue, / Ki tant par est cortoise et bien creue / Et covoitose et blance en se car nue, / Et voit le cambre ki si est portendue, / Dont li ramembre de se cheleste drue" [G. Paris and L. Pannier, *La Vie de saint Alexis . . .* (Paris, 1872), 282].) The public is called upon to participate directly in the saint's choosing. The *Vita* records the story; the OF poem reenacts it, thanks to the narrator.

Lack of space prevents a full discussion of the problem within the present context, but a brief allusion to the play of verb tenses in the passage transcribed may serve to define somewhat more clearly this reenactment. All the older manuscripts of the *Life* show a low degree of contrast between the present, imperfect, and preterite forms. This is typical of much OF poetry; the contrast, though not entirely neutralized in all positions, remains richly ambiguous. The manuscripts, to be sure, are not always consistent: MS *L* reads *Cum veit le lit*, whereas both *A* and *P* use the preterite, *vit*; the latter is obviously more in keeping with the parallel *esguardat la pulcele*. Other noteworthy inconsistencies: v. 62, *L*, *P* give *prist*, *A* gives *prent*; v. 72, *L* offers *cumandet* (*P*, *cunmande*), as against *A*'s *duna*, etc. Similar play characterizes the *rédaction rimée* quoted above: *Kant Alexis ot se femme veue . . . / Et voit le cambre ki si est portendue*. Despite these inconsistencies, a kind of tense parallelism results in each case: the formally low-grade opposition between present and past engenders an open use of both tenses in alternation, even though

49

the modalities differ from manuscript to manuscript. Such usage appears so frequently in OF texts that most efforts to characterize present:past as a categorical opposition in that language have known scant success; the linguistic problem must be related to complex literary questions of genre, rhetorical design, and the like. Thus, since all texts of the *Life* offer analogous play, one may assume that not only the scribes of MSS *L*, *A*, and *P*, but also the "original poet," profited from the syntactic and literary freedom provided him by his language and by his choice of narrative framework in order to achieve certain expressive effects.[19]

The linguistic ambiguity—or partially free variation—of the tense contrast allowed the poet to reinforce, through alternation of preterite and present verb forms, the dual perspective of narrator and protagonist within the tale's rhetorical structure. Here is how it works. The story recounts a "past action" and thereby situates it historically for the listening audience. After Alexis looked at ("esguardat") the maid, he remembers his Lord ("Dunc li remembret de sun seinor celeste"): the formal distinction reflects the narrator's telling exactly what happened and its consequence for Alexis, but, at the same time, the effective neutralization of past and present as two "sealed" semantic and syntactic categories maintains the historical setting. The public is not only introduced to what Alexis did; it also experiences what it means to him. Rhetorically, the narrator's position is strengthened in regard to his public, and the listener is made to feel he is there at the happening. The narrator retells Alexis' story, using the OF syntactic "freedom," but—and this is revealing to students of that leeway—he does so as anyone, even speaking Modern French or English, might retell, in conversation,

[19] Studies of temporality in OF and OSp texts are numerous; many contradict one another. For an intelligent discussion of some of these (along with a rigorous defense of his own well-thought position), see M.M.G. Sandmann's rev. of F. Stefenelli-Fürst, *Die Tempora der Vergangenheit in der Chanson de geste* (Vienna-Stuttgart, 1966), in *RPh*, xxi:4 (1968), 570ff.

an episode in which he has figured, e.g.: "I went to New York and I see this guy who told me he'll get me a new car, cheap." To retell such an episode is, in part, to locate it historically and, in part, to relive it, experientially. The tense order is itself usually unimportant: what matters is the relationship (hence, the equally satisfactory, "I go to New York and I seen this guy . . ."). In the *Life* the relationship is adumbrated by the poet; the scribes then follow him rather faithfully in spirit, despite their purely formal differences, though, of course, as opposed to our colloquial English example, the poem's use of the device is made to fit a consciously intricate rhetorical scheme. The relationship conforms to the devices of narrator and protagonist that, when set in the oral narrative framework of the story, share, so to speak, the expressive burden. The artistry is considerable, not at all slap-dash; it reflects a conscious *mise-en-œuvre* of highly sophisticated oral techniques. Adaptation and even improvisation remain possible, since the actual choice of tenses and where they are used, though not entirely determined by caprice, is less significant than the fact that, conjointly, both form the parallel relationship. Meanwhile, such tense play constitutes the single most effective means at the poet's disposal for penetrating and revealing his protagonist's complex motivations. The hero becomes real to his French audience. The technique is surely no less effective—and far more incisive—than, say, Chrétien's more learned use of *oratio recta* when he describes the pangs of love suffered by Alexandre and Soredamor in *Cligés* (ed. A. Micha, *CFMA* [1957], vv. 618-1038).

The narrator's presence is also felt in his many direct interventions. Since the efficacy of the story depends on his establishing a satisfactory rapport with his audience, every effort is made to build this rapport into the tale, as when he intervenes with a paraliptic variant of what Curtius, in his *Europäische Literatur und lateinisches Mittelalter* (Bern, 1949), called the "unutterable topos" (*Unsagbarkeit*), i.e., his commentary upon Alexis and his bride's joy in heaven: "Ne vus sai dirre cum lur ledece est grande!" The narrator

51

protects the confidence his hearers have in him by associating himself, and them, in the narrative process. Thus, after describing Alexis' flight from Rome, he "explains" his switch from the saint's Syrian adventure to the situation he has left behind: "Or revendrai al pedre ed a la medre / Ed a la spuse qui sole fu remese" (v. 101).

The structure and sense of the narrator's mediating role are clearly elaborated at the very start of the poem. He utilizes the fact that his story concerns an old Roman saint to establish a sense of community between his matter, his audience, and himself. The topos of the "good old days" precedes, by some twelve lines, the "beginning" of the action: "Si fut un sire de Rome la citet." We are told how good our ancestors were who "ourent cristientet," and how the saint brought joy to our Roman forebears, how his holy body (or "person") saved his parents and bride ("Par cel saint cors sunt lur anemes sal- vedes" [v. 605]), how, finally, we too may be saved by Alexis' intercession, and see at last an end to the process of decay referred to in the previous opening lines:

Aiuns, seignors, cel saint home en memorie,
Si li preiuns que de toz mals nos tolget:
En icest siecle nus acat pais e goie
Ed en cel altre la plus durable glorie! (621ff.)

In short, the narrator officiates in the ritual through which his people may become like those Romans of yore whose salvation was assured by the presence, among them, of their holy man. His role is to "create" Alexis' real presence amid the northern French community. His understanding of that role therefore underlies the kind of stylistic elaboration one notes in passing from the *Vita* to the OF poem. The variation is designed to make that poem conform more accurately and effectively to the purposes of the hagiographic pattern from which it derives its substance.

None of the amplifications in the *Life* are artistically gratuitous. On the contrary, they contribute heavily to the text's admirable economy. The bride's second *planctus* is a case in point:

"O kiers amis, de ta juvente bele!
Ço peiset mei que (si) purirat [en] terre!
E! gentils hom, cum dolente puis estre:
Jo atendeie de te[i] bones noveles,
Mais or(e) les vei si dures e si pesmes.
O! bele buc(h)e, bel vis, bele faiture,
Cum est mudede vostre bele figure!
Plus vos amai que nule creature.
Si grant dolur or m'est apar[e]üde;
M[i]elz me venist, amis, que morte fusse.
Se jo [t'] soüsse la jus suz lu degret,
Ou as geüd de lung' amfermetet,
Ja tute gent ne m'en soüs(en)t turner
Qu'a tei ansemble n'oüsse converset:
Si me leüst si t'oüsse (bien) guardet.
Or(e) par sui vedve, sire," dist la pulcele,
"Jamais ledece n'avrai, quar ne po[e]t estre,
Ne jamais hume n'avrai an tute terre.
Deu servirei, le rei ki tot guvernet:
Il ne m'faldrat, s'il veit que jo lui serve" (476ff.).

The delicacy of this depiction of her sorrow needs no commentary; the passage moreover offers a weighty psychological and thematic gloss to the Latin source. (Incidentally, it also proves that, in *oratio*, our poet was quite capable of observing strictly sequential tense relationships, when it suited his needs; MSS *L*, *A*, *P*, and *V* all agree on this score.) The bride confirms Alexis' earlier admonition that no perfect love can exist on this earth; that, in effect, "la vithe est fraisle"; that "ceste lethece revert a grant tristur," since death is the universal destiny of "ices[t] s[i]ecle"; her waiting for "de te[i] bones noveles" and her pain at seeing his "bele buc[h]e, bel vis, bele faiture" turn to decay and dust ("Cum est mudede vostre bele figure!") translate his Christian vision of what earthly

53

love must eventually come to. The expression follows medieval convention perfectly. But the passage is also a superb representation of the bride's very womanly and constant love. It contrasts totally with the ferocious *dépit* displayed by Alexis' mother in her earlier complaint. A change in the poem's tone prepares us for the salvation Alexis achieves at the end.

Miss Hatcher writes eloquently (146f.) of the bride's failure to understand, until the final section of her *planctus*, Alexis' command to take Christ as her husband, but surely one cannot expect her to do so before she sees her husband's dead body. It is his death—and his sainthood—that permits her to say: "Deu servirei, le rei ki tot guvernet." Meanwhile, she has remained faithful to Alexis in life, the only way she knew how, by being his wife. She declares that she would willingly have shared his misery, if only she had known that he was there, under the staircase; she would have ministered to him: "Ja tute gent ne m'en soüs(en)t turner / Qu'a tei ansemble n'oüsse converset." Her love may be of the flesh, but potentially, it transcends this limitation. (Note that, v. 493, whereas MS *L* gives *Ne jamais hume n'avrai an tute terre*, *A*, *P*, and *V* are more graphic: *Ne charnel* [or *charnal*] *(h)ome n'avrai*.) If she expresses herself in fleshly terms, it is because these are the only words available to her, and, being concrete, they naturally suit the purpose of the story. Human beings have at their command no other kind of words. Saints too are flesh and blood; unless their *Lives* effectively depict them as our fellow-men, their purpose as saints is undermined. The bride's *planctus* offers poignant insight into how Alexis achieved his imitation of Christ, how, by participating in the mystery of the Incarnation, his saintly history acquired relevance for those who believed in him—those among the poem's public who, like his wife, remain faithful, body and soul, thanks to his miraculous example, in serving God.

Amplificatio, a technical literary device used repeatedly in the *Life*, consistently fulfills expressive functions like those just described. Many additional examples could be cited to confirm this statement. In fact, a thorough stylistic study of the poem is called for now that we have elucidated its intentions and described its historical contexts in terms of its functional patterns. Numerous questions remain unanswered. Might not our analysis shed light on the textual problem, for example? MS *A*, we recall, stops at stanza 110. Its text therefore ends at about the same place as the *Vita*. Does this coincidence mean that *A* is more faithful to the *Urtext* than, say, *L*, *P*, or *V*? Elsewhere *A* displays substantial agreement with *L* and *P* in its treatment of the bride (thus, her *planctus* is conveyed in amplified form, and the wedding-night scene remains the same). It would appear that stanzas 110 to 125, as given in *L* and, by and large, also in *P* and *V* (the salvation, Alexis and bride in heaven), do not constitute irrelevant addenda, but rather conform to the patterns governing the *Life*'s treatment of its Latin prototype. Structurally, *A* looks artificially incomplete, as though the scribe might have compared the poem on hand with its source and decided, somewhat clumsily, to "restore" the vernacular version to its pristine Latin form by lopping off the end. Little in the previous sections of *A* prepares one for the absence of the final episodes. The rhetorical and thematic structure of the poem, when projected against the *Vita*, includes of necessity the kind of stylistic modification I have described. Without the final episodes this modification would make little sense. But our analysis has permitted us to formulate this hypothesis, not to test it thoroughly; further rigorous stylistic investigation is required before definitive confirmation may be sought.[20]

[20] If Sckommodau's reasoning is correct, namely that *A* derives from an OF *Life* situated historically half-way between the *Vita* and the presumably later version represented by *LP* (and, fragmentarily, *V*), the growth of the *Life* would tend to render the history of its structural formation far more problematic. At best, the literary historian would have to cope with a "fragmentary structure," in a sense, with a contradiction in terms. The condition of *A* which, we recall, is itself composite, "corrupt" both from the angle of Sckommodau's hypothetical *Urtext* and in regard to the construct represented by *LPV*, does not, as Lausberg pointed out, make the task any easier. From

More complete analysis of the *Life* in conjunction with a similar study of other medieval European versions might well provide insights into the patterns of legendary constructs sufficiently powerful to illuminate the historical problem of the Roman Alexis cult. There is, we stated, a definite West-European Alexis tradition; within its frame the *Vita* may be seen as the bridge between these later offshoots and the earlier Mediterranean versions, the "watershed," as we called it. Some later Greek branches of the legend may be themselves traced to Rome (Roesler, *Die Fassungen* . . . , 2-23), and there is strong evidence that, ultimately, the fourteenth-century Russian vernacular text derives from the later Latin tradition. Yet the *Vita*, though ostensibly "Roman," is in spirit nearly as Eastern as its presumed Byzantine source. This is because it is the work of clerks—cultivated men—for whom *askesis* would not, in itself, have been a strange concept. There was no need to embroider on Alexis' motives nor to dramatize the implications of the poet as do the vernacular texts. The Eastern confessor-saint simply is; it is his pure

---

the evolutionary standpoint the situation is almost hopelessly conjectural; the structuralist sees a picture, by definition, a good deal neater.

Still another point deserves mention in this connection, namely that, although the kind of speculation that has tempted Lausberg (*ASNS*, cxci) leads him to declare—extraneously, for our purposes—that the OF *Life* was originally composed for a public of nuns (*Nonnenpublikum*)—*seignors* is a misreading of *serors* (307ff.)—in championing the excellence of *L* against Sckommodau's criticism he does appeal to poetic criteria similar to those we have employed in the present study. Thus, he muses that the "original" poet did indeed amplify upon his Latin source not only at the end but throughout the work: "Natürlich hat der Dichter die lat. *Vita* amplifiziert: das tut er überall, nicht nur am Schluss" (301). Lausberg's literary criteria prompt him to imply, if not to say outright, what we have suggested, namely that the scribe of *A* preserved an amplified version, but only up to a certain point. *L* does not, it would seem, amplify upon the text contained in *A* (except at the end) because, up to that point, *L* and *A* tell pretty much the same story in pretty much the same way. The degree of poetic amplification upon the *Vita* is approximately identical.

being that counts. What he does merely symbolizes in a graphic, gestural way—in iconographic fashion—his immutable status. Such could not have been the case in the West, where, we recall, developments of the legend focus ever more closely upon the saint's relationship with his bride, and utilize the cogent dramatic possibilities inherent in that relationship to drive their points home. In the West the saint's asceticism could acquire meaning only in the historical context of its precise effect upon others. We have repeatedly pointed out that the abstract is concretized in ways an Eastern writer would doubtless find utterly superfluous. Not for a moment could one imagine a Byzantine Roland, for example, whose destiny, as a Christian hero, is rooted in what he does and does not do, with his peers, in an obscure Spanish mountain pass. The *Vita* remains too close to its Byzantine model to develop what would be developed by the OF MS *L*, Massmann's Latin manuscripts, and the MHG MSS *A*, *F*, and *H*. Yet Rome is of the West; she did provide an "authentic" Latin version of the story. By creating a truly "Roman" context for the Alexis history, the tenth-century *Vita* offered the mythico-literary framework necessary for the implantation of that history in West-European soil, as well as the authority for the kind of literary processes to which the story would be subjected. Or, put another way, the *Vita* preserved the thematic structure we described and, within the scope of the operative hagiographic paradigm, legitimized the stylistic modifications that, we saw, were carried out in order to respond effectively to rhetorical needs. Hence it would appear that the problem of the tenth-century Roman Alexis cult could be profitably approached through a careful application of conclusions drawn from a thorough stylistic study of the later vernacular tradition.

NARRATIVE ECONOMY AND AMBIGUITY

Structural complexity and rhetorical framework, techniques of amplification and perspective, as well as the other categories

I have so far utilized, allow one to circumscribe the OF *Life of Saint Alexis* and, within limits, to appreciate its rich texture. By examining certain narrational workings, we have seen how effectively the *Life* participates in its hagiographic order, how, in short, the meaning of the saint's life has been brought home to its medieval vernacular audience. Let me now return more precisely to the question of narrative means and to what, provisionaly at least, we might refer to as "narrational quality." This will help clarify further our poem's historical and intrinsic importance.

I have already mentioned in connection with the poem's economy the fact of the bride's complex structural role as inherited from the Græco-Latin composite *Vita*. Her function in the story is pivotal. She belongs to a series that includes Alexis' father and mother, but she also enjoys a special relationship with her husband that is specifically contrasted with— opposed to—her being a part of that series. She is also to be identified affectively and, in a sense, generically, with Rome. Finally, she is rendered entirely sympathetic to the audience; one must be more firmly on her side than in the case of Eufemien, not to speak of Alexis' mother. (Indeed, one's sympathy for the bride necessarily detracts from whatever favor one might be tempted to bestow upon the mother: the two characters are to a considerable degree polarized.) Through the figure of the bride, we saw, much is accomplished; thanks to her narrative role, the story reaches us with a very lively directness.

Similarly, the first-person narrator, as device, reinforces the story's verisimilitude and its relevance. A certain burden of proof is discharged by the figure of the narrator, who, in and through his own person, relates Roman antiquity and his own Norman time. It is he, moreover, who creates the perspectives and their dovetailing that, to a large extent, involve the audience in what is going on. This is achieved thanks to the means provided by the typical give-and-take of dialogue inserted into the flow of the narrative: the public is a kind of silent interlocutor. Thus the play of verb tenses in the narrative proper (e.g., the wedding-night scene), which in turn is played off against the characters' appearing themselves on stage in order to speak on their behalf, formally, and their resorting to elegant *oratio* (e.g., the bride's second *planctus*). Conditions of vernacular literary diffusion in the mid-eleventh century favor the use of the narrator device, but, as we observed, the poem exploits this device thoroughly. A constraint is made over into a resource.

Use of the narrator device did not of course originate with the *Alexis*. But how thoroughly and smoothly this device is incorporated into the work may be seen by comparing the *Alexis* with the much earlier Clermont *Passion*.[21] This latter text also utilizes a first-person narrator in order to present the story. But despite his occasional use of the first person plural, this narrator takes pains to maintain his separate identity as narrator. He remains a very clerkish figure, obviously the good pastor conscious of his own learning and, one suspects, subservient to it; he is a kind of missionary. His text, as recorded, is larded with awkward Latinisms and ecclesiastical terms. Thus, when Jesus is crucified: "Fui lo solelz et fui la luna / *post* que *Deus* filz *suspensus* fure." Only rarely does the narrator-poet achieve a genuine fusion of the learned and the vernacular; the following example, however, attains an almost tragic eloquence:

> Ad epsa nona num perveng,
> dunc escrided Jhesus granz criz;
> *hebraice* fortment lo dis:
> "Heli, heli, per que·m gulpist?"

The effect derives from the narrator's confronting us with the event itself, isolated in all its pathetic grandeur; a kind of

---

[21] The *Vie de saint Legier* would have served our purposes just as well. Thus the didactic narrator explains why he is about to tell his story: "Domine Deu devemps lauder / et a sos sancz honor porter; / in su' amor cantomps dels sanz / que por lui augrent granz aanz." He goes on: "Primos didrai vos dels honors / que il auuret ab duos seniors."

"realism" is involved. Ostensibly, the narrator ceases to "mediate," but in so eliminating himself, however temporarily, he manages to identify himself more completely with his material and his narrative task—to blend, as it were, into the stuff of the poem.

However, such success is relatively infrequent in the *Passion* and consequently, to a far greater extent than in the *Alexis,* one remains aware of a "story" being recast in palatable form by a specialist in such matters on behalf of an untrained audience. The "specialist" is more or less detached from the inner workings of the poem. Though in fact this situation also prevails in the *Alexis,* the degree to which the narrator device is successfully integrated into the poem—exploited—is incomparably greater. The narrator belongs to the work; he is never detached from the substance of what is going on. What he tells is at all times as pertinent to him as it is to his audience, not only the fact that he is narrating, or making available, the essential Christian story to a public that without him would have been deprived of the experience.

The narrator constitutes a part of the narrative economy of the *Alexis.* Yet the poet-narrator's position at the halfway point between the poem's learned sources and his audience lends itself to a certain number of ambiguities and, indeed, points to other ambiguities also linked directly to the work's narrative economy. The narrator performs the poem, as a deeply involved actor might. Nevertheless, while belonging to the group comprising the audience—the "we" he uses in the text includes himself and the public—he constitutes for that audience its only immediate channel to the story and its meaning. Unlike the narrator, whether explicit or implicit, in so-called "realist" modern novels, his presence and authority are real, even tangible. As we noted earlier, the narrator officiates in the poetic ritual; his function is priest-like:

Puis icel tens que Deus nus vint salver,
Nostre anceisur ourent cristientet,
Si fut un sire de Rome la citet;

Ric[h]es hom fud, de grant nobilitet.
Pur (h)o[e]c vus di, d'un so[e]n filz vo[e]il parler (11ff.).

The *Alexis* surely loses a great deal when read as one would read a short-story today, much as a play loses when experienced in other than stage conditions.

The ambiguities I alluded to derive, then, from the functional burden assumed by the narrator. His role is quite complex, some aspects of it at times even seeming to contradict others. On the one hand he is omniscient; he contains the story—its facts, the characters' motives, the moral sense, the values—and in a great variety of ways he transmits all these things. But, on the other hand, he takes pains to underscore his own humanity:

Las! malfeüs! cum esmes avoglez,
Quer ço veduns que tuit sumes desvez.
De noz pech[i]ez sumes si ancumbrez,
La dreite vide nus funt tresoblier.
Par cest saint home doüssum ralumer (616ff.).

The narrator sees himself, and is projected, as the vessel, the means, of Alexis' history.

The more completely one submits to how the story is told, to its narrational quality, the greater one's chance of being properly impressed by what is said. The ambiguities inherent in the narrator's position are themselves exploited by the poet for the greater glory of his *matière*. These ambiguities constitute, then, still another rich source of expressive value and intensity. The listener identifies himself with the narrator by participating with him in his dialogue. One is supposed to make oneself over into a repository of the history: "Aiuns, seignors, cel saint home en memorie" (621).

Similarly, within the economy of the *Life*, the functional burden of, say, Alexis' mother or his bride reflects complexities that are richly ambiguous. The bride's structural role is, as we saw, quite complex and these complexities are fully utilized in the narrative. Thus, she is contiguous to the mother, belonging to the same family-series and yet in opposition to it. In this way her real love for Alexis and her fidelity are literarily related to the comprehension we suspect she has, in her own way, of her husband. Meanwhile, Alexis' abandonment of frail earthly love is justified. Logically, of course, none of this really holds together, but, in literary terms, it works out admirably well. The myriad juxtapositions that make up the poem's organization permit—indeed compel—this interpretation. What Alexis' mother represents is, to all practical purposes, determined by her various positions with respect to the organization: she does much to authorize, in the poem, Alexis' wariness about attachments of the flesh. Conversely, her passionate anger and distress fill out the poem's affective dimension; there is nothing routine about her. The miracle of literature is, of course, that all these aspects are simultaneous and mutually effective.

The narrational quality of the *Alexis* is perhaps best described as compact. Compactness within the work's economy, resulting from the multi-utilization of all possibilities contained in the various elements that make up the poem's fictional structure, virtually constitutes the hallmark of the *Life*. The constraints of this kind of fiction are fully exploited. Each character, each gesture, and each event are all charged to the limit, but the story remains admirably simple and uncluttered. One is especially impressed by how the poem's technical virtuosity is entirely given over to the enactment of the hagiographical ritual, how perfectly fiction is placed at the service of religious value. The very ambiguities I have hinted at above impart a sense of the richness and the mystery that must remain at the heart of any ritual play of this sort. The same kind of poetics is put to use in the Clermont *Passion*, of course, but, as we observed, the intensity here is far greater.

Obviously, the kind of compact narrative we find in the OF *Alexis* is closely related to the style of liturgy, with its heavily symbolic colorings. When one repeats with the poem that Alexis has spent seventeen plus seventeen years in his new life (away in Syria, then back in Rome), the figure of (almost?) thirty-four years must be associated with the imitation of Christ: the resonance is liturgical in kind. The *Life* uses a liturgy-framework of reference; however amplified or muffled, the resonance is built in. And allegorical parallelisms may well play a role in this context. Thus, as Manfred Sprissler has very aptly suggested in connection with certain Latin versions of the Alexis story (*op.cit.*, 60), the saint's spiritual marriage in heaven, where he and his bride at last live in joy, recalls the wedding of the Church (*sponsa*) and Christ (*sponsus*). Again the *imitatio Christi* provides the key. In this way the *Life* makes use of the resources of the *Song of Songs* tradition. This kind of accretion fills out and deepens the narrative: the events of the story and their spiritual repercussions play on one another in the working out of the text. It is impossible to assign a clearcut purpose to each potential ramification, but one must recognize that the ramifications are there and that they are functional within the narrative operation.

The poetic framework of the *Alexis*—its "literariness," so to speak—exploits the devices and kinds of allusion I have referred to here. A heavy texture results, despite the poem's brevity and sobriety. References play off upon one another, generating through contiguity and juxtaposition (as well as the linearity of the narration) deeper insights and, surely, a more profound sense of the saint's mission. Because of this "literariness," precisely, contradictions are resolved that in other, less poetic, contexts would have been unacceptable to reader or spectator. The poetic organization permits a highly intense, even explicit, expression of the saintly ideal as this ideal was understood in historical or existential terms in mid-eleventh-century France. Poetry thus serves the myth, in all the complexity of these terms. As we have seen, however, it is only by paying extremely close attention to the details of poetic organization that one stands a chance of grasping what the *Alexis* is about. The event is clarified—it is somehow brought down on earth—in the narrative. The possibilities of the saintly paradigm, already sketched out in the Græco-Roman *Life*, are further elaborated through these poetic means. But let us not forget that, concomitantly, as the saint's truth was served in our text, so did the poem come to illustrate the possibilities inherent in the kind of narrational quality I have attempted to describe. It is true that our poet knew that fictional means could be intelligently placed at the service of a vision of history. It is no less true that his having done so (and the ways he did so) contributed immeasurably to the development of fiction.

CHAPTER II

The "Song of Roland"

INTRODUCTION

THE *Song of Roland* evolves around the image of an old king whose mission is the establishment and constant defense of an empire beloved of God. This central idea is common to the entire *Roland* tradition, including MS *O*, the splendid Oxford Digby 23, the assonanced OF-It MS *V⁴* (Venice, ms. fr. IV), as well as the variously dated rhyming versions *C* (Châteauroux), *V⁷* (San Marco, f. fr. VII), *P* (B.N., f. fr. 860), *L* (Lyons, 984), *T* (Cambridge, Trinity College, R. 3-32), and the other texts of which a good many, like the *Ruolandes Liet*, by Konrad (ca. 1132), are in foreign languages or in Latin.[1] Roland's story—his struggle, his victory and death at Roncevaux—is, so to speak, an episode in the *geste* of Charlemagne. Indeed, Einhard's report of the death, on August 15, 778, of

---

[1] These texts have been edited and/or translated (e.g., *Ronsasvals*), at times photographically reproduced in the monumental *Les Textes de la Chanson de Roland*, Raoul Mortier, General Editor, Paris: I, *La Version d'Oxford* (1940); II, *La Version de Venise IV* (1941); III, *La Chronique de Turpin et les grandes chroniques de France, Carmen de prodicione Guenonis, Ronsasvals* (1941); IV, *Le Manuscrit de Châteauroux* (1943); V, *Le Manuscrit de Venise VII* (1942); VI, *Le Texte de Paris* (1942); VII, *Le Texte de Cambridge* (1943); VIII, *Le Texte de Lyon* (1944); IX, *Les Fragments lorrains* (1943); X, *Le Texte de Conrad*, traduction de Jean Graff (1944). Let me at this point call attention to a recent, as yet unpublished, Princeton dissertation entitled LE ROMAN DE RONCEVAUX: *Prolegomena to a Study of the Manuscript Tradition of the* CHANSON DE ROLAND, by E. Heinemann (1970); the title of this work is self-explanatory. The bibliography of the *Roland* is far too lengthy to be listed here. However, I should like to recommend Pierre LeGentil's fine introductory study of the poem, *The* CHANSON DE ROLAND, tr. by F. F. Beer (Harvard, 1969).

a certain Roland, prefect of Brittany, at the hands of Basque marauders in the Pyrenean mountain pass—the earliest surviving mention of Roland—is included in his *Vita Karoli* (ca. 822), i.e., as a paragraph in Charles' life. Gaston Paris has evoked what must have been the impact of Charles' image upon those to whom we owe the *Roland* and the other songs from the *cycle du roi*:

"Il n'est pas besoin de dire que le côté impérissable de Charlemagne n'est pas celui par lequel il a frappé les peuples sur lesquels il régnait. Sa puissance, sa grandeur, sa justice, sa piété, voilà les qualités par où il était saisissable aux masses. Elles se le représentèrent généralement comme un vieillard chez lequel la sagesse n'excluait pas la force, entouré d'hommes extraordinaires qui étaient les ministres de ses volontés, régnant magnifiquement sur des pays innombrables et soumettant tous ses ennemis à ses lois. Telle est la première et la plus profonde image qu'on se fit de lui. . . ."[2]

[2] Gaston Paris, *Histoire poétique de Charlemagne*, éd. de 1865 augmentée de notes nouvelles (Paris, 1905), 450. Since the *Song of Roland* is so widely known, extensive summary is hardly necessary. Traditionally, critics divide it into four parts: I. Sent against his will on an embassy to the pagan King Marsile at Zaragoza, Ganelon elaborates a plan thanks to which the Saracens will be able to attack and, by sheer weight of numbers, overcome the Frankish rear-guard; thus will Charlemagne be deprived of the backbone of his fighting force: the twelve peers, including Roland. II. The betrayal has taken place and the Saracens are about to attack the twenty thousand Franks; Olivier begs his friend Roland to sound the *oliphant* and summon Charles, but Roland refuses; the battle is engaged, and the French are killed, one by one, though only after inflicting terrible losses on the enemy. Finally—this time against Olivier's wishes—Roland sounds the *oliphant*, so that Charles may avenge them; he sounds the horn with such force that doing so bursts his temples; the last to die, Roland lies victorious, master of the field and ready to be received in Paradise. III. Charles returns and, with the help of God, destroys Marsile's army as well as a second even more powerful Saracen force assembled by Baligant. He removes to Aix, his capital, with Bramimonde, the Saracen queen, and with Ganelon imprisoned. IV. Ganelon defends himself, alleging that he did not commit treason. His relative Pinabel offers to defend him; no Frankish knight accepts the challenge. Aude,

Gaston Paris goes on to say that the image of Charlemagne suffered a series of changes that little by little so entirely transformed him that, finally, all "signification historique" was destroyed. Yet, he adds, even those poets who contradict most flagrantly the *donnée primitive* of Charles' story "[en] subissent encore l'influence malgré eux jusqu'à un certain point."

A good deal has been written concerning the problems that lie latent in Gaston Paris' analysis. Reviewing this material, however, teaches one as much, if not more, about nineteenth- and twentieth-century intellectual history as one learns with respect to the values and meanings of the poem. Are we not after all, just like Gaston Paris' masses, also impressed by the power, the grandeur, the justice, and the piety of Charlemagne? Are we not *anguissus* before the spectacle and the idea of Roland's tragedy? Whether one speaks, precisely, of the "poet's art" or of the "voice of tradition"—or of whatever one wishes to stress—the legend, by acquiring poetic and narrative form, hardly loses historical significance. On the contrary, it takes on increased historical value—meanings from which it is impossible to escape, even today. And, even more intensely than in the *Alexis*, such value is built into the very structure of the poem; to ignore it is to condemn the work to irremediable malfunction. Consequently, one must conjoin the concepts of historical value and poetic function. In a very deep sense the *Song of Roland* is history conceived, that is, brought to the light of day, in literary and poetic terms. (In this connection compare the analogous binomials of Bédier and Menéndez Pidal: *poète-route, tradición-poesía latente.*) The history of the poem succeeds in flowing into the mainstream of civilization without, for all that, becoming an abstraction. By reviewing some characteristics of the *Roland*'s historical and political structure, we might be in a better posi-

---

Roland's betrothed and Olivier's sister, dies upon learning of her fiancé's death. Finally, Thierry accepts the duel, wins, and Ganelon is executed. The poem ends with Charles' being summoned once again to defend the borders of Christendom.

tion to restore, or to render explicit, the *signification historique* that Gaston Paris had thought forever lost.

In describing what we called the "saintly paradigm" and its relationship to the legendary material that grew up around the personage of Saint Alexis, we were able to secure a purchase on the OF *Life*. Analogously, an approach to the Oxford *Roland*[3] ought to be attempted on the basis of the "historical matter" or truth the poem was designed to convey, namely the order that is built around the person of Charles: the empire. Once again, however, caution must be observed. I do not mean to suggest that within the poem lies a political logic that in any significant way resembles the logic of an expository treatise; considered a mere apology for the imperial system, or worse, as propaganda in France for the moribund Carolingian party, the *Roland* would soon reveal itself a hopeless maze of seeming contradictions. Something, rather, of imperial doctrine is subsumed into the assumptions of reality made by the poem; the political Augustinianism[4] current in the eleventh century is welded into a work that is literarily coherent despite its seemingly contradictory glorification of the French Royal House. Irreconcilable in themselves as logical proposals, these ideas, as presented in the structure of the poem (e.g., empire, projected against the kingdom of France), complement each other and, indeed, are made to fit into a comprehensive view.

[3] There is no need to dwell on the fact that no scholar has done so much as Gaston Paris to help restore a sense of this "signification historique," despite his modesty in this respect. Also, one is struck by the high calibre of mind of many scholars who have, at one time or another, taken an interest in the *Roland*: Bédier, Faral, L. and A. Foulet, Lot, Siciliano, Menéndez Pidal, A. Castro, Becker, Spitzer, Rychner, Delbouille, and many others. Few literary works have been so favored!

[4] Among the indispensable studies of this problem, see: Robert Folz, *L'Idée d'empire en occident du Ve au XIVe siècle* (Paris, 1953); H.-X. Arquillière, *L'Augustinisme politique$_2$*, (Paris, 1955); P. E. Schramm, *Kaiser, Rom und Renovatio* (Leipzig-Berlin, 1929); F. A. fr. v.d. Heydte, *Die Geburtsstunde des souveränen Staates* (Regensburg, 1952); Ernst Kantorowicz, *The King's Two Bodies* (Princeton, 1959).

The literary artistry of the *Roland* poet—of the man, or men, or tradition(s) to which we are indebted for the juxtapositions that make the Oxford text work out the way it does—is nowhere clearer than in the tensions he creates on the basis of such ideological dichotomies. His empire, it seems to me, is a living institution compared to the nostalgic but intellectualist vision of empire present in Dante and elsewhere in the later medieval tradition.[5]

CHARLEMAGNE

Charles, king and emperor ("Carles li reis, nostre emperere magnes"[6]), incarnates his empire. But, if the poetic Charlemagne is confronted with what we know "externally" of the historical one (in Gaston Paris' sense), we see that, no more than the *Alexis*, the *Roland* is hardly concerned with precise accuracy as we nowadays have come to understand it. Nevertheless, a number of traits are common to both the poetic character and the historical personage:

La siet li reis ki dulce France tient.
Blanche ad la barbe e tut flurit le chef,
Gent ad le cors e le cuntenant fier:
S'est kil demandet, ne l'estoet enseigner (116ff.).

The portrait has been idealized, of course, but does not contradict the (equally literary) sketch given by Einhard (*Vita Karoli*, ch. xxii). Moreover, in the poem, Charlemagne is old, very old; his age is patriarchal and would tend to stem the gap separating the time he lived and the present of the

---

[5] In addition to Dante's *De Monarchia* let me cite St. Thomas Aquinas' (and others'?) *De Regimine principum*, to which I shall refer more extensively later.

[6] I quote here from the easily accessible bilingual edition made by Joseph Bédier, definitive version (Paris, n.d. [printed 1964]); subsequent line-references will be made to this edition. Other handy editions include those by F. Whitehead (Blackwell, 1947) and A. Hilka$_6$, rev. by G. Rohlfs (Tübingen, 1965). All of these rely almost exclusively on the Oxford text.

poem—a notion further justified by the *trouvère*'s use of the first-person witness, Marsile: "Men escient dous cenz anz ad passet" (524). Obviously, the poet took extraordinary liberties in his telling the emperor's *geste*. Although Charles had gone to Spain and had even fought there, the recounting of this adventure in the poem corresponds but slightly to historical fact. Legends and actual happenings blend with no apparent line of demarcation. Now then, Charles' double epithet, *reis* and *emperere*, hints at the manner of his construction; he is unique, of course, but he is "king" and "our emperor." Within the poem he is represented on two rather distinct levels as well, though at all times he does remain himself, very much a single person. Thus, on the one hand he is a man of flesh and blood, "historical" and intimate—"Li empereres se fait e balz e liez" (96)—who is, as the line suggests, at times joyful, but who, perhaps even more often, feels himself to be sad and old—"De France dulce m'unt tolue la flur" (2431)—weeping the loss of his knights, among them Roland, upon his return to Roncevaux. Yet on still other occasions Charles—one is tempted to say Charles the Emperor—is revealed as an almost superhuman personage. It is he who receives the Angel Gabriel's visits, he who has been chosen to hold in trust the vast, virtually supernatural empire upon which rest the hopes of all Christendom. His very slumber is made adjunct to this exalted status; dreams assail him and, in dreaming, he clearly participates in an activity at once mysterious and necessary to the accomplishment of the divine Will. Like Moses and the prophets, Charles retains his humanity, his real "historicity," at the same time he functions as God's spokesman. (Unlike that of the saint, Charles' role is not ostensibly modeled upon an imitation of Christ.) As a man he is more than *primus inter pares*, yet his very designation as God's workman on earth underscores his humanity. Being Charles, both "king" and "our emperor," relates him to us as at once of us and over us.

The dual character of Charles in the poem recalls a letter the historical Charlemagne is reputed to have sent Pope

Leo III. According to this document, the emperor is entrusted with a mission of combat while "the pope raises his hands toward God, so that, by his intercession, the Christian people might be everywhere and always victorious over the enemies of His holy name."[7] Charlemagne combines both functions: he combats without respite in the defence of the faith, but he is also a spiritual leader, the old king commanded by the Angel Gabriel to lead his armies to the "land of Bire," and, concomitantly in the poem, God's vicar, or spokesman, on earth. The poem's concentration upon the figure of Charles stresses the political rather more than the purely spiritual side of things. Thus, we gather, by declaring fealty to Charles' person, early ninth-century Europe as well as those who similarly respond to the universe of the poem, whether of the eleventh, twelfth, or twentieth centuries, may realize a sense of magical community for the first and last time—or for always, or both—in Western Christian history. Declaration of fealty is a kind of rite (cf., "*nostre* emperere magnes") that the narrative of the poem is designed to explain and explore. Note, incidentally, the power here of the adjective *nostre* which, unlike the more common respectful *mes/ mon*, was usually applied only to God and the Virgin (*Nostre Dame*). It was such a sense of *community*, or nostalgia for it, during the subsequent degradation into feudal *society*, that, symbolized perhaps in the relationship of Charles and the twelve peers (here, obviously, an image calqued on the New Testament), the *Roland* and other poems of the *cycle du roi* bring so poignantly to mind. (One recalls that, in his *Song of the Saxons* [ca. 1200], the later epic poet Jehan Bodel stressed the identification of the truth of the *cycle du roi* with its representation of what today we might call the meaning of the French Crown: "La coronne de France doit estre si avant,/Que tout autre roi doivent estre a li apendant" [14f.].)

[7] Quoted by Arquillière from the *Monumenta Germaniæ Historica Epistolarum*, IV, 136ff.; *op.cit.*, 115. As Arquillière puts it: "Dans cette conception théocratique, le rôle actif et dominant appartient au prince, le pape est délégué au ministère de la prière."

Within the world of the *Song of Roland* Charlemagne maintains communications between the will of God and human brotherhood, the body politic. In this way he too participates, though obliquely, in certain hagiographic patterns. But this is handled in very special ways. During his four appearances before the emperor never once does the Angel Gabriel speak of personal matters; his concern is always political. But when what he says is made over into Charles' concern, then the political is personalized, i.e., transformed into something quite real, as authentic as Charles' feelings of joy and pain, of sadness or delight. Beginning with v. 2525, just after the destruction of the Frankish rear-guard, Gabriel, in a dream, warns Charles of the battle to come:

> Karles se dort cum hume traveillet.
> Seint Gabriel li ad Deus enveiet:
> L'empereür li cumandet a guarder.
> Li angles est tute noit a sun chef.
> Par avisium li ad anunciet
> D'une bataille ki encuntre lui ert:
> Senefiance l'en demustrat mult gref.
> Carles guardat amunt envers le ciel,
> Veit les tuneires e les venz e les giels
> E les orez, les merveillus tempez
> E fous e flambes i est apareillez:
> Isnelement sur tute sa gent chet.

One of the strangest passages in the whole poem follows; Charles is permeated with the supernatural, which he understands only through premonitions and against which, very humanly, he is helpless. In a most magical context he is but a man:

> Li reis en ad e dulur e pitet;
> Aler i volt, mais il ad desturber.

It is Charles as emperor, of course, who struggles with the *granz leons,* but it is a Charles whom the poem has humanized by depicting his fear and foreboding. Then, once again, the angelic messenger appears and orders the king to undo his arms and repair to Roncevaux (2845ff.). Later, when Charles, wounded in battle against Baligant, seems to waver, Gabriel encourages him: "Reis magnes, que fais tu?" (3611). The emperor recovers his strength: "Fiert l'amiraill de l'espee de France" (3615); note the very epic double metonymic play: the "sword" of "France," identifiable with Charles on two counts—the man and his sword, and himself as France's protector. The fourth time Charles is visited by Gabriel is, of course, at the end of the poem, at which time he is once again summoned to gird his sword and set out for the land of Bire. Although personally unhappy, tired, and weeping, he will, as emperor, perform his duty to God, for such is his condition. He is emphatically not the tragic individual that Roland is and, potentially perhaps, that Ganelon might be, because, though but one man, he is politically also many.

Structurally, then, Charlemagne's role in the poem is unitary: he imposes a logic upon the various events that occur in the work (treason; victory and death of Roland; punishment, vengeance; trial and execution of Ganelon). And the logic derives both from what Charles does within the poem as well as from what he is, i.e., his historical, or real, being. The two sources of this logic are, so to speak, organically blended. Similarly, one might add, the poetic force of Charlemagne's name went a good deal further even than the precise allusions to it in the *Song of Roland* or, for that matter, in the bare framework of his biography. In the *Légendes épiques*₂, IV (Paris, 1921), Joseph Bédier collected various testimonials of Charles' popularity during the period encompassing the eighth to the twelfth centuries (437-469). He recalls Pope Urban II, exhorting the French to arms at the 1095 Council of Clermont (translation mine): "May your souls be moved and excited by the deeds of your ancestors, by the prowess and grandeur of King Charlemagne and of his son Lewis and of your other kings, who have destroyed the pagan kingdoms and pushed forward the borders of the

Holy Church" (456f.). The poetic resonance of Charles' name functions within the new—yet "traditional"—context of crusade rhetoric. In "reality," then, Charles is also poetic. Other examples quoted by Bédier or by Gaston Paris, for that matter, border upon the marvelous, e.g., nearly defeated Christian soldiers rallying about a miraculously present King Charlemagne, just arrived in their midst to lead them to ultimate victory. Such apparitions are so purely poetic that they seem to be due to, or otherwise incorporated into, the image constructed by the *Roland* poet(s).

In the poem, then, the character of Charles is rarely documented, literally authenticated, or even rounded out, because the poet had no need to do so. (It is thus that we must answer those who have criticized the poet for creating in Charlemagne a pale, uninteresting personality.) His double nature, as described above, is immediately related in the minds of those who heard the poem chanted to a tradition either oral or written (probably both) that was known, at least in broad outline, by everyone. King, emperor, old, white-haired, a man spoken to by God and for whom miracles are performed (as when, for example, the sun is commanded to halt its trajectory, vv. 2449ff.), yet, at the same time, a being whose humanity is subjected to the pains of this world—these are the elements freely drawn upon and, to a considerable degree, binarily opposed as well as exploited by the *trouvère*. (The connotations, including those of the "chosen" Christian people, suggest the patriarchal leaders—Moses, Joshua—of the people of Israel.) Charles' portrait remains selective, however. Thus, his lubricity, though mentioned by Einhard and alluded to in other poems, is never hinted at in the *Roland*, unless, perhaps, the episodes concerning Charles' *caitive franche*, Bramimonde, widow of the pagan King Marsile, whom he takes back with him to Aix and whom he has baptized (this term lends itself to *double entendre*), constitute an extraordinarily sublimated reflection of this character trait.

Hard to define, but nonetheless significant in connection

74

with what Charles represents in the poem is the tension between the real political situation of eleventh-century France and the idealized concept of unity present both in the thought of the time and in the poem. Charlemagne's structural role, we observed, is unitary; moreover, he has the same function as a historical referent. Though Hugh Capet's election to the French crown in 987 consummated definitively the political break-up of the Empire that had already advanced quite far by the accession of Otto I to the imperial throne (962), the successors of Robert the Strong considered themselves the heirs of the Carolingians, whom they called in their diplomas "antecessors" rather than "predecessors."[8] They wished to perpetuate a kind of ideal link between their state and the imperial principle and past. Charles' story authenticated their own story. Thus they had recourse to the *sacre*, a Carolingian institution, in order to stress their legitimacy. And constant reference to Charlemagne in their diplomas helped offset accusations of usurpation made by their Carolingian opponents. Moreover, the *sacre* remained symbolically powerful when used to counteract the feudal fragmentation that had been permitted to occur throughout the ninth and tenth centuries. Charles was made to serve the unitary interests of the monarchy in the old Gallo-Roman territories as well as the claims to legitimacy of this monarchy against an empire that had become increasingly Germanic. "France," as a concept, is comparable to the old "empire"—a land whose king endeavored to make his authority felt upon the feudal lords in much the same way as the emperor had done with respect to the *reguli* in former times.

Furthermore, the Capetians expended great effort in rendering their rule hereditary; each of the first several kings felt obliged to associate his son (*rex designatus*) with his

---

[8] See Ferdinand Lot, *La France des origines à la Guerre de cent ans* (Paris, 1948), 121; for a detailed discussion of these matters, by the same author, *Les Derniers Carolingiens: Lothaire, Louis V, Charles de Lorraine (954-991)* (Paris, 1891) and *Études sur le règne de Hugues Capet et la fin du Xᵉ siècle* (Paris, 1903), esp. ch. i.

own reign before his death. Here too the Carolingian *sacre* was called upon to emphasize the legitimacy of the Capetian dynasty and to assure its projection into the future. In this way even a "separatist France" generated a kind of political mystique that, far more completely than any other man or institution, Charlemagne symbolized, indeed incarnated. He constitutes the historical focus of the political myths operative in Capetian France, and, as Jehan Bodel's above-quoted prologue shows, this role, both literary and political, became traditionally associated with his person. Through the legitimacy of Charles, Capetian France found itself capable of perpetuating the ideal dimension proper to the medieval view of the body politic as a magical *communitas*, and, obviously, of articulating this ideal dimension in terms of a distinctly Carolingian heritage or symbolism. As we shall observe, the *petite France* and the *grande France*—"kingdom" and "empire"—of the *Song of Roland* were never meant to correspond to precise geographic dimensions; they are rather geographic symbols of spiritual values that the poet endeavors to fuse in his work. Charles as historical referent renders the fusion possible. "France," in the larger, "imperial" sense, is Christendom, led and sustained by Charles in a never-ending journey to virtue and salvation. Within the larger France, the geographical entity "France," a feudal concept and the nucleus of the Capetian kingdom, plays the part assigned to it, leaven to the dough: *gesta Dei per francos*. Despite the separation of Capetian France from the Carolingian Empire, the memory of Charlemagne could be utilized in the political tensions of, say, the tenth and especially of the eleventh century. The ambiguity of these tensions could be exploited: the history or myth of Charlemagne contained a truth that could and did go beyond a mere nostalgia for a golden age of the remote past as well as the considerations of *Realpolitik* indulged in by a legitimacy-conscious Capetian dynasty. Enough reality adhered to the myth that it easily became a political ideal whose possible implementation was not to be lightly cast aside.

76

What might be called the "binary impulse," the force that actualized Charles' meaning in terms particularly appropriate to poetic, or epic, expression, derives, of course, from the crusades: "The pagans are in error [*unt tort*], the Christians are righteous [*unt dreit*]!" There is no need to seek out complicated reasons explaining why the popular imagination of 1070 chose Charlemagne as the prototype of the crusading king. Already in the year 1000 (after a century of minor wars and skirmishes throughout Europe) war between Christians and Muslims broke out in Italy; the struggle was carried on in Spain and, later, was brought to the Orient. The first expedition, organized in large part by Cluny, took place in 1063; it included many French participants. In 1095 Pope Urban II convoked the Council of Clermont at which the crusade policy that was to lead to the conquest of Jerusalem in 1099 was worked out. In these crusades France played a major role: the four principalities that made up, in 1099, the entirety of the conquered territories in the Holy Land were French ("French," Aquitanian, and Norman). Yet frequently men of great importance in the crusading ranks were *adoubés*, i.e., soldiers who had undergone rites of "military consecration." These *chevaliers*, whose allegiance was not to a feudal lord but rather to an international order in which could be found a curious mixture of Roman discipline and Germanic fidelity (*Treue*), multiplied throughout the eleventh century.

This notion of knighthood derived perhaps from the old concept of *miles Christi*;[9] it implied, in theory if not always in practice, a hierarchy of values located above the feudal system and the belief that effective action against Islam re-

[9] This idea is advanced by Paul Zumthor, *Histoire littéraire de la France médiévale* (*VIe-XIVe siècles*) (Paris, 1954), 100; "[chivalry] donnera, à un certain idéal de droiture. . . , une forme fixe, susceptible de multiples développements littéraires et profondément enracinée dans l'ancienne conception métaphorique du *miles Christi* . . . elle donnera, au niveau de l'individu, poids et corps à la notion de Chrétienté."

quired political unity rather than feudal separatism. The "dubbed knight" was expected to be the servant of all Christendom, not of any given lord. The sheer size of the Christian military adventure brought poignantly to mind the need for a strong, united front in Europe. No single "nation" could suffice in the task. Though at times given political entities—kinds of "nation"—bore the brunt of the military activity, they usually did so in the name of Christendom or of the empire, as did certain tenth-century Leonese kings, who called themselves "emperors" in their diplomas. The medieval mind never did conceive of the crusades as a "national" venture. Thus, the European dedication to crusade activity involved, on several counts, a truly symbolic identification with the Empire of 800. (This identification occasioned numerous anachronisms in the *Roland* itself, which combines in an ideal temporal dimension—an *ævum*—concerns of a "Carolingian past" and of a later era; the literary tradition perpetuates this anachronistic state—the mythology—well into the thirteenth century. The legends or myths informing, e.g., Villehardouin's view of crusading and his account of the taking of Constantinople, are replete with such anachronisms or "timelessness." In Joinville's *Vie de saint Louis* the focus is quite different; he merits close study for that reason.)[10]

The temporal problem, i.e., Charles' historicity vs. his abstraction out of time ("over two hundred years old"), pervades the complex relationship between Charles and Roland. Roland the nephew is conscious of being his uncle's

---

[10] In connection with this problem of time I think it may well be relevant to ponder Alfred Adler's careful application of the distinction between the "figurative" (related to Neoplatonic and Augustinian thought) and the "individualized" (or Aristotelian and Thomist doctrine) to, respectively, the *Queste del saint graal* and the *Mort Artu*. Time in the former tends to resemble *ævum* and the "figurative" nature of the *Roland*, whereas the second of these two works suggests a more precisely delimited and—for lack of a better term—"real" chronology. See "Problems of Aesthetic versus Historical Criticism in *La Mort le roi Artu*," PMLA, LXV (1950), 930ff.

vassal, i.e., of blood relations and a feudal connection. But it is a feudalism transposed into an ideal *communitas*; both vassal and lord are engaged in the accomplishment of a transcendental mission. Roland the *miles Christi* best serves his task by professing allegiance to Charlemagne. The poem presents the structure of the kind of inspired feudalism in which the ideal Christian knight of every century serves to the best of his ability an ancient, indeed immortal, Charlemagne. There is nothing in Roland with which the eleventh-century feudal knight could not ideally identify himself. And his well-defined place in the social structure would permit proper relative self-identification on the part of listeners and observers of the poem—both "within" (e.g., Aude, Roland's *fiancée*, who dies when she hears the news of his death at Roncevaux) and "without" (the public). Along with Olivier and the other peers, Roland constitutes a link between the *ævum* incarnated by Charlemagne and earthly time. Even today, I venture to say, it is through Roland and Olivier—as well as through Aude and Thierry—that we, as readers of the poem, approach Charlemagne. We approach them all together, of course, through their relationship, i.e., the archetypal construct of lord, twelve "peers," and faithful vassal. (Interestingly, Ganelon—whose punishment is accomplished, thanks to Thierry—advised Marsile to "get at" Charles precisely through the twelve peers; Charles' destruction, he averred, would follow soon upon that of this relational construct. He was, of course, mistaken.)

EMPIRE

The emperor's personal mission and the mission of the empire derive from God. Both are sacred, yet both are worked out by and through men. (Another manifestation of epic binarism—from now on I shall refer repeatedly to the mechanics of this binarism.) As the secular arm of the Church, the empire organizes the material and spiritual resources (courage, morale) of the age in the struggle against

79

the Infidel. Because he is Charles' principal support, the knight must impose upon himself a pure and humble morality; this is the lesson implicit in Roland's personal tragedy and even in Ganelon's destruction. *Corruptio optimi pessima* finds a counterpart in the epic formula—here applied to Baligant, Charles' archenemy—"Deus! quel baron, s'oüst chrestientet!" (3164). The knight's sword is a gift from heaven; his strength therefore depends on how completely he follows God's will. The empire, Christendom, stands for a strong state, in the medieval sense of "strength," capable of responding to the needs of a Europe launched upon the crusades. The *Song of Roland* portrays such an empire. How does it do so?

Although "empire" (*emperie*) appears only once in the Oxford manuscript, a number of terms designating political entities are used with various degrees of frequency. The most common of these are *reialme* (<REGIMINEM + REGALEM), *regne* (REGNUM)—especially *regne* and *regnet*—though *regnet*, being a bit more concrete (REGNATUS/—M means "thing or area governed"), perhaps has feudal overtones of "fief." Moreover the poet uses the terms rather indiscriminately, applying them both to Christendom ("France *le regnet*" [694]) and to the (Spanish) Saracens ("d'Espaigne *le regnet*" [1029]). It is curious that whereas Charles is consistently referred to as *reis* and/or *emperere*, *emperie* is not used to describe his territory. There is no opposition between *reis* and *emperere*; so far as I can see, the titles seem to be rather complementary. Indeed both *reis* and *emperere* are frequently used not only by themselves but also in conjunction as epithets or partial epithets in apposition to *Carles* or to *Carlemagne*, as in the following randomly picked cases: *Carles li reis, nostre emperere magnes* (1); *Li empereres Carles de France dulce* (16); *Carlemagne le rei* (81); *li emperere Carles* (740, 2846); *Carles* (or *Carlemagnes*) *li reis* (2892, 3750). *Reis* being the more familiar and more "French" term in the eleventh century, one might hazard a guess that the poet rendered the word *emperere* a bit more familiar to

his audience by such indiscriminate substitution. The similarity of position within the phrase or with respect to *Carles* contributed to a kind of semantic contagion in which the familiarity and loyalty engendered by *reis* spread as well to the grander, more foreboding (and perhaps foreign!) word *emperere*. Charles is thus both king (i.e., French feudal lord) and emperor (above feudal relationships); he is at once subjected to and superior to the laws and uses of feudal political organization. Does not this word-play tend to confirm that the eleventh- or twelfth-century audience probably felt that Charles derived from it and yet surpassed it?

Moreover *emperere*, in constant semantic juxtaposition to *reis*, conferred upon the latter word a special nuance, a grandeur that did not quite correspond to the everyday reality of medieval kingship. The feudal terminology with which the poem is rife undergoes a decided poetic metamorphosis equivalent to the idealism of the political vision expressed in the poem. It cannot be said that the poet is merely groping for a vocabulary that he takes, meekly and gratefully, from whatever source his poverty-stricken language puts at his disposal. The transformations occurring in the poem are too consistent to be the handiwork of chance and happy coincidence. Thus, when Charles is about to receive Marsile's messengers:

> Cil sunt muntez ki le message firent;
> Enz en lur mains portent branches d'olive.
> Vindrent a Charles, *ki France ad en baillie* (92ff.).

Charles' relationship to the italicized phrase is clearly feudal; the situation is one which anyone in medieval France would understand and even feel a part of. The expression *ki France ad en baillie* could only be applied metaphorically to the empire and would be so applied in order to render the concept more familiar and home-like; taken in a transcendental sense, it might be viewed as an expression of political Augustinianism. Interestingly enough, previous to this mention of France in MS *O*, the other references to *dulce France* are consistently imperial: *Li empereres Carles de France dulce* (16); *En France, ad Ais, s'en deit ben repairer* (36); *Francs s'en irunt en France, la lur tere / . . . Carles serat ad Ais, a sa capele* (50ff.). "Aix" as capital of "France," "Carles" as "emperor" of "sweet France," and the interchangeability of *Francs* and *Franceis*—the poem indicates upon each occasion that Aix-la-Chapelle is the capital of the France whose head is *nostre emperere* Charles.

As has been frequently pointed out, *France* itself is used in several possible meanings; the poet took full advantage of the semantic instability of the terms as well as of the ambiguities present in the dichotomy *France:empire*. Aix-la-Chapelle was never a French city, although it was, certainly, a Frankish one and, moreover, Charlemagne's historical capital. By the process of contagion I have just sketched, Aix does indeed become a truly French capital, and, even more important, the French capital becomes Aix; the capital of France acquires values that are "imperial." By the same token, *Franceis* and *Francs* merge: Frenchmen are heirs to Frankish—eventually Roman—imperial universalism. But, thanks to the poetic genius displayed in the *Roland*, the *Franceis* do not for that lose their identity which, since Charles' death, they have forged for themselves. The classing of the *échelles*, or order of battle, of *cil de France* (2999) in the Baligant episode breaks down into ten groups ordered as follows: (1) *Franceis*, (2) *Franceis*, (3) *li vassal de Baivere*, (4) *Alemans* (*si sunt d'Alemaigne*), (5) *Normans*, (6) *Bretuns*, (7) *Peitevins* and *barons d'Alverne*, (8) *Flamengs* and *barons de Frise*, (9) *Loherengs* and *cels de Borgoigne*, and (10) *baruns de France*. At first glance it would seem that this nomenclature is hopelessly confused, but such surely is not the case. Scholars have nevertheless puzzled over the problem. If, on the one hand, *cil de France* include the *barons de Frise* or *Alemans*, the term *France* would naturally tend to mean the old Carolingian empire at the moment of its greatest extension and of which Capetian or, for that matter, modern France would be but a small part. And the poem distinguishes between *Franceis* and *Normans*, an invalid, anachronistic distinction for pre-invasion Carolingian times. He is therefore neither consistently historical (eighth century) nor contemporary (eleventh century). Ferdinand Lot has attempted to describe the France of the poem and has taken stock of these difficulties:

"À côté des passages, si nombreux, où la France s'identifie à l'Empire, on voit que, dans l'idée de l'auteur, c'est le pays qui va du Mont-Saint-Michel jusqu'aux Saints (c.-à-d. Xanten ou Cologne, sur le Rhin), de Besançon jusqu'à Wissant sur la Manche. . . . Mais les 'Français' se distinguent, non seulement des gens d'Outre-Rhin et d'Outre-Loire, mais des 'Frisuns' (Hollandais), mais des Bourguignons (vallée de la Saône et du Rhône), mais des 'Loherengs,' . . . mais des 'Flamengs,' mais des Bretons, mais des Normands. . . . Ce sont les habitants du pays qui va de la Meuse à la baie du Mont-Saint-Michel et aussi à la Basse-Loire, puisque le comte Geoffroi d'Anjou porte l'oriflamme."[11]

On the one hand, then, "France" as the empire; on the other, what he has elsewhere called "la France de la fin de l'ère carolingienne et du début de la période capétienne." In short Ferdinand Lot has demonstrated the existence of, and confusion between, a "greater" Frankish *France* and another, smaller, political entity, and has shown that both correspond to equally true political realities. He is mistaken, however, in assigning them definite times and values, since such rigor on his part overlooks the fact that, in the *Roland*, the "confusion" was deliberately intended—or at least exploited—since the political vision is expressed here in poetic, not positivistically historical terms.

Neither "France" cancels out the other; the ambiguities, built, as we observed, on the opposition of *France:empire* as well as on the confrontation of *now:then* (for all oppositions

[11] F. Lot, *Études sur les légendes épiques françaises, V: La Chanson de Roland* (*À propos d'un livre récent*), first printed in *Rom*, LIV (1928), 374f., reprinted with the same title in a separate volume, "Introduction" by R. Bossuat (Paris, 1958), 275f.

are also by definition juxtapositions), constitute a source of richly poetic (and, once again, properly epic) expression. Rendering these ambiguities explicit tends to destroy them, but in what follows here I shall explicate merely in order to illustrate, with these examples, a certain functioning—the functioning of what the late don Ramón Menéndez Pidal, for different reasons, called "un poema historiográfico."[12]

If the "confusion" between the words *Franc* and *Franceis* in the year 1080 (or earlier) is linguistically comprehensible, given the poem's context, it is not any more difficult to see that the poet wished also to confuse Charles' empire and contemporary France; a throwback of a century or two would have incurred no difficulty for his audience. The past gives the present greater relief, but also a fusion takes place, quite simultaneously; a past history is dramatized by its narrational resituation in the present time. What then could be more natural than to conceive Charlemagne's empire physically in the geopolitical terms of the eleventh century? (Analogously, the *Alexis* poet makes sure his audience gets its proper bearings when he identifies his Roman story with "our ancestors.") The ambiguity of the notion of *France*—a concept floating, so to speak, in the temporal flow separating the year 800 from 1100 (and beyond)—is consequently an artistic *tour de force* of the first magnitude. The *Song of Roland* is very much concerned with the here-and-now, but, by constantly identifying France with Charles and his Christian empire, it succeeds in destroying that part of time which might be construed as a limitation. (That is the reason for so much scholarly confusion.)

Both Roland and Olivier are French, from the smaller

[12] Cf. Menéndez Pidal, *La* CHANSON DE ROLAND *y el neotradicionalismo* (Madrid, 1959), 429: "La razón permanente del interés épico es, pues, la apetencia historial de un pueblo que se siente empeñado en una empresa secular. La epopeya no es un mero poema de asunto histórico, sino un poema que cumple la elevada misión político-cultural de la historia; es un poema historiográfico. . . ." Let us recall also at this point J. Frappier, "Réflexions sur les rapports des chansons de geste et de l'histoire," *ZRPh*, LXXIII (1957), 1-19.

France. Their prowess as well as the favored position given
the *Franceis* in the imperial army exalt French heroism and
sense of origin. The poem seldom misses an opportunity to
sing the glories of France:

> La disme eschele est des baruns de France.
> Cent milie sunt de noz meillors cataignes;
> Cors unt gaillarz e fieres cuntenances;
> Les chefs fluriz e les barbes unt blanches,
> Osbercs vestuz e lur brunies dubleines,
> Ceintes espees franceises e d'Espaigne;
> Escuz unt genz, de multes cunoisances.
> Puis sunt muntez, la bataille demandent;
> "Muntjoie!" escrient; od els est Carlemagne.
> Gefreid d'Anjou portet l'orie flambe;
> Saint Piere fut, si aveit num Romaine;
> Mais de Munjoie iloec out pris eschange (3084ff.).

Never once does the poem even hint that these men might be
used to serve the secular or material advance of the French
kingdom, even within the empire. All military conquests are
achieved exclusively on behalf of the faith. After the capture
of Zaragoza, Charles orders his army to break the idols and
heathen images in the pagan temples while his bishops bless
the water to be used for the baptism of the vanquished pagans.
The French forces, acting as a kind of spearhead with respect
to the entire imperial army, are nevertheless completely as-
similated into it. Through their valor *cil de France* deserve
well of their native land by serving to propagate the true faith.
The poet of the *Song of Roland* constructs a political edifice
designed to be at once universal and Christian, but whose
spiritual and military center remains clearly France. Thus
Charles is both the Christian emperor and the king of France;
his political roots remain, so to speak, both Roman-Frankish
as well as Germanic-feudal. In no way do these concepts
clash in the poem as they so frequently did in medieval and
more recent history. The two notions are made to complement
one another.

Although subordinate to the idea of empire, the concept of a nascent French nationalism is given wide scope in the poem. It is encouraged to seek its highest expression within Christian universalism: *gesta Dei per* (Gallic) *francos*—no higher sense of national mission is conceivable. The attitude of the *Song of Roland* may therefore be contrasted with that, say, of Dante faced with the rise of the Italian communes. For Dante Florence's rise toward independence constituted a direct threat to Christian unity; his religious monism, like that of the *Roland* too, required a counterpart of political monism. Without an Empire all would be disorder and fratricidal war on the face of the earth. Less burdened by the heavy memory of Rome (to which Dante devoted one-third of *De Monarchia*), our poet was able to reconcile the new national energy and the imperial ideal. He was able to put this energy to good use whereas, in the fourteenth century, Dante could only fulminate against Florentine avarice.

Another term of great interest in the poem is the frequently occurring *chrestientet*. The word is first used during Ganelon's speech to Marsile:

E dist al rei: "Salvez seiez de Deu,
Li Glorius, qui devum aürer!
Iço vus mandet Carlemagnes li ber,
Que recevez seinte chrestientet;
Demi Espaigne vos voelt en fiu duner"(428ff.).

The second appearance of the word occurs some lines later, once again in a speech by Ganelon, this time directed to Charlemagne himself. He explains why Marsile cannot hand over the *algalife* to the emperor:

De Marcilie s'en fuient por la chrestientet
Que il ne voelent ne tenir ne guarder (686f.).

The next instance reminds one of the first. Marsile implores help from the old *amiraill*; he threatens to go over to the other side if aid is not forthcoming:

E, s'il nel fait, il guerpirat ses deus
E tuz ses ydeles que il soelt adorer,
Si recevrat seinte chrestientet,
A Charlemagne se vuldrat acorder (2618ff.).

In the thick of battle Charles speaks as follows to Baligant:

Receif la lei que Deus nos apresentet,
Chrestientet, e pui t'amerai sempres (3597f.).[13]

Finally, at the close of the poem, Bramimonde *creire voelt Deu, chrestientet demandet* (3980); the emperor *en Bramidonie ad chrestientet mise* (3990).

In each of these cases *chrestientet* is closer to Eng. *christianity* than to MFr. *chrétienté* (a term more adequately rendered by "Christendom"). In the *Roland*, certainly, *chrestientet* possesses no precise geopolitical value, although in one instance it might be construed to suggest one. The occasion is Turpin's passionate speech to the rear guard at Roncevaux shortly before battle is joined:

"Seignurs baruns, Carles nus laissat ci;
Pur nostre rei devum nus ben murir.
Chrestientet aidez a sustenir!" (1127ff.).

In all previously quoted occasions in which the term was used, *chrestientet* is inserted into the context of conversion. It is something that the pagan *has* or *receives*—like baptism—in order to merit salvation. Indeed, *chrestientet* is essentially synonymous to *chrestiene lei*, another frequently used formula. Not so in Turpin's speech, however; no conversion is intended, *chrestientet* means here the faith and the laws according to which Christians (**chrestiene gent*) live.

It may be said, I believe, without fear of distortion that

---

[13] One recalls the previous reference to Baligant: "Deus! quel baron, s'oüst chrestientet!" (3164). This frequent epic formula is echoed in the first part of the *Cantar de mio Cid*: "¡Dios, que buen vasallo, si oviese buen señore!"

Turpin's speech indicates the semantic path later to be taken by Fr. *chrétienté*. The context here is political—at least it has strong political overtones. King and religion are, so to speak, mentioned in the same breath. Once again the poem skillfully used contiguity to rub values belonging properly to one term off on another. Not only is dying for the king made equivalent to sustaining *chrestientet*, but sustaining *chrestientet* is accomplished by dying for the king. It is hinted that the true head of *chrestientet*—for the term definitely implies an organic institution—is precisely the king.

Nevertheless, the poem is never obvious. The equivalences are invariably expressed with subtlety. Thus the act of conquest implies immediately two things: the pagans are baptized and declare homage to Charles as their king. Baptism and political fealty are the inseparable consequences of surrender, implying thereby the closest possible association between becoming *chrestien* and a subject of Charles' empire. By imparting a political (and imperial) coloring to his religious faith as well as a sacerdotal value to the political order, he equates pagan surrender with an accession to higher realms. But, as I have suggested earlier, the poet had ample historical justification for his standpoint. Charles' own empire was so conceived (cf. the numerous baptisms of the Saxons). The poem goes still further, for times have changed: *Franceise gent* generates the concept of **chrestiene gent*, although the latter is never explicitly stated. The idea of "nation" is caused, so to speak, to interfere with the notion of *chrestien*, and the latter's universality is applied to *franceis*.

This particular case of contamination is accomplished in a way that, by now, has become quite familiar. The poem uses the terms *chrestien* and *franceis* in what might be described as almost identical contexts with only one clearly defined nuance distinguishing between them. Both terms serve to identify the subjects of the emperor; *Franceis* is used most frequently, but *chrestien* also appears quite often: *De chrestiens voelt faire male vode* (918); *Paien unt tort e chrestiens unt dreit* (1015); *Mult grant dulor i ad de chrestiens* (1679); *Li chrestiens te recleiment e crient* (3998). However, when *chrestien* is used as an adjective, it invariably modifies *lei* (*chrestiene lei* [85]; *la lei de chrestiens* [2683]), whereas *franceis*, of course, indicates geographic provenance: *franceise gent* (396, 2515) and *ceintes espees franceises e d'Espaigne* (3089). The term *lei* (except when used in the adverbial *a lei de*) possesses no immediate or pure secular value whatsoever, although, interestingly enough, it is applied to the pagan faith (*La lei i fut Mahum e Tervagan* [611]; *Tutes lor leis un dener ne lur valt* [3338]). *Franceise lei is thus equivalent to *chrestiene lei*, by implication if not by fact—a most curious state of affairs. *Lex*, originally a secular concept, but certainly influenced by the Old Testament tradition (Moses, etc.), also becomes a "magical" one; in this poem it is used in a context both secular and magical, and it is best translated as "religion." It is as though the poem were attempting to render the secular more magical and the magical somehow more secular.[14]

THE PAGANS

The dynamics of epic binarism also underlie the role played by the pagans in the *Song of Roland*. Many debatable, even doubtful, things have been said or written concerning the political, social, and religious institutions of the Saracens. The obvious parallelisms between Charlemagne's empire and the Saracen nation have been frequently alluded to and described. The pagans are usually "explained away." Thus, the poet—or the tradition—has been blamed for his naïveté calquing the Saracens upon a Christian model. At times he has been justified, but once again on grounds of naïveté: How

[14] "Law" in its modern sense of code of operational justice seems to be one of the semantic facets of *dreit* and *dreiture* in the poem, although, of course, nowhere does the modern concept of law come through clearly in any single word.

89

could he be expected to remain faithful to a political structure of which he had no real knowledge? He did not know enough to be accurate.

It will not do to approach this problem from the standpoint of what we know about the Saracens nor, for that matter, from the assumption of naïveté and folk-like simplicity. The poem itself must orient us. Clearly, the pagan body politic and religious viewpoint can hardly be considered either authentically Spanish or Muslim, except insofar as they, being pagans, ought to be opposed to Christendom. The pagans function as one of the terms of the opposition I alluded to earlier. It is in this context that one must grasp the fact that they worship a Trinity composed of Tervagant, Mahum, and Apollin (names that are epic stock and trade). Like their Christian adversaries, they too speak of *dulce France* and, amusingly, of *seinte chrestientet*. Although the poem utilizes foreign words to designate several of their titles (e.g., *amiraill, algalife*)—thereby showing that the poet was hardly averse to a bit of authentic local color when it suited his purpose—the pagans borrow heavily from Christian terminology: Marsile is *reis* and he is aided by his *baruns*, a special group of whom closely resemble the twelve peers (cf. *laisse* v). One recognizes here the familiar workings of opposition-juxtaposition and semantic (or structural) contamination.

Verses 3214-3264 describe the three groupings of ten pagan *escheles*. As in the case of the Frankish army, each of these *escheles* is made up of one nationality. Several of these are fantastic and/or anachronistic; some are unidentifiable today, but others seem closer to home: Slavs (*Esclavoz*), Huns (*Hums*), Turks (*Turcs*), Persians (*Pers*), and the like. There is even an *eschele* of demonic *feluns* whose skin is so tough they need neither *osberc* nor *elme*. At the beginning of the poem this Saracen unity was not so apparent. King Marsile, one of the pagan rulers, fought his own war against Charlemagne's army. Only after Charles' return to Spain following the disaster of Roncevaux and Marsile's defeat does empire measure itself against empire (I use "empire" here in its meaning of a political organization comprised of and superior to simple states).

Baligant, the only character who can be compared to Charles—indeed, in keeping with the notion of the dynamics of the epic binarism, I should say that the presence of Charles required and created a "slot" for Baligant[15]—is introduced rather late in the poem:

> Li reis Marsilie s'en purcacet asez:
> Al premer an fist ses brefs seieler,
> En Babilonie Baligant ad mandet (2612ff.).

He is the *amiraill* ("emir"), the head of Islam. Like Charlemagne, he is old: *Tut survesquiet e Virgilie e Omer* (note the "pagan" image). Before helping his beleaguered coreligionary and "vassal," he must summon troops from forty *regnez* (i.e., kingdoms obedient to him), and organize a vast navy to transport them, their baggage, and their animals from Alexandria to Spain. Similarly, of course, Charles had to bring his army from Aix; both rulers are fighting in border country. The poet spares no effort to depict Baligant's grandeur:

[15] The Baligant episode has been at various times attributed to later *remanieurs* or otherwise considered somewhat extraneous. Critics include such scholars as T. A. Jenkins, R. Fawtier, and L. F. Benedetto. The authenticity—i.e., old age—of the episode has been affirmed by, among others, P. Aebischer, "Pour la défense et l'illustration de l'épisode de Baligant," *Mélanges Hoepffner* (Paris, 1949), reprinted in *Rolandiana et Oliveriana* (Geneva, 1967), 211-220, and by M. Delbouille, *Sur la Genèse de la* CHANSON DE ROLAND (Brussels, 1954), "De l'Authenticité de Baligant," 32-61. The episode seems to be required by the inner logic of the poem. Even Bertoni, who held that the work would be better without it, was forced to admit that were one to amputate the Baligant episode from the *Roland*, "sa suppression laisserait des 'filaments brisés'!" (quoted by I. Siciliano, *Les Origines des Chansons de geste*, tr. par P. Antonetti [Paris, 1951], 88). Structurally, without Baligant the poem makes little sense; this fact helps support the preeminence of MS *O* in the *Roland* tradition.

91

> En sun destrer Baligant est muntet;
> L'estreu li tint Marcules d'ultre mer.
> La forcheüre ad asez grant li ber,
> Graisles les flancs e larges les costez;
> Gros ad le piz, belement est mollet,
> Lees les espalles e le vis ad mult cler,
> Fier le visage, le chef recercelet,
> Tant par ert blancs cume flur en estet;
> De vasselage est suvent esprovet;
> Deus! quel baron, s'oüst chrestientet! (3155ff.).

We are made to understand over and over again that, in Baligant, Charles has a worthy opponent. At Baligant's command the pagan host bows down before the standards of its gods as do the Christians during prayer. But there is, in this juxtaposition, a striking contrast between Baligant's invocation of *noz deus* and Charles' previous supplication:

> Des Canelius chevalchent envirun;
> Mult haltement escrient un sermun:
> "Ki par noz deus voel aveir guarison,
> Sis prit e servet par grant afflictiun!"
> Paien i bassent lur chefs e lur mentun (3269ff.).

Here are Charles' words:

> "Veire Paterne, hoi cest jor me defend,
> Ki guaresis Jonas tut veirement
> De la baleine ki en sus cors l'aveit,
> E esparignas le rei de Niniven
> E Daniel del merveillus turment
> Enz en la fosse de leons o fuz enz,
> Les .iii. enfanz tut en un fou ardant!
> La tue amurs me seit hoi en present!
> Par ta mercit, se tei plaist, me cunsent
> Que mun nevold poisse venger Rollant!" (3100ff.).

Charles' prayer resembles formally the prayers for the dying; it is movingly humble. As a Christian he puts his trust in the

92

Lord, a God whom he can address individually and whom he can exhort in terms of the history of other persons whom He has saved. The harangue of Baligant's priest, on the other hand, implies no god of love or freedom, but rather tyrants exacting a price for their protection. The opposition is many-layered. Essentially, however, what is lacking to the pagan view is any concept of charity, whereas the Christians, though rude warriors too and far from perfect, possess, in their filial relationship to God, a kind of *douceur* or softness born of love. Within the dramatic structure of the poem the pagans are clearly the villains and, of course, cannot be made out to be too sympathetic within that structure. There is no real Homeric sympathy for a Priam or a Hector here, except in that each pagan, including Baligant, may be seen as a kind of "potential Christian." Nevertheless, though both their religion and their "empire" are condemned, it behooves us to under-stand how this evil is depicted by the poet and what it means.

Pagan "evil" is not inherent in the person (witness Brami-monde's conversion); it is rather contingent upon their serving and submitting to false gods. As we noted, these false gods have little to do with authentic Muslim belief—the Moorish local color offers merely a symbolic structure for the poet's Christian ideology. The pagan divinity is essentially negative, conceived simply in anti-Christian terms; the poem exhorts us, as Christians, to steer clear of them. The polarity itself imparts sense to its members.

Locked in desperate hand-to-hand combat, Baligant and Charles symbolize the dichotomy of the two empires:

Ceste bataille ne poet remaneir unkes,
Josque li uns sun tort i reconuisset (3587f.).

Baligant states his position in this dramatic moment:

Dist l'amiraill: "Carles, kar te purpenses,
Si pren cunseill que vers mei te repentes!
Mort as mun filz, par le men esciente;
A mult grant tort mun païs me calenges.

Deven mes hom [en fedeltet voeill rendre]
Ven mei servir d'ici qu'en Oriente" (3589ff.).

For an eleventh-century audience these words, in opposition
to what Charles stands for, must have evoked what we today
might call the secular materialism present in the feudal or-
ganization—residual paganism allied to the fast-developing
secularization that, already in eleventh-century France, threat-
ened the mythical, "magical" status of institutions. There is
no mention of holy war in Baligant's speech, no allusion to the
Church, no concern for the struggle between the two faiths,
though, of course, a kind of "behavior" is contrasted with the
authenticity of Christian belief. The only relationship spoken
of by Baligant—by a man addressing the alleged murderer
of his own son!—is that of a master to a servant; his words,
incidentally, sound much like a diabolic temptation. What is
expressed, however, is a purely feudal relationship with no
transcendental aims. May Baligant's empire be described,
then, as a kind of compendium of diverse territories connected
by an oath of feudal service and held together mainly by fear?
Such would seem to be the case, especially after one hears
Charles' answer. Charles speaks of Baligant's proposition as
though accepting it would be a sin, but all he asks of his army
is his conversion; no purely personal ambition is stated:

Carles respunt: "Mult grant viltet me semblet:
Pais ne amor ne dei a paien rendre.
Receif la lei que Deus nos apresentet,
Chrestientet, e pui t'amerai sempres;
Puis serf e crei le rei omnipotente" (3595ff.).

Charles expresses the desire of receiving his worthy opponent
—worthy in that he too may be saved—in a community
formed by divine love. He would like to accept him as a
brother. Herein lies the difference between the notion of
empire, as conceived within the poem, and a simple union of
feudal states based on fear and force. In this passage—and
thanks to the structural configuration I have described here—

we are invited to see in Charles' ultimate victory, a victory accomplished with the active help of God, an attack directed not so much against Saracen enemies as against those among the faithful (the poem's contemporaries as well as all of us) who were perhaps forgetting that a political organization not primarily designed for God's service is a detestable and corrupt thing.

Medieval political theory usually saw the organization of the state in terms of precise goals always intimately related to salvation. Thus, St. Thomas Aquinas is most explicit in this respect. In his view men unite in order to live the good life. To govern is to lead:

"Est tamen præconsiderandum, quod gubernare est, id quod gubernatur, convenienter ad debitum finem perducere. Sic etiam navis gubernari dicitur, dum per nautæ industriam recto itinere ad portum illæsa perducitur. Si igitur aliquid ad finem extra se ordinetur, ut navis ad portum; ad gubernatoris officium pertinebit non solum ut rem in se conservet illæsam, sed quod ulterius ad finem perducat. Si vero aliquid esset cujus finis non esset extra ipsum, ad hoc solum intenderet gubernatoris intentio ut rem illam in sua perfectione conservaret illæsam" (*De Regimine principum*, I, xiv, in *Opera omnia*, XVI [New York, 1950], 236).[16]

Lead where? to virtue: "Ad hoc enim homines congregantur ut simul bene vivant, quod consequi non posset unusquisque singulariter vivens. Bona autem vita est secundum virtutem. Virtuosa igitur vita est congregationis humanæ finis" (*ibid.*). Here indeed is a sense of mission, though hardly a transcendental one. The following text brings us to the nonsecular *imperium*:

"Hujus autem signum est quod hi soli partes sint multitudinis congregatæ qui sibi invicem communicant in bene vivendo. Si enim propter solum vivere homines convenirent; animalia et servi essent pars aliqua congregationis civilis. Si vero propter

[16] According to the *Enciclopedia cattolica*, XII (Vatican City, 1954), 255, the text of *De Regimine principum* ought to be attributed to St. Thomas up to Book II, ch. iv.

acquirendas divitias, omnes simul negotiantes ad unam civitatem pertinerent; sicut videmus eos solos sub una multitudine computari qui sub eisdem legibus et eodem regimine diriguntur ad bene vivendum. Sed quia homo vivendo secundum virtutem ad ulteriorem finem ordinatur, qui consistit in fruitione divina, ut supra jam diximus; oportet eumdem finem esse multitudinis humanæ qui est hominis unius. Non est ergo ultimus finis multitudinis congregatæ vivere secundum virtutem, sed per virtuosam vitam pervenire ad fruitionem divinam" (237).

St. Thomas goes on to declare that if human beings by virtue of their own strength could achieve this end, it would incumb upon the royal power to lead them: "Tanto autem est regimen sublimius, quanto ad finem ulteriorem ordinatur." But, he adds, such a government is in the hands of the King who is not only man but God, Jesus Christ. Consequently, according to the New Law of the Gospel, kings must submit to the leadership of the priest, in particular to the authority vested in the pope. Though he departs here from the ideology of the *Roland*, St. Thomas stresses unity, employing an argument frequently invoked in the Middle Ages: "Ipsa tamen hominis unitas per naturam causatur: multitudinis autem unitas, quæ pax dicitur, per regentis industriam est procuranda" (xv, 238).

Thus, St. Thomas incorporates the level of virtue (the secondary, temporal, or purely "human" level) into the superior level or purpose of "divine fruition" to which the king must endeavor to lead his people. The fact that the very meaning of redemption involves complete immersion of the temporal into the spiritual indicates that *res publica* must be conceived in terms of the higher good. A political organization unable to lead toward this higher good would, in terms of this dialectic, be the worst of all. Though he does not approve of pluralistic government, St. Thomas has kinder words for the republic or an aristocracy than he does for a regime dominated by a single man but not given over to the pursuit of justice (i.e., salvation):

96

"Sicut autem regimen regis est optimum, ita regimen tyranni est pessimum. Opponitur autem politiæ quidem democratia: utrumque enim, sicut ex dictis apparet, est regimen quod per plures exercetur; aristocratiæ vero oligarchia, utrumque enim exercetur per paucos; regnum autem tyrannidi, utrumque enim per unum exercetur. Quod autem regnum sit optimum regimen, ostensum est prius. Si igitur optimo opponitur pessimum, necesse est quod tyrannis sit pessimum" (iii, 227).

Finally, he distinguished between the multitude of free men (*multitudo librorum*) and the multitude of slaves (*multitudo servorum*), the former being, of course, the Christian community. To what end are the enslaved subjects of the tyrant led? To the personal profit of their ruler, not to any purpose of common good.

The symmetry of St. Thomas' exposition is already present and structurally relevant in the *Song of Roland*. Charles' empire is composed of a union of free men who, under God and their emperor, strive for both human and divine justice. Conversely, the Saracens live in abject tyranny. Their gods, patterned on the biblical Mammon, are projections of human greed and lust. Thus, e.g., in the thick of battle, Baligant promises Apollin, Tervagan, and Mahumet that he will have statues of pure gold raised to them if victory is given to his forces:

"Mi Damnedeu, jo vos ai mult servit:
Tutes tes ymagenes ferai d'or fin . . . " (3492f.).

Exhorting his troops, the emir promises them women and wealth provided they fight well:

Li amiralz la sue gent apelet:
"Ferez, paien: por el venud n'i estes!
Jo vos durrai muillers gentes e beles,
Si vos durai feus e honors e teres" (3396ff.).

In a parallel speech Charles also promises land, but the context is quite different. And we may be sure that this contextual dichotomy was meant to be noticed:

Li emperere recleimet ses Franceis:
"Seignors baruns, jo vos aim, si vos crei.
Tantes batailles avez faites pur mei,
Regnes cunquis e desordenet reis!
Ben le conuis que gueredun vos en dei
E de mun cors, de teres e d'aveir.
Vengez voz fils, voz freres e voz heirs,
Qu'en Rencesvals furent morz l'altre seir!
Ja savez vos cuntre paiens ai dreit" (3405ff.).

Charles speaks of self-sacrifice and of *dreit* (a difficult word
to gloss); nothing of the sort is invoked by Baligant.

Earlier in the poem, before Baligant's intervention, the
pagans' relationship to their gods is shown in detail. After
their defeat, Marsile and Bramimonde rush to a crypt with
twenty thousand men in order to desecrate Apollin, Tervagan,
and Mahumet:

Ad Apolin en curent en une crute,
Tencent a lui, laidement le despersunent:
"E! Malvais deus, por quei nus fais tel hunte?
Cest nostre rei por quei lessas cunfundre?
Ki mult te sert, malveis luer l'en dunes!"
Puis si li tolent sun sceptre e sa curune,
Par les mains le pendent sur une culumbe,
Entre lur piez a tere le tresturnent,
A granz bastuns le batent e defruisent;
E Tervagan tolent sun escarbuncle
E Mahumet enz en un fosset butent
E porc e chen le mordent e defulent (2580ff.).

The passage serves to set in relief Charles' reaction to Ro-
land's death:

Ne poet muer n'en plurt e nes dement
E priet Deu qu'as anmes seit guarent (2517f.).

The pagans serve gods who have promised them money,
power, and sensual pleasure—all things of this world to

which no magical value adheres. Their régime, externally like the Christian empire, is set up merely to obtain these purely material satisfactions. It is therefore a tyranny. It is against this backdrop of tyranny that Charles' empire is projected. Within the structure of the *Roland*—a structure based on epic, not novelistic, alternatives—this political dichotomy permits no nuance or shading: The Christian empire is good, the pagans "unt tort." The shading occurs elsewhere, in the very process of contrast. As we observed, on a non-institutional or individual level the poet does stress a certain inherent human merit in persons within the pagan camp; they are corrupt only by virtue of the false gods they serve. And Ganelon too, after all a Christian, is corrupted by his passions and ends up serving false gods as well. Fidelity to Charles, then, is something more than mere feudal homage, although the pattern of showing one's faith is borrowed from the feudal mode. By the same token, pagan tyranny must, I believe, be appreciated here above all as an *internal* danger within Christendom despite the fact that it is ostensibly depicted as emanating from without. On the purely human level Baligant is a man—and, as such, admirable from several viewpoints—irrevocably condemned because not only is he without God, he refuses to receive Him. (And unlike the case of Milton's Satan, the structure of the *Roland* does not allow any suggestion of heroism in Baligant's refusal.) It is moreover perfectly logical that Marsile, who dies of chagrin at his ultimate defeat, is snatched away by demons (3647). The point is obvious, perhaps, but its very lack of subtlety underscores the godlessness of the pagan position and the fact that the Saracens are being judged specifically for their godlessness. The point could hardly be lost on an eleventh-century audience.

It is at this juncture that the greatness of the poet's art appears staggering. He uses a symbolic structure—Charles' empire and its struggle—derived both from traditional history and contemporary political theory (at once "imperial" *and* national in direction) in order to depict a *communitas* of

Christian heroes. It is this sense of the heroic Christian *communitas*, worked out, as we saw, in specific binary frameworks, that engenders the underlying epic force and value of the *Chanson de Roland*. As Américo Castro has put it: "La *Chanson* muestra el paradigma del orden supremo que enlaza el mundo visible y el mundo invisible."[17] The roots of the poem plunge deep into ground its listeners could conceive of as real: France, the crusades, Charles himself, feudal society, the empire, the divine order of creation. Yet by no means can one justify calling it, in the restricted sense of the term, a "French epic." Rather, its universality is such that it both confers upon and extracts from the concept of *France* (a poetic symbol) a value of vital participation in a Christian grand design. Spiritual meanings are imparted to geographical terms in such a way that the reader (or listener) is called upon to recognize the danger of "Saracenism" within himself. Similarly, the audience partakes fully in Charlemagne's endeavor, which, in turn, seems to be a kind of endless journey of penance, an extraordinary pilgrimage. Charles *is* emperor, but an important feature of the poem is its telling us what being *nostre emperere* implies.

Whereas it is true that Charles, like Roland and the other characters, is, as Américo Castro put it, a "result of the abstract and absolute expression of his being," his being holds our interest—even on the aesthetic plane—thanks to his incessant journey at the head of Christendom. The myth prevails. The abstractness of the imperial ideal and its Saracen

---

[17] Américo Castro, *La realidad histórica de España* (Mexico, 1954), 265. I disagree, however, with Professor Castro's subsequent distinction: "El poeta [of the *Roland*] mantiene rigurosamente separados el mundo de su experiencia inmediata y el plano poético en que flota su fantasía" (268). How, indeed, may one level be rigorously separated from the other? What is important is the connection between the two. Thus, I find more satisfactory E. Auerbach's notion of the *rapport* between the "reality of the flesh" and "authentic . . . reality." The connection between the two and, in a sense, the justification of the former lie in its "figurative" role; see *Scenes from the Drama of European Literature* (New York, 1959), 72.

100

counterpart are fully utilized in the poem, but, like the historical Charlemagne himself, they are transfigured. Both are relocated in a new and vital dimension of reality, albeit a magical one, a reality, in short, seeming to have little to do with the bread-and-butter concerns of everyday life. Yet the reality of the poem has so much to do with these petty concerns that it can transform a vulgar border skirmish in a mountain pass into a drama of salvation. The oppositions and juxtapositions that, in conjunction with one another, make up the empire establish it, quite precisely, as a poetic creation in the deepest possible sense of the term. The oppositional patterning reaches down, even, into the landscape at Roncevaux, in the haunting refrain:

Halt sunt li pui e tenebrus e grant, AOI.
Li val parfunt e les ewes curant (1830f.).

The poetry subsists, for that matter, in the Cornelian love of Aude:

. . . "Cest mot mei est estrange.
Ne place Deu ne ses seinz ne ses angles
Après Rollant que jo vive remaigne!" (3717).

The meanings I have hinted at in this discussion of the Christian vs. Saracen dichotomy are thus worked out through the same process of "contagion" or "contamination" that we observed in the resolution of France vs. Empire. Because these meanings—values—are hardly amenable to simple summary, because one must experience them in the relationships I have tried to isolate as well as in their concomitants—relationships one appreciates for their own sake—the coherence of the *Song of Roland* is fundamentally poetic. In this work the operative myth is poetic history. The degree of fusion of these two "components" is noticeably greater even than in the *Alexis*, where, as we noted, fiction, essentially, was placed at the service of an historically understood myth. In the *Roland* what is referred to—the reality of the poem—is even more entirely a matter of the kinds of patterns prevailing in the

101

discourse. These patterns organize the matter and impose their truth.

This patterning contains the fundamental artistry of the *Song of Roland* (even that of the Oxford version). Individual phrases are permeated with the principle of such patterning, but, of course, this does not preclude considerable expressive variation. The *Roland* is verbally much looser than the *Alexis*, with its tight stanzaic structure. As is well known, the diction relies heavily on formulaic stylization, though its tradition is probably every bit as much written as oral. The extraordinarily intricate and forceful structural patterning we have examined allows, indeed favors, it would seem, the freer, formulaic diction, with its amplifications, reductions, addenda, and the like. As a poem, then, the *Roland* behaves analogously to the Alexis legend. It is convenient and right to state that the *Song of Roland* exists in a number of very different MSS, whereas the OF *Alexis* legend exists in a number of poems (some of which, in turn, have various MSS).

The time has come to be somewhat more technical. Let us examine the structural operations of the binary patterns as these may be observed in the assembling of themes, characters, and certain scenes. The relationship of "authority" and "being" will provide a valuable and fruitful framework.

AUTHORITY AND BEING

It is Charles who incarnates *auctoritas* in the *Song of Roland*. It is also he who, more than any other person, provides the lastingness characteristic of *ævum*, the poem's temporal dimension. But his *auctoritas*, though deriving directly from God, is seldom deployed directly upon his subjects; Charles is not a despot. Rather it is they who reflect it and give it earthly meaning. For example, Charles is wise and nearly all-knowing. He is warned by a dream of the coming disaster at Roncevaux, and when Ganelon proposes Roland to lead the rear-guard, Charles answers:

. . . "Vos estes vifs diables.
El cors vos est entree mortel rage" (746f.).

A little later he weeps when Roland asks him for his bow.
Yet he is powerless to stop the tragedy. He is not, so to speak,
involved in action until the crescendo of the Baligant episode.
Then, during the judgment of Ganelon, he becomes once
again a pure authority.

Seldom have the judgment and punishment of Ganelon
received the critical attention they merit. The episode is
announced quite formally: "Dès ore cumencet le plait de
Guenelun" (3704), though, in fact, the death of Aude is
artfully interpolated, with v. 3734, before things get under
way. Ganelon is the victim of no summary execution. To be
sure he is removed from Spain to Aix-la-Chapelle, where he is
tied ignominiously to a post in front of Charles' palace and
where he is the butt of harassment on the part of serfs:
"N'ad deservit que altre ben i ait" (3740). The narrator
shares Charles' need of vengeance; we are conditioned for
Ganelon's destruction and, indeed, led to believe all will go
well. The king summons his barons and the trial "De Guenelen,
ki traïsun ad faite" (3748) begins:

"Seignors barons," dist Carlemagnes li reis,
"De Guenelun car me jugez le dreit!
Il fut en l'ost tresqu'en Espaigne od mei,
Si me tolit .xx. milie de mes Franceis
E mun nevold, quo ja mais ne verreiz,
E Oliver, li proz e li curteis;
Les .xii. pers ad traït por aveir."

But, quite dramatically, Ganelon answers:

Dist Guenelun: "Fel sei se jol ceil!
Rollant me forfist en or e en aveir,
Pur que jo quis sa mort e sun destreit;
Mais traïsun nule n'en i otrei."
Respundent Franc: "Ore en tendrum cunseill."

103

A new polarity emerges: Charles against a resurgent Ganelon. The traitor takes the initiative and the drama is heightened:

Devant le rei la s'estut Guenelun.
Cors ad gaillard, el vis gente color;
S'il fust leials, ben resemblast barun.
Veit cels de France e tuz les jugeürs,
De ses parenz .xxx. ki od lui sunt;
Puis s'escriat haltement, a grant voeiz:
"Pur amor Deu, car m'entendez, barons!
Seignors, jo fui en l'ost avoec l'empereür,
Serveie le par feid e par amur.
Rollant sis niés me coillit en haür,
Si me jugat a mort e a dulur.
Message fui al rei Marsiliun;
Par mun saveir vinc jo a guarisun.
Jo desfiai Rollant le poigneor
E Oliver e tuiz lur cumpaignun
Carles l'oïd e si nobilie baron.
Venget m'en sui, mais n'i ad traïsun."
Respondent Francs: "A conseill en irums."

The roles are reversed. Ganelon has taken revenge on a Roland who had done him out of his "gold" and "riches" (another "materialist" reference!); he did not betray Charles. The feudal apparatus seems tailor-made to Ganelon's purposes. His family protects him. Pinabel offers to defend Ganelon against all comers; whoever accuses Ganelon of treason must fight the champion. No one dares take up the challenge. On the contrary, whisperings among the barons favor exonerating Ganelon: "Let Ganelon off this time, let him serve the king in love and faith; Roland is dead, you will never see him again; neither gold nor riches [again!] will bring him back" (3800ff.). Much to his disgust they propose this to Charles (*laisse* CCLXXVI), with but one dissenting voice, that of Thierry, the brother of Geoffroy of Anjou.

One of the most significant passages in the poem follows upon this expression of crisis, *laisse* CCLXXVII:

104

Quant Carles veit que tuz li sunt faillid,
Mult l'enbrunchit e la chere e le vis,
Al doel qu'il ad si se cleimet caitifs.
Ais li devant uns chevalers, Tierris,
Frere Gefrei, a un duc angevin.
Heingre out le cors e graisle e eschewid,
Neirs les chevels e alques bruns le vis;
N'est gueres granz ne trop nen est petiz.
Curteisement a l'emperere ad dit:
"Bels sire reis, ne vos dementez si!
Ja savez vos que mult vos ai servit.
Par anceisurs dei jo tel plait tenir:
Que que Rollant a Guenelun forsfesist,
Vostre servise l'en doüst bien guarir.
Guenes est fels. . ."

Thierry offers to combat Pinabel.

Charles' authority takes on real meaning in what Thierry stands for: his being. *Auctoritas* is, so to speak, translated into action. The "binary impulse" of the poem—both in depiction of Charles' cause against Ganelon as well as in the interplay of the king's authority and the deed of his subject—provides the necessary framework for an extraordinarily profound idea. Note the description of Thierry, one of the few personalized portraits in the poem. (Charles, we recall, is shown as a warrior patriarch, Baligant is anti-emperor; Roland, the perfect *miles Christi*, and Ganelon, his opposite number, proud, handsome, evil.) Thierry is thin, slightly built, and slender; his hair is dark, as is his complexion; he is neither very tall nor excessively short. (Conversely, in Thierry's own words, his opponent, Pinabel, is proud: "Granz ies e forz e tis cors ben mollez" [3900].) Quite clearly, within the series of portraits given by the poem, Thierry is obviously designed to represent a kind of Everyman, a typical Frenchman with whom a member of the audience might physically identify himself. Charlemagne depends on this obscure, unprepossessing subject of his. Without

105

Thierry—without this *Français moyen*, without you and me—
Roland would not have been avenged and the mighty Charles
would have been cruelly defeated. Thierry's victory prompts
the Franks to cry out:

> ". . . Deus i ad fait vertut!
> Asez est dreis que Guenes seit pendut
> E si parent, ki plaidet unt pur lui" AOI (3931ff.).

Ganelon is executed and the poem ends with Charles' final
dream. Ganelon's trial and judgment, however, confirm the
wide-reaching quality of Charles' authority and, in a sense,
the moral quality of the *Chanson*. Furthermore, the episode
ties together some of the narrative threads; these range, in the
passage, from the functional dichotomies to the subtle associa-
tion of material wealth (witness the frequent references to
"gold" and "riches") with opposition to Charles. Everything
proceeds smoothly. The poem is able to exploit according to
its own genius the constraint of feudal—or Frankish—tradi-
tional justice. Charles' righteousness is vindicated in a way
that puts into practice what the poem represents. Finally,
thanks to Thierry's example, we understand once and for all
the purpose of character, of what I have called "being."

Charles' authority permeates the scene of battle at Ronce-
vaux no less thoroughly than in the episode we have just
examined. The epic structuring requires us to see that it is, as
it were, Charles' will that the French rear guard combat the
pagan hosts of King Marsile. Roland's ultimate salvation, just
like Ganelon's punishment, occurs as a vindication of Charles'
authority (and intuition), just as, on a still higher level of
action, Charles' victory over Baligant is at once testimony to
his faith in God and proof of the moral tasks entrusted to him.
His empire is consequently not only a community of the
heroic, but also, and perhaps even more strikingly, a com-
munity of the free—"free" in the theological sense of being
capable of choosing redemption. Meanwhile, from the view-
point of the poem's construction, Charles' omniscience, though
at times imprecise, fulfills an important purpose. It reminds

us of the tragic events before they actually happen and it provides these events with a properly supernatural setting. We are able to concentrate adequately upon the *exemplum* of fidelity and freedom the events eventually depict. Knowing beforehand what will happen to Roland, we are all the more impressed by the grace he learns to merit and to receive.

More ink has been spilled on the Roncevaux episode than on any other in the *Song of Roland*. Scholars have debated lengthily whether, in not sounding the *oliphant*, Roland does not sin with excessive pride or desmesure.[18] If one examines the episode in terms of the authority-being configuration we have outlined, Roland's behavior is fully justified. Let us see how this is technically achieved.

At the beginning of the episode we know who Roland and Olivier are: two of Charlemagne's twelve peers, two close friends and companions in arms. Roland is engaged to Aude, Olivier's sister. Roland is already very familiar to us. One remembers the proud, somewhat impetuous, but entirely loyal young man who clashed, at the beginning of the poem, with Ganelon in suggesting him for the dangerous job of ambassador to Marsile. (We recall too that Ganelon wished above all to get back at Roland—as well as to save his own skin—when he betrayed his erstwhile companions to the Saracens.) We know less about Olivier. He exists above all when paired off with Roland.[19] Like Roland, he is of "merveillus vasselage" (1094). As the Roncevaux episode pro-

---

[18] This very debated issue is adequately summarized by J.-Ch. Payen in *Le Motif du repentir dans la littérature française médiévale (des Origines à 1230)* (Geneva, 1967), esp. Pt. I, ch. ii. By and large I find myself in agreement with Alfred Foulet (*RPh*, x [1956-57], 145ff.), who shows, in effect, that, far from having sinned with pride, Roland possessed a true sense of what had to be done at Roncevaux.

[19] The very idea of pairing reappears in the fairly numerous instances of brothers named "Roland" and "Oliver," as recorded by Rita Lejeune in "La Naissance du couple littéraire *Roland* et *Olivier*," *Mélanges H. Grégoire*, II (*Annuaire de l'Institut de philologie et d'histoire orientales et slaves*, X [1950], 371-401). Cf. D. McMillan, *MLR*, XLVII (1952), 334ff.

gresses—that is, as the French rear guard (a portion of Charles' empire: its spearhead, in fact) combats Marsile's Saracens (an opposing part of Charles' enemies)—we become further acquainted with him. Olivier assumes relevance in counterdistinction to Roland within the framework of the Christian viewpoint. His "being" is clarified, then, both with respect to Roland and with respect to the battle against the pagan foe. (By the same token, Roland, too, assumes a sharper identity for us.) The Roland-Olivier dichotomy is worked out within the context of the Christian-Saracen opposition; it is designed to further the plot and, I believe, to render certain Christian values more explicit.

Not without serious premonitions of disaster, Charles and his Franks take off for France, leaving the twelve peers and twenty thousand French behind in the rear guard (*laisses* LXVI-LXVIII); eleven *laisses* are given over to describe the pagan preparations. These culminate in the following lines:

> Granz est la noise, si l'oïrent Franceis.
> Dist Oliver: "Sire cumpainz, ce crei,
> De Sarrazins purum bataille aveir."
> Respont Rollant: "E! Deus la nus otreit!
> Ben devuns ci estre pur nostre rei.
> Pur un seignor deit hom susfrir destreiz,
> E endurer e granz chalz e granz freiz,
> Sin deit hom perdre e del quir e del peil.
> Or guart chascuns que granz colps i empleit,
> Que malvaise cançun de nus chantet ne seit!
> Paien unt tort e chrestiens unt dreit.
> Malvaise essample n'en serat ja de mei" AOI (1005ff.).

What next occurs is nothing short of a narrative *tour de force*. Olivier observes the arrival of the Saracen army from atop a hill or mountain. He sees their mass, their gleaming and bejeweled helmets, their shields, their yellow enameled breastplates, and their pennanted lances. There are so many, says the narrator, that he cannot judge their number, and, overwhelmed, Olivier himself repeats: "Jo ai paiens veüz:/Unc mais nuls hom en tere n'en vit plus" (1039f.). He is afraid that on this day he and his companions may be defeated (1046).

The first of three confrontations between Roland and Olivier takes place in *laisse* LXXXIV: Olivier urges Roland to sound the *oliphant*; it is still time to summon Charles and the main body of the imperial army. All together they would make short shrift of the Saracens. But Roland refuses: "May it not please God that my family be blamed because of me nor *dulce France* fall into baseness." The argument continues. Olivier has seen the pagans with his own eyes; he knows their strength: "Nus i avum mult petite cumpaigne" (1087). Roland answers: "Melz voeill murir que huntage me venget" (1091).

Up to now the poem has simply polarized the two friends around the issue of whether or not to call Charles. At the beginning of *laisse* LXXXVII the polarization is given value: "Rollant est proz e Oliver est sage." "Prowess" is opposed here to "wisdom," though, as we noted earlier, both men are of "merveillus vasselage." (Just as the two friends are most contrasted, reason justifying the eventual reconciliation is provided.) Roland commands; the battle is engaged. Archbishop Turpin and the peers support their captain; Olivier fights as bravely as the others. His *sagesse* prompts him to speak bitterly to Roland (*laisse* XCII), but his *vasselage* causes him to urge on his fellow *baruns*. He is no Ganelon. Roland kills Aelroth, his "structural counterpart," Marsile's nephew. But, one by one, the French are struck down; *laisses* CIX-CXI hint at this loss. In *laisse* CXII the second confrontation between Roland and Olivier is already suggested. This time Roland takes the initiative in speaking to his friend:

". . . Oliver, compaign, frere,
Guenes li fels ad nostre mort juree.
La traïsun ne poet estre celee;
Mult grant venjance en prendrat l'emperere" (1456ff.).

109

Roland's tone is softer, one is tempted to say wiser, here than earlier; he is *preux*, however, and his softness and wisdom are a function of his being, of his *prouesse*. (In *laisse* cxv Turpin takes up Roland's argument: "Pur Deu vos pri que ne seiez fuiant,/Que nuls prozdom malvaisement n'en chant" [1516f.].) The battle continues. In *laisse* cxxviii a curious reversal takes place: Roland deplores Charles' absence. He asks:

> "Oliver, frere, cum le purrum nus faire?
> Cum faitement li manderum nuveles?"
> Dist Oliver: "Jo nel sai cument quere.
> Mielz voeill murir que hunte nus seit retraite" AOI
> (1698ff.).

The polarity is maintained: Roland decides to sound the *oliphant* and summon Charles, but Olivier objects that to do so now would bring disgrace on "trestuz vos parenz." Roland ought to have sounded the horn when there was still time to save the rear-guard. Now it is too late. Roland persists in his decision. Olivier, furious, swears to break off Roland's engagement to his sister Aude: "Ne jerreiez ja mais entre sa brace" (1721).

Olivier, the *sage,* explains his viewpoint: *Vasselage* and good sense are not folly, measure is better than *estultie*, and the French have died uselessly because of Roland's *legerie*. He goes right to the heart of the matter and blames Roland's *prouesse*, i.e., his very nature: "Vostre proece, Rollant, mar la veïmes!" (1731). Turpin intervenes in the quarrel (but Roland has said nothing), explaining to Olivier that Charles' army will at least bury the dead, saving them from being eaten by pigs and dogs. Roland sounds the *oliphant* with such strength that his temples burst. Charles and the French hear him; they prepare to return to Roncevaux.

The third and last confrontation between Roland the *preux* and Olivier the *sage*, is, of course, the most poignant of all. Few French remain alive. Olivier himself is mortally wounded in the back by a sneak attack. He calls out to Roland: "A grant dulor ermes hoi desevrez" (1977). Roland sees his wounded comrade, and, in sadness, he falls in a faint on his horse. Olivier can no longer see, so he does not recognize his friend. Thinking Roland is an enemy, he strikes him on his golden helmet, breaking it open to the nose-piece, but not hitting his head. Ironically, though without realizing it, Olivier resumes his former quarrel with Roland by coming to blows. Roland does not understand, but "softly, sweetly" he asks:

"Sire cumpain, faites le vos de gred?
Ja est ço Rollant, ki tant vos soelt amer!
Par nule guise ne m'aviez desfiet!" (2000ff.).

Olivier answers:

". . . Or vos oi jo parler.
Jo ne vos vei, veied vus Damnedeu!
Ferut vos ai, car le me pardunez!"

The almost dialectical movement of the three confrontations ends, then, in *prouesse* and *sagesse* rising above their respective categories. Their humanity takes over. Roland gives his pardon "here and before God," and the narrator explains:

A icel mot l'un a l'altre ad clinet.
Par tel amur as les vus desevred (2008f.).[20]

Both Olivier and Roland are free, just as Thierry will be; all serve Charlemagne and, in fact, through what they are (and do), they vindicate this authority. It seems to me that the polarity of Roland and Olivier helps affirm this freedom by contrasting it with Ganelon's traitorous rebelliousness at the same time that it provides deeper insight into the nature of *prouesse*. Olivier's *sagesse* is certainly not "wrong" (though

[20] Here is Bédier's translation of these lines: "À ces mots, l'un vers l'autre ils s'inclinèrent. C'est ainsi, à grand amour, qu'ils se sont séparés."

111

the analogous, but cowardly, wisdom of those who, when faced with Pinabel, preferred to dismiss charges against Ganelon points out its shortcomings); it is simply that Roland's *prouesse* is "more right." Ganelon, not Roland, is guilty of the massacre. But even more significant is the manner in which the whole passage, in all its complexity, demonstrates how the community of the free, that is, those who reflect most purely Charles' authority, must be based on love. The oppositions become juxtaposition, a fusion, at the moment of Olivier's death. A considerable complexity accrues to the *prouesse* and *sagesse*—the categories—incarnated by Roland and Olivier. A certain "jelling" occurs that tends to individualize these characters; they acquire full dimension as human beings. Once again, the poem remains faithful to its structure, managing to exploit marvelously what might well have been an overwhelming constraint. The individuality of the persons is affirmed by the same means used to explain the ramifications of the community, and, of course, the two play off on one another.

This sense of Roland's humanity is essential to the tragic implications of the events immediately subsequent to Olivier's death. About a tenth of the poem—some four hundred lines— follow the loss of Olivier and precede Charlemagne's arrival at Roncevaux. Apart from a number of verses that describe the death of Gautier de l'Hum and, especially, of Turpin, the entirety of these *laisses* is dedicated to Roland: to a Roland who has just taken leave of Olivier, i.e., of earthly friendships, and who fights on, knowing that he too must die, probably before his emperor returns. He is a completely sympathetic figure. Even those scholars who had found him guilty of *desmesure* speak, in this connection, of his repentance and regeneration.

There is no need to dwell on the last battles. Suffice it to say that after pronouncing Turpin's funeral prayer, Roland feels "que la mort li est près" (2259). He prays for the dead peers and, to Gabriel, on his own behalf. A setting is given— a natural, very epic-like stage—in which Roland's tragedy is played out. "High are the mountains, and very high the trees; four marble columns gleam there, and Roland falls down to the green grass." One recalls once again the obsessive refrain:

Halt sunt li pui e tenebrus e grant, AOI.
Li val parfunt e les ewes curant.
Sunent cil graisle e derere e devant
E tuit rachatent encuntre l'olifant (1830ff.).

Roland's solitude is heightened by this lyrical tone and tragic setting. His "being" is redefined with considerable power as he attempts to dash his sword, Durendal, to pieces; the sword acts metonymically to suggest, of course, Roland's chief meaning. But, as though that were not enough, Roland addresses his sword—himself—and recalls his own history: he has served Charles throughout the world. *Auctoritas* and being are here rendered explicit in their relationship as Roland prepares to die. Even in death, however, he acts out what, in life, he was summoned to do. The pagans have fled; Roland lays himself under a pine tree, facing Spain; he is the victor in this extraordinary battle. Only then, in *laisses* CLXXIV and CLXXV, does he confess himself to God. The rhythm is beautifully handled. In CLXXIV the narrator informs us:

Cleimet sa culpe e menut e suvent,
Pur ses pecchez Deu en puroffrid li guant AOI (2364f.).

In the following *laisse* Roland himself speaks:

"Deus, meie culpe vers les tues vertuz
De mes pecchez, des granz e des menuz,
Que jo ai fait dès l'ure que nez fui
Tresqu'a cest jur que ci sui consoüt!" (2369ff.).

And then comes the magnificent *laisse* CLXXVI, in which, highly condensed, the scene is recapitulated: Roland lies beneath the pine facing Spain; he remembers the many lands he has conquered, *dulce France*, the men of his lineage, finally, Charles, "sun seignor, kil nurrit." But he does not wish to forget his own salvation; he prays a very moving prayer of

113

the dying, begging forgiveness of the God "who resurrected Lazarus from death and who protected Daniel from the lions." The *laisse* ends with Gabriel taking the glove Roland had proffered to God, and with Saint Michael and an *angel Cherubin* who carry his soul up to Paradise. Roland's salvation is at the same time, then, a kind of epiphany, a revelation and manifestation of his being in these tragic circumstances.

The inner workings of the poem—its techniques of binary opposition and juxtaposition—bring out, starting with *laisse* CLXXVII, a very interesting development in Charles himself. No "time" elapses: "Roland is dead, God has his soul in heaven; the emperor reaches Roncevaux" (2397f.). Roland's humanity, so to speak, rubs off on Charles. Charles becomes here the person "who raised" the young Roland in his household: "U estes vos, bels niés?" And, as he weeps, so grieve the rest of the Franks the loss of their sons, their brothers, their nephews, as well as their friends and their "lige seignurs." At the very moment when the action of the poem is about to focus directly on Charles himself—for the next two thousand lines or so it is he who incarnates, with God's help, his own authority (revenge upon Marsile, the Baligant episode)—he is cast in an entirely human role. By well serving Charles, Roland has risen to salvation; in avenging, with incredible sadness, the death of his nephew, Charles lives his humanity, humbly, as it were, in space and time. *Auctoritas* has become flesh, even though, as we remarked earlier, space and time here are magical. We are prepared for the synthesis given at the very end of the poem, when, after having judged Ganelon (thanks to a Thierry who, in a sense, "imitates" Roland and the dead heroes of Roncevaux), Charles is called upon once again to summon his hosts (us?) in defense of Christians who "te recleiment e crient" (3998). He remains very much a man; his response is convincing:

> Li emperere n'i volsist aler mie:
> "Deus," dist li reis, "si penuse est ma vie!"
> Pluret des oilz, sa barbe blanche tiret (3999ff.).

114

POETRY AND VALUE

However trivial it might sound, one must never tire of repeating that the sense of the *Chanson de Roland* is intimately related to the way the work is put together, that, indeed, the poetry of this epic contains as well as modulates the values it expresses. The relationship between poetry and value may be stated in this fashion: the poem is just as responsible for creating the myths it propounds as these myths are responsible for generating the poem. As we noted earlier, poetry and history are even more perfectly fused in the *Roland* than in the *Life of Saint Alexis*. In the *Alexis*, fiction is employed to recount a legend in such a way that certain kinds of ritual responses may take place. Conversely, in order to grasp even minimally what is going on in the Oxford text, one must submit to its poetic order. The task is not always easy, especially for today's reader who cannot really experience the poem as it was meant to be experienced, namely, sung or chanted before a more or less populous audience.

Now that we have established the general structural patterns of the work and the relationships of these patterns to the meaning, it would be well, I think, to discuss in greater detail some of the specifically poetic techniques operative in the *Roland*—some of the devices of form that seem characteristic of the poem and that do much to prove its artistry. In a number of instances, as we shall see, certain constraints are made over into resources. In others the poem makes use of given epic archetypes, though it is not always clear as to how these were first known to its redactors.

The principle of hierarchy must be considered not only as an element of theme but also as an element of construction—and, consequently, also of rhetoric—in the *Song of Roland*. One thinks especially of the hierarchy involving, at its summit, Charles, then Roland and the peers; next, the Frankish army and empire (personalized in the knight Thierry); and, finally, the audience. Ideally, we are to identify ourselves with Roland, as Thierry does, and one of Thierry's purposes in the poem is

115

to help us do so. Through the intricate relationships expressed by the hierarchy (and analogously to the role played, say, by Alexis in his marriage), the audience is drawn directly into the poem. By understanding these relationships—Charles to Roland as much as Roland to Charles, etc.—the audience is called upon to function within the poem. Similarly, the ideal of empire is clarified: it too is hierarchical and dynamic. The principle of hierarchy provides a framework and a progression that gives substance and movement to the plot and the episodes.

Yet, interestingly, much of the poem's charm and, so to speak, its existential "thickness" lie in its highly varied modulation of this "framework" and "movement." Aude's speech and death, coming at the very moment in which Ganelon's trial is about to begin, do not merely add a delicate, sadly feminine touch; the episode serves narrationally to recall most vividly Roland's death and the effects of Ganelon's treason. Aude's touching fidelity underscores the seriousness of the betrayal. The maiden is totally opposed in tone and in feeling to what occurs sequentially both before and after *laisse* CCLXVIII, but just as she "est a sa fin alee" (3723) so she reminds us of her fiancé who, his hands joined together, also "est alet a sa fin" (2392). We are psychologically prepared for the trial.

Modulation of the narrative line is frequently (and very effectively) achieved by juxtapositions of the Aude-trial sort. The narrative sequence—Ganelon's judgment—progresses, but the interpolation of the Aude episode within this sequence provides color and relief, a kind of narrative and indirect commentary, and simultaneously it ties up a potentially loose end of plot. The character Aude, we recall, was used earlier in order to define more sharply the fraternal nature of Roland's and Olivier's friendship; at this juncture she serves to highlight the poignancy of their death and the quality of their fidelity.

An even more characteristic type of narrative modulation is brought about by subtle exploitation of the *laisse* structure.

116

This important question deserves somewhat fuller treatment than I can grant it here. Let me therefore recommend at the outset perusal of at least two studies: Jean Rychner, *La Chanson de geste: essai sur l'art épique des jongleurs* (Geneva-Lille, 1955), especially ch. v, "La Structure strophique des chansons," 68-125, and Angelo Monteverdi, "La Laisse épique," in *La Technique littéraire des chansons de geste*, Actes du Colloque de Liège (Paris, 1959), 129-139 (p. 140 contains discussion of this report). Also a few brief reminders may be appropriate here before continuing.

The *Song of Roland* is made up of *laisses*—two hundred and ninety-one of them in Bédier's edition (other editions differ somewhat)—which in turn are composed of a varying number of assonanced decasyllables. According to Monteverdi, only one *laisse* contains at least thirty-five lines, thirty-odd have more than twenty, one hundred and seventy-eight have between ten and twenty, and eighty-one have less than ten (129). The epic *décasyllabe* breaks down into two hemistichs of four plus six syllables, but considerable play is permitted since, after the fourth or tenth syllable, a mute /e/— and sometimes two, as in *virgEnE*, *jovEnE*—is allowed: *Charles li reis / nostre emperere magnEs.* Verses are lengthened or shortened this way, and the monotony is broken.

According to Rychner, the gamut of OF *chansons de geste* may be polarized around two main types, i.e., the kind that "respects" the integrity of the *laisse* and that leans toward lyricism, as opposed to the more purely narrative unit. The *Song of Roland* respects the *laisse* more than any other poem. Each *laisse* tends to display a narrative, dramatic, and/or lyric unity; the *laisse* is the basic "element" of the work. The poem is built up, then, of relatively independent units that participate in the main contexts of the poem at the same time that they enjoy considerable structural autonomy. In turn, this structural autonomy of the *laisse* constitutes a significant distinctive feature of the poem as a whole. Though the individual *laisses* together compose the poem and ought to be viewed in terms of the poem as a whole, to a very considerable degree

117

it makes sense to proceed in the opposite way too, namely, to describe the manner in which the poem can and does operate upon the *laisse*.

Important narrative modulation is due, of course, to the constraints of oral diffusion. Thus, e.g., epic formulas are useful not only to *jongleurs* who must chant from memory long stretches of verse, but also for an audience unable to cope with the intricacies of a less familiar or less redundant diction. Similarly, repetition, as in the *laisses similaires*, serves to underscore events or actions of great importance, and, in some instances, making sure the entire audience has grasped a given point itself constitutes a technique of emphasis. The *laisses similaires* behave, as it were, adverbially with respect to the movement, or action, of the narrative. Few critics have complained of repetitiousness in the *Roland*, however. The poem converts the constraints imposed by the conditions of diffusion into an expressive resource that in no way detracts from the work's merit. The *laisses similaires* may be approached from various standpoints. Thus, they often function with respect to the progression of the narrative (usually slowing its pace somewhat, imparting dimensions of greater depth or breadth to the events, etc.). In other cases they modify the tone; the language becomes more lyrical, the stylizations add more pronounced affective coloring. The degree and precision of repetition should also be taken into account. Some *laisses* sequences show greater similarity than others, others restate in different terms the same material, still others throw back to previous *laisses* by repeating a key verse or formula. Sometimes the effect is incantatory. (What Rychner has called "parallel *laisses*" function analogously.) Ironies, emotional play, expressive variety (as when, e.g., what the narrator had previously described "objectively" is now acted out and reported directly by a character) are all rendered possible or, at the very least, reinforced by *laisses similaires*. Here again a certain "thickness," a kind of fictional "body," results, which, in my view, provides much of the poetic authenticity and value of the *Song of Roland*.

118

To the extent that one is aware, first of all, of the principle of these modulations, secondly, of their workings, one receives a more profound sense of the poem's meaning. (The reader or spectator articulates in this way relationships suggested by the poem.) Yet, one can plumb these depths indefinitely without ever exhausting the possibilities hidden there; the tight hierarchies of the work are qualified, then, in this open-ended way. Meanwhile, however, none of these modulations is in and of itself utterly indispensable. The poem is consequently not so much many-levelled as it is multi-layered, or perhaps better: multi-clustered. Various values adhere to an inescapable and central nucleus. By skimming off the top (i.e., even by barely making out what the *jongleur* is singing, at some distance) one can manage to understand what is happening, and, thanks to the nature of the diction, one can participate with the minimum necessary efficiency. The greater autonomy and variety of the *laisse* in the *Roland* may thus be contrasted with the regular strophic pattern of the *Alexis*. Dependent, as we saw, on ritual hagiographic patterns that impart structure to the legend, this strophic pattern differs in kind from the looser, more flexible, and essentially modulated *récit* presented in and by the *Roland* sequence of *laisses*.

Let us take a closer look at a case in point. The event—it is virtually a theme—of Roland's death is first suggested, of course, by the legend itself (which must be viewed as a "component" of the poem, though its structural role is not susceptible of precise delimitation). But the opposition that eventually leads to this death is first articulated in the poem when, in *laisse* xiv, Roland tells Charles: "Ja mar crerez Marsilie!" (196), and, in the following *laisse*, Ganelon takes up the same term in his response to Roland: "Ja mar crerez bricun!" (220). Premonitions of disaster accompany Ganelon's dropping Charles' glove and, of course, Ganelon's plot with Blancandrin (*laisse* xxix) and later with Marsile (xliff.) confirms these premonitions. The poem comments upon these events to come; thus, in *laisse* lv, after Roland has given the sign to break camp and the four hundred thousand Franks prepare to

119

leave for their country, we hear: "Deus! quel dulur que li Franceis nel sevent!" AOI (716). Charles' dream follows immediately: Ganelon wrenches Charles' lance away from him, the emperor is attacked by an unnamed animal and a leopard, but defended by a furious hound. The next day, when Ganelon nominates Roland to lead the rear guard, Charles, forebodingly, accuses him of *mortel rage*. In *laisse* LXVI the refrain "Halt sunt li pui e li val tenebrus" occurs for the first time and, in *laisse* LXVIII, Charles cannot keep himself from weeping; the French fear for Roland and the peers: "Guenes li fels en ad fait traïsun" (844). The connection between what we know (from the legend as well as from the poem), what will happen, and what Charles and the Franks fear is explicitly stated. But once Roland's death has been, so to speak, fully established and articulated in a kind of implacable conditional time, it is once again narrationally modulated. *Laisse* LXIX introduces Marsile's nephew Aelroth, an "anti-Roland," who asks of his uncle a boon: "le colp de Rollant" (866). If Roland's death by betrayal is certain, so is, as well, his victory. The juxtaposition of these two *laisses* tells us this, for we know that Aelroth will not defeat Roland, and the poem deliberately capitalizes on our knowledge.

Before the battle is joined, then, Roland's death is effectively linked to both Ganelon's treason and the Frankish victory. The battle itself, with its dichotomy of Christians and Saracens, its polarization (and reconciliation) of Roland and Olivier, not to forget the setting of high mountains and deep valleys, plays out these connections. But, curiously, as it does so, the battle provides spiritual meaning to Roland's death.

The process, clearly, is one of dovetailing; the narrative rhythm exploits the high degree of autonomy of the *laisses*. Yet we go from the suggestive plays of Roland's "Ja mar crerez Marsilie!" (*laisse* XIV), as answered by Ganelon's "Ja mar crerez bricun" in *laisse* XV, and the more intense opposition of the type expressed in the above-quoted *laisses* LXVIII and LXIX to the amazingly high-powered and marvelously rich series of *laisses* in which, almost one by one, the French are cut down. The betrayal literally takes effect as the field is strewn with the French dead. In a kind of metonymic way Roland "dies" too, in that the organism of which he is a part is slowly destroyed during the pagan onslaughts. The *douze pairs* are no more. Meanwhile, however, by a kind of epic *tour de force*, Roland takes the place of his dead companions. He is progressively glorified while, through the death of his *cumpainz*, he is in fact diminished. The very setting of Roncevaux becomes a stage, with props, for his death and epiphany. The immediate "cause" of his death—his sounding the *oliphant*—occurs in *laisse* CXXXIII, as this process of glorification in diminishment has already been well under way for some time, but he does not actually give up the ghost until *laisse* CLXXVI, about six-hundred lines later. Meanwhile, Olivier dies and, last *cumpain*, Archbishop Turpin who, in *laisse* CLXII, blesses the dead and, just before dying himself, tries to help Roland in *laisse* CLXV. It is certainly no accident that the last to precede Roland in death was his priest. By the time Roland's soul is carried off to Paradise, the personal, political, and, indeed, the cosmic implications of his death are clarified. However, at no time are these implications expressly given; they derive from the juxtapositions of the *laisses*.

The technique of dovetailing carries with it—built in as it were—both visible and potential confusions of time and space. Chronologies are disturbed, indeed made light of, as are the locations of actions and their consequences. Similarly, clusters of fact and modifications adhering to given events tend to comprise different orders of reality; naturalistic detail readily combines with the supernatural, or with dreams and even the narrator's interpolations. Perspectives are blurred, often blended, at times, seemingly, quite gratuitously—much more so, even, than in the *Alexis*. Such blending has probably prompted most judgments (stemming from a nineteenth-century obsession with neat evolutionary patterns?) that describe the poem as technically "naïve," "simple," "artless," or "popular." This is surely why Rychner equated the degree of autonomy of the *laisses* with "lyrical tendencies" and with "lack of respect" for the narrative. However, if indeed the constraints of oral diffusion favored the organization of the poem into highly autonomous *laisses*, it nonetheless follows from what we have observed that his organization does not necessarily imply lack of sophistication. Not only is it "respected," the narrative line of the *Song of Roland* is structurally quite sound. In fact, as I have tried to point out, its very security encourages the kinds of modulations I have described. If temporal sequences other than the logic starting with Ganelon's betrayal and culminating in his trial and execution are, in fact, disturbed, it must be for deliberate cause. Normal sequential chronologies are simply less important than the authentic temporality of the poem: *ævum*, of course, and what might be called the "concrete" time of events—a time possessing its own relational logic. Thus, Roland's death takes place in a diachrony that presumably extends back earlier than the duration of the poem: a blood feud? Its synchrony encompasses, if not the poem, at least the Roncevaux episode. As an event, it exists in relation to other "events." We have examined some of these relationships and, we saw, they constitute an important segment of the fictional texture (as well as "texturing") of the poem.

A work of history, conceived, like the *Roland*, in the framework of eternity and, so to speak, related directly to its audience, can consequently better convey the higher integrity of concrete events than, one suspects, many a modern novel. What at first glance looks like confusion turns out to be, in most cases in the Oxford text, a more adequate order, that is, a form perfectly suited to value and to structural possibilities. What makes *laisse* CLXXVI so sublime a poem is, naturally, hard to summarize. It is, I am tempted to say, everything I have mentioned so far. Once more it is asserted that Roland is lying beneath a pine tree, his face is turned towards Spain, he remembers his past life—all these things are repetitions, including the fact that he must confess and that he does so. His prayer is an even more beautiful restatement of the prayer given in CLXXV (surely, in fact, the "same" prayer, but here "related" somewhat differently). Once again he is visited by angels. However, the last line is entirely new; it justifies and, narrationally, makes sense of all the rest: "L'anme del cunte portent en pareïs" (2396). The whole *Chanson de Roland* lies latent in this *laisse*, which, when it is sung, brings back to us the entire "event" of the hero's death and, of course, its justification, what it leads up to: Roland's salvation. The poem operates upon the *laisse* as fully as the *laisse* functions within the poem.

Laisse and poem partake of the same epic "binary impulse" that other constructs in the *Song of Roland* also illustrate. Here as elsewhere there are grounds to stress the high degree of fusion and unity that characterize the relationships operative in the work. Far more difficult of access and far less amenable to explanation are certain archetypal epic figures that also play an important role in the economy of the poem. One thinks, e.g., of the Roland-Olivier pair; it surely reflects the same sort of construct illustrated by Achilles and Patrocles. Duke Naimes, Charles' aged and venerable counselor, reminds one inevitably of Homer's Nestor, who takes, like Naimes, a prominent part among the heroes in council and battle alike. Even Charles himself, deriving his strength from powerful belief, is constructed along the essentially mythic lines provided by the Old Testament rulers and prophetic tradition. He is the archetypal king, to be sure, but he is also a kind of Moses or Joshua. His Franks are chosen people; they are to be contrasted with those pagans who, like Marsile's uncle, Marganices, come from "une tere maldite" (1916). The prevalence of this tradition explains in part why the "epic sympathy" for a worthy foe is quite different in the *Roland* from what it is in the Homeric texts. The traitor figure, here epitomized by Ganelon, also constitutes an epic archetype, this time, perhaps, of essentially Germanic and Celtic provenance. One is every bit as conscious, surely, of Ganelon's playing out the traitor's role, of filling, so to speak, a structural "empty slot," as one is, say, of Roland's heroic destiny.

123

The list of renegades and traitors in the OF *chansons de geste* is at once extensive and indicative of this archetypal figure's importance. In *Ami et Amile* (ca. 1200), for example, the two heroes are paired in friendship, like Roland and Olivier —even more so, since they were not only born the same day and identical in appearance, but conceived the same day! The two friends serve Charlemagne, but they must contend with Hardré, the traitor, who is indeed of the *lignage des traîtres* and who seeks to undo Charles' high regard for them. (In *Jourdain de Blaye* Hardré's nephew, the traitor Fromont, is accused of being of the *lignage de Ganelon.* Whereas the "good" wife of Renier claims that "mi parent furent Rollans e Oliviers" [ed. Dembowski, v. 1431].)

These archetypal figures serve important purposes within the epic framework. In them one finds a blend of generic traits (all epics use such figures), legendary and historic meaning summarized and symbolized in a character, and, finally, perhaps concrete examples of constants of human behavior or conduct. Ganelon is quite individualized in the Oxford text; indeed "personal" reasons as much as, so to speak, "generic" reasons—i.e., his traitor's role—prompt him to act as he does. At the same time he is fully integrated into the legendary construct that is Charles' empire; his family is virtually a political faction in Charles' capital. And, lastly, he "contains" the complex strands of behavior—the motivation, the spite, the pride, the egotism—that we associate willingly with traitorous action. The ways he blends these traits make of Ganelon an authentic epic type, one whose "category" and whose "individuality" complement each other perfectly. The epic type differs from a hagiographic character like, e.g., Eufemien, whose status, or "category," as the saint's father is brought home to us because his historicity is depicted convincingly. Ganelon's success as an epic character and his personality are properly fused. The epic archetype is thus more complex than his hagiographic counterpart. This is not surprising when one recalls that the structure of the saint's life subordinates the other characters to the saint; they exist in relation to him. Although they too are highly abstract as characters, the archetypal figures in an epic like the *Song of Roland* must display ostensible independence in a fashion not permitted their hagiographic counterparts.

The *Song of Roland* is fictionally more complex than the OF *Alexis*. Historicity is less a means here than an indispensable goal of the fiction, whereas, we observed, in the *Alexis* without the illusion of historicity the hagiographic values would not have been adequately conveyed; the *Alexis* is more ostensibly didactic. In the *Roland* the "collaboration" of poetry and value is so close, so tightly knit, that one's attention is channelled constantly and evenly from the one to the other. By focusing upon poetic constructs, the audience is led into a more profound understanding of the work's meaning, and, conversely, one's appreciation of that meaning and its ramifications illuminates the poetic techniques employed. Yet the *Song of Roland* remains epic, not novelistic; literature serves the myth. Structural ironies that one must associate with, say, certain later romances—e.g., Chrétien de Troyes, the Tristan *Folies*—are startlingly absent from the *Roland*. Experiencing this poem means that one does what one can: one submits to its order, i.e., one grasps the narrative line and the principle of modulation. The mythic framework is inescapable. Then, depending on one's capacity or ability (and in the eleventh or twelfth century, probably on one's proximity to the *trouvère* or *jongleur*), one works out the various "clustered" relationships to which I have referred. The poem offers degrees of depth available simultaneously to the individuals making up a congregated audience, a bit, say, like a Molière play, which, if we are to believe much recent criticism, also "functions" by calling its spectators' attention primarily to the ways it has been put together. Important facts, or data, are stated and restated, each time, however, with more or less significant modulations of the kinds we have examined.

Whereas the *Life of Saint Alexis* constitutes a marvelous example of vernacular literature—that is, of fictional means placed intelligently at the service of a vision of history—of

125

truth, organized poetically, the Oxford *Song of Roland* comes closer to what might be called the ideal of popular literature. The events of Saint Alexis' life are clarified in the OF narrative and, to be sure, the poem's audience was far more "popular" than the clerical public to which the Bollandist *Vita* was addressed, but, precisely, the greater fictional complexity of the *Roland* renders this poem more autonomous, less dependent on the external didactic framework so indispensable to the mythic paradigm of the *Alexis*. In the *Roland*, to a much greater extent, the poem provides its own order which, of course, each of us is called upon to reconstruct in his own way and according to his own ability. The audience is heterogeneous and its very heterogeneity is effectively incorporated into the poem's operations. The "popular" character of the *Roland* lies, then, in the fact of one's personal reconstruction along with the poem's structural allowance for its audience's heterogeneity.

Such "popularity" is akin to that of Romanesque architecture,[21] the rise of which, incidentally, is roughly contemporary to the poem contained in the Oxford redaction. The "Roman" allusions of this architecture remind one of the poem's constant reference to imperial unity; the fervor of the Crusades had much to do with the flowering of the epic as well as with the building of churches. Also, both the architecture and the *Chanson* partake analogously of the same drive toward transcendence. Even more importantly, however, the *Song of Roland* and much Romanesque design share a similar "unrestricted" public, a public explicitly made up of composite social classes. There is nothing "child-like" or "naïve" in this popularity; whatever simplicity may be ascribed to the *Roland* derives surely from the same careful craftsmanship we owe the Autun sculptors. Furthermore, it serves the same purpose, namely, to make the entire construct accessible to the widest possible community. One no more exhausts the

[21] This structural and spiritual kinship is very suggestively studied by Fern Farnham in "Romanesque Design in the *Chanson de Roland*," *RPh*, xviii (1964), 143-164.

resources of the *Song of Roland* than one assimilates all the possibilities in the Angoulême cathedral. Yet, just as one's eye and mind are directed by certain architectural relationships to certain key parts of that cathedral, so are one's ear and spirit brought to fix on a number of high points in the poem. Though perhaps for different reasons, the entire audience realizes the central importance and high beauty of Roland's prayer:

> "Veire Patene, ki unkes ne mentis,
> Seint Lazaron de mort resurrexis
> E Daniel des leons guaresis,
> Guaris de mei l'anme de tuz perilz
> Pur les pecchez que en ma vie fis!" (2384ff.)

Nothing could be more simple, yet no words could be more significant.

It is useful to see in the *Song of Roland* the culmination of an expressive tradition that, as Mrs. Farnham suggested, is summarized in the term "Romanesque design." I believe as well that it is equally useful to place the poem in its true and effective popular context. The Romantic critics were surely right to associate the poem with the People, or *Volk*, but they articulated this relationship in an unsatisfactory way. Perhaps scholars should once again address themselves to this problem. We should not forget the opening words of the Strasbourg Oaths:

> Pro deo amur et pro christian poblo et nostro
> commun salvament

Here, in the middle of the tryptich, one finds, I suspect, the concept that underlies the audience of the *Song of Roland*.

CHAPTER III

Chrétien de Troyes

INTRODUCTION

AFTER years of having been ignored or shunted aside as extravagant Gothic curiosities or as childish fairy tales, the romances of Chrétien de Troyes and similar compositions of the twelfth and thirteenth centuries have at last begun to reach modern literary circles and to earn their respect. To be sure, specialists have long ago succumbed to the charm of Chrétien's work, but only in recent decades could this appreciation be shared by a wider public; translations of several romances were made available, for instance, recently in the inexpensive Livre de Poche collection. Of course, a number of modern artists, among them Richard Wagner and T. S. Eliot, found in the tradition of medieval romance sustenance that they put to good use in their own work. Ironically, however, they once again made of the genre a victim of its own success by absorbing it in this way.

In the first place, we recall, after many avatars, Chrétien's work was eventually incorporated into the Renaissance narrative of an Ariosto, the heroic poetry of a Tasso, and, above all, the new fiction of a Cervantes. The process of this lengthy absorption deserves further study; it is crucial to the understanding of European narrative fiction. It offers the curious example of the consciously well-wrought and *signed* text—the work, usually, of a single author who is especially proud of his handiwork—entering, first through poetic enlargements then through anonymous prose recastings, a kind of literary public domain that future authors, who will also sign their work, might exploit, technically and substantively, as they needed. Chrétien's success, as well as that of contemporaries

128

like Marie de France, helped cause the oblivion into which they eventually fell. T. S. Eliot's *The Waste Land* depends far more on the legendary and formal traditions to which Chrétien's work belongs than on the romances as such. Indeed, certain misunderstandings cloud early twentieth-century efforts to understand Chrétien. Despite his love for the medieval literature of France and Italy, Ezra Pound, in judging Chrétien, fell into what we might call the fairy-tale trap:

"The work of Crestien de Troyes has been lately translated by W. W. Newell, and is available to all.

"The tales move more swiftly than the similar tales in Malory's 'Morte d'Arthur.' Crestien has a fine eye for the colour of medieval pageantry and some fidelity to nature. The tales are to-day what they were to Dante: 'The very beautiful legends of King Arthur.' . . . They belong to that vast body of pleasant literature which one should read when one feels younger than twenty. There are few people who can read more than a dozen or so of mediaeval romances . . . without being over-wearied by the continual recurrence of the same or similar incidents. . . ."[1]

Some contemporary scholars have evinced greater interest in the specifically literary qualities of Chrétien's romances than had usually been the case in the past. Gustave Cohen speaks regularly and rightly of Chrétien as France's first novelist, though he does not do much to show what, precisely, is novelistic in Chrétien's work. Literary questions have also interested critic-scholars like Eugène Vinaver, the late Erich Auerbach, and Jean Frappier. Though none of these learned men neglect other aspects of literary history—the origins, the Celtic problem, editorial questions, dates—they clearly recognize the validity, even the primacy, of poetic concerns. In this respect they share some of the interests expressed by Pound in the manifesto-like Preface to *The Spirit of Romance*, although, as historians, they seek above all to

[1] Ezra Pound, *The Spirit of Romance* (London-New York, [1910], 81).

understand and to explain, not to draw up parallels between former kinds of poetic art and present-day schools.

Very recently, a tendency to pay even greater attention to Chrétien's artistry may be singled out. Books, dissertations, and articles have been dedicated to such matters as irony, description, "structural style," and the like in one or more of the five great romances of certain attribution. One may indeed speak of a mild boom in scholarly studies devoted nowadays to Chrétien de Troyes.[2] Significantly, Chrétien turns out to be *literarily* congenial to a wider spectrum of readers today than, perhaps, ever before. All this, of course, goes far to justify including his work in the purview of our introductory study. Not only is Chrétien de Troyes typical of an important stage in the history of the Old French narrative; his work stands very much on its own intrinsic merits too. Furthermore, it may well have something meaningful to tell us concerning narrative fiction—something at least as significant to our time as what we learned in reading the *Alexis* and the *Roland*.

Of Chrétien's romances the *Chevalier au lion* (ca. 1179), or *Yvain*, as it is now usually called, has been frequently praised by *cognoscenti* for the variety of its episodes, the perfection of its symmetry, and the delicacy with which it treats

[2] Some of the more important of these relatively recent studies include: Gustave Cohen, *Un grand Romancier d'amour et d'aventure au XIIe siècle; Chrétien de Troyes et son œuvre* (Paris, 1931 [1948₂]); Wilhelm Kellermann, *Aufbaustil und Weltbild Chrestiens von Troyes im Percevalroman*, Beiheft ZRPh, LXXXVIII (Halle/Saale, 1936); R. S. Loomis, *Arthurian Tradition and Chrétien de Troyes* (New York, 1949); Stefan Hofer, *Chrétien de Troyes: Leben und Werke des altfranzösischen Epikers* (Graz, 1954); Jean Frappier, *Chrétien de Troyes* (Paris, 1957 [1965₃]; Nouvelle édition revue et augmentée, illustrée, 1968); J. H. Reason, *An Inquiry into the Structural Style and Originality of Chrétien's* YVAIN (Washington, 1958); Jean Frappier, *Étude sur* YVAIN *ou* LE CHEVALIER AU LION *de Chrétien de Troyes* (Paris, 1952 [1968₂]); F. Douglas Kelly, *Sens and conjointure in the* CHEVALIER DE LA CHARRETTE (The Hague, 1966); Peter Haidu, *Æsthetic Distance in Chrétien de Troyes: Irony and Comedy in* CLIGÉS *and* PERCEVAL (Geneva, 1968).

matters of the heart.[3] It ranks with the *Chevalier de la char-rette* (*Lancelot*) and the *Conte du graal* (*Perceval*) among the poet's masterpieces, and some claim it is superior to these; Chrétien finished neither *Lancelot* nor *Perceval*. The text of *Yvain* is somewhat more easily available than that of the other romances.[4] Finally, scholars—e.g., Auerbach, in *Mimesis* (1946, tr. 1953)—have used *Yvain* to epitomize twelfth-century courtly romance; from various standpoints it is a uniquely interesting narrative text. For these reasons, though I shall refer both generally and extensively to the whole of Chrétien's work when appropriate, I shall concentrate particularly upon *Yvain*.

A fully informed appreciation of Chrétien's romances, including *Yvain*, must be based on an understanding of these works in terms of the possibilities open to courtly romance and to other types of narrative current in Chrétien's time. What kinds of narrative structure respond best to what Chrétien set out to do? How might one go about describing them?

Exhaustive answers to these questions would require a study of major monographic proportions. Despite many erudite and critical investigations of OF courtly literature, we

[3] Thus, Mario Roques opens the Introduction to his CFMA (Classiques français du moyen âge) edition with the following remarks: "*Yvain* . . . est tenu pour le meilleur des romans de Chrétien par la variété de ses épisodes, l'intérêt de ses situations psychologiques et la délicatesse de ses études du sentiment" (iii). And Jean Frappier: "*Yvain* est, avec *Érec*, le roman le mieux construit de Chrétien" (*Étude sur* YVAIN, 23).

[4] The principal editions include: Wendelin Foerster, *Kristian von Troyes, sämtliche Werke*, II (Halle, 1887), and, in *Romanische Biblio-thek*, V (Halle, 1891 [1926₆]); T.B.W. Reid annotated Foerster's edition in a volume published by the Manchester University Press (1942 [1948₂]); Mario Roques, *Les Romans de Chrétien de Troyes*, IV, CFMA (Paris, 1960); a recent, highly annotated text, based on B. N. fr. 794 was prepared jointly by J. Nelson, C. W. Carroll, and D. Kelly (New York, 1968). The text is also available in modern French translation: André Mary, LE CHEVALIER AU LION *précédé de* ÉREC ET ÉNIDE (Paris, 1923 [1944₂]).

still know little about the possibilities "open to" the romance genre. Furthermore, our techniques for analyzing narrative structures, especially the medieval varieties, remain rudimentary. Terminological difficulties complicate matters. Thus "courtly romance" and MF "roman courtois" emphasize differences between say, the poems of Chrétien and the *chansons de geste*—differences that are rather more soft-pedaled by G. "höfisches Epos." Problems of all sorts arise.

The very magnitude of the issues warrants, I think, an experimental, even eclectic, approach. Let us attempt here to establish, if only provisionally, the conditions determining the kind of fiction *Yvain* and certain congeners represent. With this much accomplished, we may more safely go on to discuss several assumptions upon which this fiction rests, as well as a few conclusions that may justifiably be drawn. We shall utilize the *roman* (and given specimens of *roman*) to examine specific texts, and, conversely, we shall employ specific texts in order to understand better the nature and workings of Chrétien's *roman*.

I propose, then, to follow a multi-directional approach; my categories are intentionally at once somewhat arbitrary and loose. In the process, however, we should make some progress, despite the severe selectivity our study imposes. Four areas seem particularly promising. First, I shall examine and attempt to circumscribe the "literary consciousness" that pervades the kind of writing at which Chrétien excelled, and aspects of the traditions to which this consciousness belongs. Next, I shall look at a number of technical questions relating to the romance genre and the kind of "story" romance purports to be. This will help us define as cogently as possible Chrétien's "literary attitude." Certain useful distinctions should emerge at this juncture. Thirdly, I expect to analyze with considerable care and detail the nature of and function of Chrétien's "novelistic scene"; I shall deal extensively with the delicate episode during which Yvain falls in love with Laudine. Nevertheless, rather minute analysis of other scenes —e.g., the Immodest Damsel in *Lancelot*, the Drops of Blood on the Snow in *Perceval*—will be necessary in order to circumscribe more precisely Chrétien's accomplishment in *Yvain*. Finally, some brief words on what might be referred to as "celebration" in Chrétien are indispensable: myth, women, knighthood and *clergie*, as well as the entire notion of *san* and "novelistic world." Here I shall rely on evidence drawn from all the romances. Using these approaches, I hope to respect fully the artistic integrity of Chrétien's carefully designed works, without, however, sacrificing either what has been up to now accomplished in the previous chapters of this book or the help other selected texts can furnish. We must always bear in mind that isolated data, extracted from texts with little or no attention paid to the text as a whole, usually turn out to be trivial at best or useless.

LITERARY CONSCIOUSNESS

Chrétien de Troyes, like Flaubert or Proust, is a highly conscious artist. Furthermore, his literary consciousness is built into his work on all levels; it ranges from specific statements concerning his artistry or his intentions to a highly developed and easily observable exploitation of literary techniques, many of which were taught in twelfth-century schools. What might be called the "specificity" of Chrétien's literary consciousness concerns us particularly. Thus, in relating how he has gone about composing a given romance, he means frequently to guide his reader or listener. (Chrétien's "listener," unlike those who "heard" the *Song of Roland* performed, is in fact a reader: He either reads directly himself or—more probably—he is being read to; the contact involves the process of reading.) *Érec et Énide* (ca. 1170) offers the classic example of such guidance. Here Chrétien describes how he has derived (*tret*) from a mere *conte d'avanture* a "molt bele conjointure," something utterly different from the corrupt and silly tales hawked by minstrels "who make their living telling stories" to their noble and royal patrons. His own *estoire* will therefore live as long as Christendom—"de ce s'est Crestïens

133

vantez" (26).[5] The refined audience should make every effort to grasp the *conjointure*. Similarly, *Cligés* (ca. 1176) opens with a self-conscious statement of Chrétien's literary accomplishments: What he has done justifies, in a sense, what he intends to do. He is a master craftsman whose past wares prompt confidence in his future undertakings. Also, in one of the most celebrated passages in all medieval literature, Chrétien names his source, an "ancient book," one of those writings through which we know the deeds of the Ancients and have consequently become heirs to *chevalerie* and *clergie*. *Cligés* will thus equal, or surpass, any ancient work. Chrétien articulates here the topos usually called *translatio studii*. As in *Érec et Énide*, we have in *Cligés* also a preliminary story— that of Alexandre and Soredamor—which prefigures and, in a way, controls that of Cligés and Fénice, the romance's protagonists. Furthermore, as all critics have been quick to point out, *Cligés* unfolds in a context imbued with reminiscences of the Tristan story; literary feedback supplies one of its chief elements. Once again, the reader must be worthy of the task; he must make a strong effort to understand this "literature."

Not surprisingly, the dedicatory prologue to the *Charrette* (ca. 1179) also illustrates Chrétien's literary consciousness in an analogous way. Easily the most debated of Chrétien's critical pronouncements, this text also directs the audience

---

[5] Throughout the following pages line citations to Chrétien's works refer, when appropriate, to the frequently reprinted and accessible *CFMA* editions (*Érec et Énide, Yvain*, and *Lancelot*, ed. by Mario Roques; *Cligés*, ed. by A. Micha); references to *Perceval* correspond to William Roach's TLF edition (1956). Other textual references will be stated immediately after the quotation. Let me note at this juncture that in addition to the translations cited in fn. 4, there exist modernized French versions of *Érec et Énide* (tr. R. Louis, 1954), *Cligés* (tr. A. Micha, 1957), *Lancelot* (J. Frappier, 1967), and *Perceval* (L. Foulet, 1947; S. Hannedouche, 1969₂). English versions of all these, except *Perceval*, may be found in W. Wistar Comfort, tr., *Arthurian Romances* (London-Toronto-New York, [1913]); *Perceval* has been translated by R. White Linker, *The Story of the Grail* (Chapel Hill, [1952]).

by explaining how the romance came to be written and by analyzing further Chrétien's conception of his task. In *Lancelot* the circumstances of composition represent part of the romance's hard core. Chrétien claims to have received both *matere* and *sen(s)* from his patroness, Marie de Champagne; he takes credit only—but significantly—for the fictional elaboration of this material.[6]

[6] The exact meaning, or intention, of *matere et sen(s)* is quite elusive. Most editors have sought to distinguish between *sans* in v. 23, i.e., the understanding furnished by Chrétien himself (". . . sans ne painne que g'i mete") and the *sen(s)* or *san* (*sen*) of v. 26, which was, so he claimed, provided by the Countess Marie. In the 1914 ed. of their *Wörterbuch* W. Foerster and H. Breuer defined v. 26 *san* (<Frk. **sin*; cf. It *senno*) as "Princip, Motiv (des Romans)" and *sans* (<SĒNSU), generally, as "Verstand, Klugheit"; in the 1933 ed. v. 26 becomes "Auffassung (eines Romans)," though both *san* (<**sin*) and *sans* (<SĒNSU) are frequently synonymous. It would seem that, though by the thirteenth century (perhaps earlier) the progeny of SĒNSU and **sin* had virtually merged—due to semantic affinity (also perhaps because of the lateral homophonic pressure of *san*[c] <SANGUINE?)—enough play remained to permit Chrétien to assign different meanings to the two obviously parallel forms.

Not only do the Chrétien MSS fail to offer consistent spellings of *san, sen, sens*—e.g., the as yet unpublished fragment Garrett 125 (Princeton) gives v. 26 *sens*—but other texts of the time offer similar confusion. In Constans' SATF edition, v. 3 of *Troie* reads: *Que nus ne deit son sen celer*, though MSS *M²BD* each give *sens*. However, the ambiguity does seem to be one-way, since, v. 18, all MSS agree on *sens: E coneü par lor granz sens*; the rhyme with *toz tens* also reinforces this agreement. We ought also to note, in the *Lancelot* Prologue, the repetition of *painne* in vv. 23 and 29 and, in the latter, *s'antancïon*, which surely throws back to v. 23. Chrétien, then, contributed his understanding whereas the Countess, he avers, provided, along with the subject-matter (*matere*), the central idea. (The opposition obtaining between vv. 23 and 26 is protected by the context despite the spelling confusion—*sans~san, sens~sen*—one finds in the MSS.) But what of *matere et sen(s)*? W. A. Nitze, *Rom*, XLIV (1915-1917), 14-36, identifies *san(s)* with "la *sciance* ou *sapience* qui vient de Dieu" and claims (1) that, for Chrétien, the value of his work depends on how well he uses this quality, and (2) that this belief has its source in the Book of Wisdom. Nitze also alludes to the etymological problem (fn. 5); in *MPh*, XXVII (1929-30), 462, he sug-

135

Finally, the opening lines of the *Conte du graal* (ca. 1181) —the dedication to Philip of Alsace—elaborates upon the old "sow and reap" topos: Chrétien sows in fertile ground, so fertile, in fact, "qu'il ne puet [estre] sanz grant preu" (10).

---

gests replacing *san* by *sans* (<SĒNSU); cf. T. P. Cross and Nitze, *Lancelot and Guenevere* (Chicago, 1930), where *sens* is viewed as equivalent to *interpretatio* or *expolitio*. Note Frappier's essential agreement: *sen* "est l'esprit de l'œuvre, l'interprétation morale des aventures, l'idéal qu'elles visent à illustrer, ou, plus simplement, leur intérêt psychologique et humain" (62). Roques translates *san* as "idée essentielle"; see also E. Hoepffner, " 'Matière et sens' dans le roman d'*Érec et Énide*," *AR*, XVIII (1934), 433-450. D. W. Robertson, Jr., in *SP*, XLVIII (1951), 669-692, agrees that *matere* means "subject-matter," but proposes that *san* (CORTEX or SENSUS) be downgraded to suggest the "surface meaning"; this view burdens the poet with the task of imbuing the story with a deeper allegorical sense. When, in v. 29, Chrétien confesses to have added to the *matere et sen(s)* "sa painne et s'antancïon," Robertson sees him showing his awareness that such a task is incumbent upon him: *antancïon* signifies SENTENTIA, i.e., "doctrinal content." Robertson's interpretation, though bristling with erudition, is rejected by F. Lyons (*ibid.*, LI [1954], 425ff.), who, for linguistic reasons, equates *antancïon* (*entention*) with "endeavor, care, application"; she renders *sa painne et s'antancïon* as "his effort and careful attention," much as had done E. Vinaver (*The Works of Sir Thomas Mallory*, I [Oxford, 1947], lxv, n. 1).

Finally, Jean Rychner has sought to turn the tables, first in a hint that he included in his review of Frappier's translation of *Lancelot* (*RPh*, XVII, 711), then in three articles that develop his thesis as well as study its implications. In "Le Prologue du 'Chevalier de la charrette,' " *VRom*, XXVI (1967), 1-23, Rychner claims that Chrétien "n'a pas fait lui-même la distinction entre la 'matière' et le 'sens' de ses œuvres, et qu'il n'a pas dit que Marie de Champagne lui avait donné le sujet et l'idée maîtresse du *Chevalier de la charrette*" (1). The second article, "Le Prologue du *Chevalier de la charrette* et l'interprétation du roman," *Mélanges Rita Lejeune*, II (Gembloux, 1969), 1121-1135, Rychner examines the consequences of his revision. He is on solid ground, I think, when he rejects the traditional interpretation (going back to Gaston Paris) that dissociates "une signification et un récit qui lui est étranger." In my opinion, however, he does not go quite far enough; the poetic structuring of the work imparts, through and of itself, what the poem "means"; what it celebrates may be seen as akin to what Rychner calls, tantalizingly, its

Flattery addressed to Philip blends with a certain sententious-
ness; the religious tone of the work is established (God, the
Gospel, charity, and—a misquoted—Saint Paul are named,
in some cases repeatedly). Again Chrétien stresses his role in
putting together the romance; he is proud of his handiwork:

Dont avra bien salve sa paine
CHRESTÏENS, qui entent et paine
Par le comandement le conte
A rimoier le meillor conte
Qui soit contez a cort roial:
Ce est li CONTES DEL GRAAL,
Dont li quens li bailla le livre.
Oez coment il s'en delivre (61ff.).

Recent scholarship has done much to reveal what must
have been the ambiance in which Chrétien's kind of literary
awareness flourished. The twelfth century was, so to speak,

"signification d'ensemble" (1135). The same timidity appears in the
third article, "Le Sujet et la signification du 'Chevalier de la char-
rette,'" *VRom*, XXVII (1968), 50-76, where Rychner "confesses" that
"j'ai essayé de m'expliquer sur la poésie et la beauté auxquelles je
suis sensible DANS le *Lancelot* plus peut-être que sur une signification
exacte DU *Lancelot*" (76). That is the whole point; we shall return
to these issues briefly in the section of our study devoted to *Celebra-
tion*.

For the moment, however, let me suggest that structurally Chré-
tien's prologues usually are fully integrated into the poetic fabric of
his romances: they help us read the text and they usually correspond
in a functional way to what the romance is about. Thus, in *Cligés*, the
bookish clerkliness of Chrétien's listing his works by title and his
adumbration of the *translatio studii* topos hint at the role bookishness
will be called upon to play in that work. Similarly, as we shall see in
due course, the motifs of charity, of reality vs. appearance, and the
contrast between Alexander and Philip of Alsace all foreshadow what
will happen in the *Conte du graal* (e.g., the opposition between
Gauvain and Perceval). In my judgment Chrétien, in the Prologue to
Lancelot, elaborates upon the notion of clerkly service: he serves *his*
lady, the Countess Marie, as Lancelot, the knight, will be called upon
to serve Guenevere. *Clergie* thus goes hand-in-glove with *chevalerie*
in pursuit of the ideal of *dépassement*.

literary to its fingertips; scholastic formalism had not yet come to dominate the intellectual scene, as it would, in Paris at any rate, a century later.[7] Of course, we observed in previous chapters the authentically poetic character of earlier vernacular texts like the *Alexis* and the *Roland,* as well as the contrived—even learned—nature of much diction in these poems. What I am about to say must not be construed as a denial of the true literary nature of these texts. However, in romance and for reasons I shall try to clarify, literary self-consciousness performs a function qualitatively distinctive from what occurs in *Alexis* and *Roland.* As poets must do with the materials at hand, Chrétien utilizes values pertaining to the literary and social ambiance within which he lived and worked.

Literary self-consciousness is thus in part a matter of civilization. Even in earlier times the cultivation of letters was very much an attribute of the refined life. We recall Alexis' birth, his baptism and infancy, but particularly his education. Whereas the Bollandist *Vita* does speak of the young Alexis' training at the feet of masters of the liberal arts and his

[7] In addition to E. Faral's *Les Arts poétiques du XIIe et du XIIIe siècle* (Paris, 1962₂) and E. R. Curtius' *Europäische Literatur und lateinisches Mittelalter* (Bern, 1948), Eng. tr. by W. R. Trask (1953), to which I refer repeatedly in these pages, let me cite as well É. Gilson's studies of medieval intellectual and spiritual history: *Héloïse et Abélard* (Paris, 1938; Eng. tr. by L. K. Shook, 1953), *La Philosophie au moyen âge* (Paris, 1947₂); *Saint Bernard; un itinéraire de retour à Dieu* (Paris, 1964). Though these—and other uncited—works provide much insight into the literary ambiance of the twelfth century, as well as into its transformation and bifurcations during the thirteenth century, the processes of transformation to which, say, romance-type narrative was submitted remain little known. The crisis of the narrative genres and of the literary spirit, especially in the period 1190-1220, requires study; "literature" is, so to speak, overwhelmed by philosophy and theological concerns. On the one hand a kind of trivialization occurs, on the other the development of allegorizing revitalizes vernacular *belles-lettres* against the backdrop of a triumphant (and anti-grammatical) scholastic philosophy and theology.

knowledge of philosophy, the OF *Life* links his education to
his social station; he goes through what boys of his class go
through:

> Puis ad escole li bons pedre le mist:
> Tant aprist letres que bien en fut guarnit;
> Puis vait li emfes l'emperethur servir (Rohlfs$_4$, 33ff.).

A gentleman is versed in letters and arms. The same idea
is richly developed in Alexandre de Paris' *Roman d'Alexandre*
over a century later; position and a kind of learning are
directly associated:

> Alixandres fu preus et de grant escïent;
> Ce conte l'escripture, se la letre ne ment,
> Que plus sot en set jourz que uns autres en cent.
> La nouvele est alee deci en Ocident;
> De ne sai quantes terres i sont venu la gent,
> Li mestre des escolles, li bon clerc sapïent,
> Qui vouloient connoistre son cuer et son talent.
> Aritotes d'Athenes l'aprist honestement;
> Celui manda Phelippes trestout premierement.
> Il li moustre escripture, et li vaslés l'entent,
> Grieu, ebrieu et caldieu et latin ensement
> Et toute la nature de la mer et du vent
> Et le cours des estoiles et le compassement
> Et si com li planete hurtent au firmament
> Et la vie du siecle et quanqu'a lui apent
> Et connoistre reison et savoir jugement,
> Si comme rethorique en fet devisement;
> Et en aprés li moustre un bon chastïement,
> Que ja serf de put ere n'et entour lui souvent,
> Car maint home en sont mort et livré a torment. . .
> > (ed. Armstrong, Elliott Monographs, 37
> > [Princeton, 1937], vv. 326ff.).

A similar opposition is explicitly drawn up in the Prologue
to the *Roman de Thèbes*, whose author, after developing the
commonplace that no man of learning should hide his knowl-

edge (after all, what would we have done if Homer, Plato, Virgil, and Cicero had hid their light under a bushel?), clearly associates *belles-lettres* and aristocracy:

> Ainz me delét a aconter
> Chose digne de remembrer.
> Or s'en voisent de tot mestier,
> Se ne sont clerc o chevalier,
> Car aussi pueent escouter
> Come li asnes al harper.
> Ne parlerai de peletiers,
> Ne de vilains . . . (ed. Constans, I, *SATF*, 31
> [Paris, 1890], vv. 11ff.).

This last text puts us on the track of yet another significant component of the literary consciousness we seek to understand. The very matter recounted in *Thèbes* is described as "chose digne de remembrer." Obviously, indisputable worthiness was built directly into the raw material of Saint Alexis' life—by definition, so to speak—though the OF poet (unlike the Bollandist *Vita*) takes pains to tell us that in the good saint's times the "world was good." And Charlemagne's *geste* is inherently the noblest of all, as Jehan Bodel will point out in the forematter to his *Saisnes*. The dignity of the subject-matter is taken for granted. The *Thèbes* poet, however, must articulate this worth and, as we observed, link the subject-matter to his audience as well as to the learned clerks whose function it is to purvey this lore.

These various threads of argument are taken up by Marie de France in the Prologue to her *Fables*. Like *Thèbes*, this text also opens with the topos summarized by Curtius among the "topics of the exordium" as "The possession of knowledge makes it a duty to impart it" (*European Literature and the Latin Middle Ages*, tr. Trask, Harper Torchbooks [New York, 1963], 87). But Marie goes on to say that one's literary work preserves the good books of past philosophers, what they "troverent / E escristrent e remembrerent" (ed. Ewert and Johnston, Blackwell's French Texts [Oxford, 1942], 5f.).

140

Quite naturally, the finest rulers (e.g., Romulus) have found the *bons proverbes* quite congenial, including the noble king (?)—"Ki flurs est de chevalerie, / D'enseignement, de curteisie" (31f.)—who entrusted her with the task of rendering Æsop into vernacular verse. Such poetry, Marie claims, is useful. Did not Romulus show his son *par essample* how he might beware of those who would deceive him? Here, then, what is "digne de remembrer" is what proves to be of good moral use. (We recall that, in his discussion of this topos, Curtius cites a number of cases in which poetry, or study, was praised because it kept the young person from idleness, hence from vice.) Alexandre de Paris elaborates on the same idea:

> Qui vers de riche istoire veut entendre et oïr,
> Pour prendre bon example de prouece acueillir,
> De connoistre reison d'amer et de haïr,
> De ses amis garder et chierement tenir,
> Des anemis grever. . . (1ff.).

Alexandre's history is *riche* and exemplary, worthy of those who are capable of being interested in the values it illustrates, and of potential utility to such an audience. As the romancer declares: "D'Alixandre vous voeil l'istoire rafreschir" (11). In the very next stanza he devotes some thirty-odd verses to explaining what he means; his poetic art and his exemplary purpose are intricately and inseparably blended. He will write in verse and in the vernacular so that lay folk may "profit"; he will pay as much heed to his ending as his beginning, not like "cil trouveour bastart" who "font contes abessier," and who resemble

> . . . l'asnon en son versefïer,
> Qui biaus est quant il nest et mainte gent l'ont chier;
> Com plus croist, plus ledist, et resamble aversier (34ff.).

The connection is explicit in these lines:

> Mes encontre ces vers doit la teste drecier
> Qui veut de bonnes meurs son cuer asouploier (42f.).

141

Our poet is interested in "de bonnes coustumes estruire et enseignier" (60), and this instruction is conceived in terms of his understanding of his literary ability, his literary consciousness.

In the above-quoted prologue, Marie also mentions her "travail e peine" (35); she is fully aware of her part in this transmission of knowledge, and she too works this awareness into the fabric of her text. But these ideas are developed most fully by Benoît de Sainte-Maure in the prologue to his *Roman de Troie* (ca. 1165), some 144 verses in the Constans edition (I, *SATF* [Paris, 1904]). The familiar commonplace introduces the theme:

> Salemon nos enseigne e dit,
> E sil list om en son escrit,
> Que nus ne deit son sen celer,
> Ainz le deit om si demostrer (1ff.).

We too may have "pro e honor" provided we demonstrate what we know just as our ancestors did. Indeed, had those who studied the seven arts and the philosophers' treatises chosen to remain silent, civilization would have suffered:

> Se fussent teü, veirement
> Vesquist li siegles folement:
> Come bestes eüssons vie;
> Que fust saveirs ne que folie
> Ne seüssons sol esguarder,
> Ne l'un de l'autre desevrer.
> Remembré seront a toz tens
> E coneü par lor granz sens,
> Quar sciënce que est teüe
> Est tost obliëe e perdue (11ff.).

Knowledge that is well understood "germe e florist e frutefie" (24). Benoît next describes how he has gone about his work; he will not be guilty of hiding his *sen*: "E por ço me vueil travaillier / En une estoire comencier" (33ff.). He will take his Latin source and will put it *en romanz* so that those who

142

"n'entendent la letre / Se puissent deduire el romanz." The story is most

> . . . riche et granz
> E de grant uevre et de grant fait.
> En maint sen avra l'om retrait,
> Saveir com Troie fu perie,
> Mais la verté est poi oïe.

Truth, then, is at issue here, and in the following hundred lines Benoît tells the story of the transmission of the Troy legend. Both in content and in form, the narrative follows essentially the topic of *translatio studii*; it is structured according to this topos, not, of course, according to authentic records. Thus, Homer ("clers merveillos / E sages e esciëntos" [45f.]) described the destruction of Troy, but his version was hardly exact. Nor could it have been true, since Homer was no eye-witness. Besides, his work met with opposition in Athens because of the "merveillose folie" in his contention that gods and goddesses fought with men during the war. Nevertheless, Homer was so highly esteemed that "sis livres fu receüz / E en autorité tenuz" (73f.). The notion of *translatio*, we see, allows for a critical attitude on Benoît's part, a certain philological aloofness, as it were. We go next to Rome, at the time of the most aristocratic Sallust ("Que l'on teneit si a poissant, / A riche, a pro de haut parage" [78f.]). Sallust's highly literate nephew, Cornelius, found in Athens by chance "l'estoire que Daires ot escrite" (91) and translated it into Latin "par son sen e par son engin" (122). A rather lengthy digression tells who Dares was—born and bred at Troy, a soldier and "cler merveillos / E des set arz esciëntos" (98f.), the perfect eye-witness. We know all this to be quite false, of course, but most indications point to Benoît's believing what he has written; he will, he declares, follow "le latin . . . et la letre" (139), and add nothing.

Artistry, truth, social standing, value, as well as a clear—though specialized—notion of the historicity of fiction blend, then, both characteristically and coherently within what might be described as Benoît's vision. As the anonymous poet of the *Énéas* and Wace had done before him, Benoît exploits the learned myth of the Trojan origins of the Britons. Yet, we must agree, this is hardly the historicity of the *Song of Roland*, nor, for that matter, do the other components here turn out to be related in quite the same way. The myths are differently structured.

Modern critics have complained at Benoît's lavish displays of science and learning, the many pompous and pedantic disquisitions with which he lards his seemingly endless text (in a fashion that recalls somewhat the lengthy battle descriptions of inferior *chansons de geste*). Yet the point is exactly that such learning, or displays thereof, can provide for Benoît's need to work his literary consciousness into the tissue of his composition. The absence of these displays, then, would be far more surprising than their presence; philological concern and sheer knowledge constitute indispensable ingredients of the romance. (The same is true of other texts—like the *Alexandre*—belonging to the *matière antique*. We recall once again Jehan Bodel's adjectives: *sage et de sens aprendant*.) In Benoît's work such concern is far closer to the surface of his text than, say, the *bele conjointure* which, in Chrétien de Troyes, furnishes a kind of counterpoint.

Testimony dealing with the formation of the types of literary consciousness one observes in the twelfth century may be sought in a number of sources. Of these the *Metalogicon* of John of Salisbury (ca. 1155) is both well-known and particularly rich in suggestions. John of Salisbury accords primacy to grammar among the liberal arts (end of Bk i), claiming that without literary training no true education is possible. A page from ch. xxiv of Bk i (ed. Webb, 55) is particularly famous. Here John describes quite charmingly the teaching methods, around 1130, of Bernard of Chartres, "exundantissimus modernis temporibus fons litterarum in Gallia." The doctrine of imitation is propounded: one imitates the masters in order one day to become worthy of imitation oneself. The method involves textual analysis, with special emphasis on how the text is "joined," on what John of Salisbury calls the *iuncturas dictionum* (cf. Chrétien's *bele conjointure*). Other details, too numerous to mention here, only confirm further what is apparent in John of Salisbury, namely, that for the twelfth century, literary artistry—seen largely as technique—is a matter of the highest priority and importance, with moral and philosophical implications. It is intimately associated with the very essence of the life of the spirit, as well as with the pretensions of the aristocratic class served by this artistry; *chevalerie* goes back to Rome and Greece (and Troy), so does *clergie*—both are now in France. (We should note at this point, if only in passing, that these attitudes incur the deepest suspicions of a Bernard de Clairvaux, who points out the dangers to proper Christian orthodoxy of romance and its values; but we must not forget that Saint Bernard himself was formed in the *belles-lettres* tradition, as, of course, was Abelard, his philosopher antagonist.)

The opening lines to Chrétien's *Érec et Énide* (ca. 1170)— the very text in which we find the poet describing his task as deriving "d'un conte d'avanture / une molt bele conjointure" (13f.)—utilize, like so many of the prologues we have reviewed, the topic concerning the clerk's duties:

> que reisons est que totevoies
> doit chascuns panser et antandre
> a bien dire et a bien aprandre (10ff.).

Chrétien's motivation is good, he seems to be telling us, and his work will live on; he shares fully in Bernard of Chartres' scheme of values:

> Des or comancerai l'estoire
> qui toz jorz mes iert an mimoire
> tant con durra crestïantez;
> de ce s'est Crestïens vantez (23ff.).

Despite his explicit acceptance of the kind of literary doctrine we have described so far—despite, in other words, a literary awareness that seems on many counts to be identical

145

to that of, say, Benoît de Sainte-Maure or the *Alexandre* poet
—Chrétien's material in *Érec et Énide* differs very consider-
ably from the *matière antique*. His subject-matter is Arthurian.
Chrétien does not stress his role as cultural intermediary in
Érec et Énide as, of course, he will do at the start of the
largely Greek *Cligés*. Indeed, though praising his clerkly
function, he downplays the initial topic somewhat; by neglect-
ing one's knowledge one risks "tel chose teisir / qui molt
vandroit puis *a pleisir*" (7f.). The moral urgency is much less
strong in Chrétien's "molt vandroit puis a pleisir" than in
Benoît's analogous remarks. As a consequence of this differ-
ence in subject-matter, Chrétien is led to stress, even more
than Benoît or Alexandre de Paris, the literary craftsmanship
he must provide. Nevertheless he is quick to point out the
matchless nobility of his characters; they reflect the same ideal
of civilization one finds in our other texts. Similarly, Chrétien
will partake fully in the expressive, or technical, traditions
illustrated by *Énéas*, *Troie*, *Thèbes*, and *Alexandre*; the im-
ages, the procedural devices, the conventions, and the outer
forms remain remarkably alive. Indeed, we observed, *Cligés*
indissolubly links *clergie* and *chevalerie* in one of the most
explicit and poetically rich renderings of the *translatio studii*
topic to have survived in the OF vernacular (25ff.).

The plain fact that Chrétien worked with an Arthurian
subject-matter in *Érec et Énide* and elsewhere must be under-
stood in all its implications before one may go on to analyze
the mechanisms of his literary consciousness. For Chrétien's
romances differ in many ways from the *matere de Rome*, and
it is largely in the use to which he put Arthurian legend that
the important differences may be best grasped.

To understand better, then, the differences that accompany
Chrétien's sharing the literary consciousness of the romancers
we have so far looked at, we should do well to review the two
chronicle-romances of Wace: the *Roman de Brut* (ca. 1155)
and the *Roman de Rou* (ca. 1160-1174). (We recall that, in
1174, Henry II invited Benoît de Sainte-Maure to write the
history of the dukes of Normandy, at which point in all

probability Wace gave up this work himself. Benoît's call, however, reminds one that "history" and "romance" were hardly distinct genres in the twelfth century.) Similarities between Chrétien and Wace have been such as to encourage scholars to seek out influences and borrowings. In his *Chrétien de Troyes* (Paris, 1968₂), Jean Frappier devotes a number of pages (26ff.) to these questions; M. Pelan studied *L'Influence du* BRUT *de Wace sur les romanciers de son temps* (Paris, 1931), with Chrétien receiving much attention (17-70). Indeed, Miss Pelan's suggestion that "Wace était modèle littéraire plutôt que source" (70) sets us off, I think, on the right track. To Chrétien Wace offers the means of intensifying the novelistic character of his narratives. Part of this problem falls within the category of literary consciousness.

In the *Brut* Wace tells the *verité* of those "ki Engleterre primes tindrent" (ed. Arnold, I, *SATF* [Paris, 1938], 4). He recounts the legend of the Trojan origin of the Britons: Brutus, grandson of Æneas, is banished from Italy; he finally removes to England, where he founds London, "New Troy." Wace reviews the history of the British kings (including King Lear). According to a recent edition (Arnold and Pelan [Paris, 1962]), some 4728 lines (B.N. fr., 794)—about a third of the 14,866 lines constituting the 1938 text—are given over to the life and times of King Arthur, clearly the central figure in the work. Wace's *Brut* translates and adapts Geoffrey of Monmouth's widely circulated *Historia regum Brittaniæ* (1137). Wace's role here is analogous in all respects to that of Benoît in *Troie*; a *translatio* certainly takes place. Remarks by Arnold and Pelan are interesting in this connection: "Dans les manuscrits on trouve souvent réunis soit le *Brut* et les 'romans antiques' (voir *Eneas*, éd. S. de Grave, pp. iv-v) soit le *Brut* et les romans courtois (voir le ms. de Guiot): cela indique peut-être que toutes ces œuvres s'adressaient au même public, attiraient les mêmes amateurs" (*op.cit.*, 33). Each of these romances belongs substantively and formally to the *translatio* type.

Not only does Wace endow the Arthurian material with

147

OF narrative form (e.g., the romance octosyllable, a wide variety of literary devices); he circumscribes a kind of novelistic attitude that betrays a literary consciousness quite close to that of Chrétien. Here is a significant text:

En cele grant pais ke jo di [the Arthurian Golden Age],
Ne sai si vus l'avez oï,
Furent les merveilles pruvees
E les aventures truvees
Ki d'Artur sunt tant recuntees
Ke a fable sunt aturnees.
Ne tut mençunge, ne tut veir,
Tut folie ne tut saveir.
Tant unt li cunteür cunté
E li fableür tant flablé
Pur lur cuntes enbeleter,
Que tut unt fait fable sembler (9787ff.).

Wace protests the deformations perpetuated by those whom, in *Érec*, Chrétien will call "cil qui de conter vivre vuelent" (22). But even more important, he builds into his own narrational perspective a certain doubt, an ambivalence toward the authenticity of his tradition: "Ne tut mençunge, ne tut veir." The tales are shady; their truth is hard to penetrate. Indeed, this "truth" is doubted precisely because Wace claims to serve the *verité* of the Britons—the very pretext is quintessentially novelistic. Thus, Wace is led to utilize this doubt in a typically novelistic way when recounting the story of Arthur's death. We find the source topos, of course; it reinforces the narrator's credibility: "Arthur, *si la geste ne ment*,/ Fud el cors nafrez mortelment" (13,275f.). This also permits the narrator's intervention. Arthur is taken off to Avalon to be cured: "Encore i est, Bretun l'atendent,/ Si cum il dient e entendent" (13,279f.). Arthur will return, but Wace reaffirms his perspective: "Maistre Wace, ki fist cest livre,/ Ne volt plus dire de sa fin/ Qu'en dist li prophetes Merlin." Wace's attitude reinforces the doubt inherent in the event: "sa mort dutuse serreit" (13,286):

148

Tut tens en ad l'um puis duté,
E dutera, ço crei, tut dis,
Se il est morz u il est vis (13,238ff.).

We recall that Geoffrey, Wace's source, avoids such novelistic construction: "Sed et inclytus ille rex Arturus letaliter vulneratus est, qui illinc ad sananda vulnera sua in insulam Avallonis advectus, cognato suo Constantino, filio Cadoris ducis Cornubiæ, diadema Britanniæ concessit" (XI, 2).

In yet another famous instance Wace speaks of Breton fables, indirectly citing them as sources in his description of the Round Table:

Pur les nobles baruns qu'il out,
Dunt chescuns mieldre estre quidout,
Chescuns se teneit al meillur,
Ne nuls n'en saveit le peiur,
Fist Artur la Roünde Table
Dunt Bretun dient mainte fable.
Illuec seeient li vassal
Tuit chevalment e tuit egal . . . (9747ff.).

(No mention of the Round Table is to be found in Geoffrey's *Historia*.) Wace's incorporation of this detail into his story is best seen in rhetorical terms, as part of the coherent rhetoric of his fiction. The description of the Round Table illustrates and amplifies the theme of Arthur's courtly excellence. The anecdote reinforces the contact here between the subject-matter of the story and its audience; it flatters Wace's patrons at the Norman court of England and, concomitantly, it serves to celebrate the dignity of Wace's work. This kind of identification is frequent in *Brut*; one need only compare Geoffrey's description of court ceremonies—in which elegance and sumptuousness already are praised—with Wace's counterpart. See Geoffrey's *Historia*, IX, 13-14, and compare his presentation with that offered by Wace's "Fêtes de cour" (10,237ff.). Wace's story brings in, utilizes, and thereby *expresses* his patrons' social ideal.

149

But Wace's relationship with his audience is articulated with even greater forthrightness in the *Roman de Rou*. His frankness ought not to be confused with mere cynicism, however, since the dignity of Wace's own work is at issue here:

Jeo parouc a la riche gent,
Ki unt les rentes e le argent,
Kar pur eus sunt li liure fait
E bon dit fait e bien retrait (ed. Andresen [Heilbronn, 1879], 163ff.).

This passage concludes an extended series of lines in which "Maistre Wace" aspires to be known as one who "mult dit bien." The romancer describes his work and, at the same time, keeps his distance from those values it expresses that belong essentially (or ostensibly) to the men and women to whom he dedicates his work. Wace is, in a sense, "of" his audience; he does not "belong to" it. A dovetailing occurs, but no real identification. All sorts of ironies ensue. Indeed, Wace suggests in proper romance fashion, true civilization could never do without the clerk:

Pur remembrer des ancesurs
Les feiz e les diz e les murs,
Les felunies des feluns
E les barnages des baruns
Deit l'um les liures e les gestes
E les estoires lire a[s] festes.
Si escripture ne fust feite
E puis par clers litte e retraite,
Mult fussent choses ubliees . . . (1ff.).

This motif is developed subsequently in a number of highly literary ways: Names change—and Wace cites about thirty of them!—over time and space ("Man en engleis e en norreis/ Hume signifie en franceis" [59f.]), and, without writing, we should know nothing of all this past. One would indeed be hard-pressed to find traces of erstwhile majestic cities:

"Meis par les bons clers ki escristrent/ . . . Sauum nus del uies tens parler" (104f.). Wace makes sure we get the point.

Undoubtedly, Wace's literary consciousness sums up much of what we have observed to be true of the twelfth-century romancers, including Chrétien de Troyes himself. But in Wace what we have noticed is brought even more closely to the surface than in the practitioners of the *matière antique*. This is in great part true because of the historical "truth"— what one might be tempted to call the "close-to-home" quality —of his subject-matter: what is "digne de remembrer" (to use the phrase from *Thèbes*) are the "deeds, the sayings, and the customs" of our "ancestors." Wace is involved in the fostering of the *translatio* myths that, though predominantly social and moral, are partly political and familial. The product of his craft is even less gratuitous than that of the *Alexandre* poet or of his rival Benoît de Sainte-Maure. Because it concerns his audience more intimately, Wace's text involves, on the part of the author, a greater commitment, a firmer moral engagement, and, consequently, a strengthened narrator figure: a learned witness, someone closer in spirit (though by no means identical) to the *Alexis* narrator. Yet, conversely, what serves to link his public and his subject-matter—the Norman court is "heir" to Arthur, not Wace— tends to separate poet and *matière*. The *Alexis* and *Roland* poet-narrators intervened between tale and public, to be sure, but they fully belonged to both. Wace the chronicler-romancer is indispensable at once to his material and to his audience; however he may not be entirely identified with either. His identity resides in his craft: it is he who "speaks well."

Our romancers may be authentically and properly viewed as philologists, as men of letters concerned primarily with the very stuff of literature. This concern lies at the heart of their work. All romancers took the trouble to explain the moral and scientific value of literature, and many referred extensively to their own role in the transmission of such value. Their explanations and references do much to situate

151

literature within the value schemes of the new refined aris-
tocracy of France and England, as well as to delimit the
function of a partly secularized clerical class. The *Alexandre*
poet and the author of *Thèbes* are creative philologists in that
their literary "study"—their discipline—finds its way into the
texture (substance and form) of their art. It is there for all
to see and to admire, in its proper place. However, the more
modern the subject—Wace's Arthurian and Norman ma-
terial is "modern"—the more thoroughly novelistic the philo-
logical attitude, or literary consciousness, tends to be. The
romance form takes on a new character. Wace, we noticed,
put his literary awareness to work, incorporating it more in-
tensely into the rhetorical structuring of his poems. His narra-
tor is at once "reliable" and "ambiguous"; he is critical of
fables but nonetheless makes free poetic use of them when
it suits his purposes. (Indeed he recalls his childhood when
he used to listen to story-tellers.) The poet serves his *matière*
and his audience by stressing his craft: how, in other words,
he has put things together. What counts for him is, in fact,
the fiction. One marvels at Jehan Bodel's critical acumen
when, in *Saisnes*, he refers to the *effect* the Breton tales pro-
duce, their "vain and pleasant" form, which he contrasts with
the "wise" content of the *matere de Rome* and the noble
"truth" of the story of France. Wace is clearly aware of play-
ing with truth; that issue arises again and again. Yet none of
his inventions—accretions, modifications of Geoffrey, inter-
ventions—can be explained as well as when confronted with
the requirements and purposes of his kind of fiction.[8] His
ultimate success may be gauged by the effects his ironies have
had on certain modern readers. The late J. P. Tatlock de-

[8] This conclusion is reached by Margaret Houck, *Sources of the*
ROMAN DE BRUT *of Wace*, UCPMPh, V:2 (University of California,
1941): "Most of the alterations made by Wace in Geoffrey's narra-
tive have their source in his characteristic technique of storytelling
and his poetic individuality; that is, in his style as a narrative poet"
(167).

scribed him as "enquiring, critical, honest," while Gaston
Paris spoke of his "amour sincère de la vérité." Miss Houck
was closer to the point when she wrote that "Wace was a
writer by profession" (163), and, in this connection, it is
most worthwhile to bear in mind how Chrétien de Troyes
will further utilize techniques and procedures developed by
Wace (cf. M. Pelan, *op.cit.*).

Present throughout Chrétien's work, the kinds of literary
consciousness, or specific awareness, I have tried to describe
are nowhere more crucially important than in *Yvain*. In this
text Chrétien's novelistic irony may be found at its purest. A
few words concerning these matters will conclude this sec-
tion of our study.

As was the case in Wace's *Brut*, Chrétien's narrator in
Yvain is both reliable and ambiguous; he is even more in-
tensely both of these. Thus, at the very start, we have a
throwback to the kind of literature represented by *Alexis*
and *Roland*. Arthur, the good king of Britain, whose prowess
teaches us to be "preu et cortois," holds court "a cele feste
qui tant coste, / qu'an doit clamer la Pantecoste" (5f.). This
focusing on Arthur, his court, and, so to speak, a historical
situation reminds one of the opening to the Oxford text of
Roland: "Carles li reis, nostre emperere magnes, / Set anz
tuz pleins ad estet en Espaigne." Charles too holds court, at
"Cordres," whereas, we learn, Arthur is at "Carduel en
Gales." Woven into this depiction is the "Good Old Days"
topos, a fine, traditional commonplace of the exordium, a
variant of what we find at the beginning of *Alexis*: "Bo[e]ns
fut li si[e]cles al tens anciënur." In Arthur's time Love was
prized and properly served, but now it has declined: "Or
est Amors tornee a fable / por ce que cil qui rien n'en san-
tent / dïent qu'il aiment, mes il mantent" (24ff.). As in
Alexis, this topic allows the narrator to connect his material
and his audience—to link them effectively—as well as to
claim his work worthy: "Mes or parlons de cez qui furent, /
si leissons cez qui ancor durent, / car molt valt mialz, ce

153

m'est a vis, / uns cortois morz c'uns vilains vis" (29ff.). And the narrator goes on to praise even more highly the courtesy and grandeur of King Arthur.

By saying all these things at the beginning of his poem, Chrétien puts the memory of *Alexis* and *Roland* to work; he associates his poem with this illustrious narrative tradition, and, by so doing in the exordium, he confers value upon his enterprise. *Yvain* is meant to represent a narrative mode that treats the Arthurian history as *Alexis* had treated the stories of saints and *Roland* the epic of France. (Whether it was indeed possible in late twelfth-century France to consider Arthurian material as though it were authentic in this way is a matter of conjecture—it was surely a question of degree— but Chrétien certainly, even obviously, makes the effort or plays seriously at doing so. Nevertheless, I repeat, he does so within the framework of a purely "literary" consciousness; the literature quite ostensibly takes precedence over the myth.) In this manner the narrator is shown to be reliable; what he tells, in large part because of how he tells it, is worthy of remembrance.

Though Chrétien's public was indubitably fond of a good story and, perhaps, at times even took itself seriously enough to see, mirrored in the goings-on of Arthur's court, an image of what it too aspired to achieve, Chrétien himself, like Wace, could hardly go so far. Inserted into the beginning lines from *Yvain* that we have examined here are a number of curious and even disquieting side remarks: the "feste *qui tant coste,* / qu'an doit clamer la Pantecoste"; "car molt valt mialz, ce m'est a vis, / uns cortois morz c'uns vilains vis." The rhyme *tant coste: Pantecoste* stresses a bizarre, unexpected (though not untrue) *rapprochement*. Similarly, the proverb-like bit of bravura that a dead gentleman is worthier than a live boor constitutes the kind of cheap flattery a courtly poet may be expected to indulge in so as to insure his audience's complicity, but it jars with the rest of the context, especially with what follows:

154

Por ce [i.e., "therefore"] me plest a reconter
chose qui face a escouter
del roi qui fu de tel tesmoing
qu'an en parole et pres et loing;
si m'acort de tant as Bretons
que toz jorz durra li renons
et par lui sont amenteü
li boen chevalier esleü
qui a enor se traveillierent (33ff.).

Both these side remarks constitute judgments on the narrator's part. However, they are personal judgments and they stem from his own experience. Because their value derives entirely from the narrator's validity as a witness (another topos!), these judgments are unlike the "historical" judgment contained in, say, the above-quoted vv. 33-41. A kind of undercutting is at issue here. The narrator subverts the modes within which the poem ostensibly functions. Similar subversion occurs, quite decisively, in the narrative itself. No sooner does the narrator finish praising, almost ritualistically, Arthur's courtesy than he must describe how, to the total surprise of his stunned guests, the king gets up from table to join Guenevere in bed; and "demora tant delez li / qu'il s'oblia et endormi" (51f.). While her husband sleeps on, a thoroughly awake Guenevere leaves the bedroom in order to hear Calogrenant, who had begun to tell a small assembly of knights "un conte, / non de s'annor, mes de sa honte" (59f.). At the appearance of the queen, Calogrenant stands up, respectfully, but Keu, "qui molt fu ranponeus, / fel et poignanz et venimeus" (69f.), insults him for doing so. A vulgar quarrel ensues, involving even Guenevere ("—Certes, Kex, ja fussiez crevez, / fet la reïne, au mien cuidier, / se ne vos poïssiez vuidier / del venin don vos estes plains. / Enuieus estes, et vilains" [86ff.]). Meanwhile, the young Yvain distinguishes himself by his moderation. In short, the behavior of Arthur, his queen, and a representative body of gentlemen

155

belies the heroic and polite ideal praised in the judgment. Observed conduct contradicts, or undercuts, myth. The narrator remains reliable—we are his accomplices (even more than we are accomplices to what in fact is being said)—but considerable ambiguity is brought into the narrator's position. A new complexity results. Arthur and his court remain glorious, but all this undercutting modulates our relationship to that glory.

The mediation of the fiction, which we saw essentially as a means in *Roland* and in *Alexis*, becomes here a kind of goal or purpose in itself. Chrétien shifts our loyalties from the events of his "history" (and our participation in them) to the narration itself, which we must unravel. It dawns upon us that what *Yvain* is all about may be grasped only when we are willing and able to play the literary game Chrétien has set up, when, in other words, we understand that Chrétien's literary awareness not only enables us to penetrate the Arthurian world he recreates but that it constitutes as well the prime device obliging us to maintain our distance from that world. *Yvain* is novelistic; it is not historically straight, like *Roland* and *Alexis*, nor technically speaking is it entirely confined to romance, like, say, the *Alexandre* poems. Bad manners are contrasted with courtly ideology and in the contrast itself, in the very process of contrast (narrator, myth, legend, observed behavior, scenic structure, etc.), the novelistic perspective is established. And, I repeat, the fact that all this occurs precisely at the point where romancers—including Chrétien himself—and other narrative poets customarily declare their intentions, namely, in the exordium or beginning of the poem, reinforces still more novelistically what can only be called Chrétien's generic intent.

MATTERS OF TECHNIQUE

We have seen how, in *Yvain*, Chrétien's novelistic perspective is enunciated by the development of certain attitudes already present in Wace as well as by what in fact turns out to be the poeticization, or internalization, of the exordium motifs one finds in straight "historical" works and also in contemporary romances. *Yvain* poeticizes the commonplaces with which, as we observed, so many of the "wise" texts of the *matière antique* begin, e.g., the suitability, or pairing, of letters and good manners. Chrétien's own *bele conjointure* is proclaimed implicitly by virtue of being built right into the astonishing juxtapositions with which *Yvain* opens and which determine its unfolding. (Even Arthur's knights and ladies are astounded when he leaves the table!) In short we have already looked into problems of novelistic or compositional technique.

But now that we have established the primacy of these matters, we must examine them even more closely. I propose to focus especially upon *Cligés*, the romance dating from ca. 1176, according to A. Fourrier, and consequently the one to precede immediately *Lancelot* and *Yvain*. (Most authorities agree that *Lancelot* and *Yvain* were probably composed at about the same time, possibly even jointly, between 1176 and 1181, so that it makes sense to consider *Cligés* as the proper predecessor to *Yvain*.)[9] Even more significant, however, is the fact that *Cligés*, as Frappier has suggested, is surely the romance in which Chrétien displays the greatest technical virtuosity. This work shows what he was capable of in that range, and it does so in a fashion that will permit us to understand better his accomplishments in the later texts. Furthermore, *Cligés* is perhaps the purest and most accomplished "romance" among Chrétien's creations, the one work that takes the romance possibilities (in this sense as opposed to novelistic ones) about as far as they will go. Conversely, *Lancelot* and, to a lesser degree, *Perceval* may, I believe, be usefully seen as attempts to deepen and render more "serious" the romance form. Chrétien attempted this deepening by making use of the novelistic means that he perfected in *Yvain*, but

[9] See J. Frappier, *Chrétien de Troyes* (Paris, 1968), p. 145, and, mentioned by Frappier, A. Fourrier, in *Bulletin bibliographique de la Société internationale arthurienne*, no. 2 (1950), 69ff.

that, of course, were not entirely suitable to his goals in either *Lancelot* or *Perceval*; *Cligés*, meanwhile, remains more completely gratuitous.

A brief plot summary may be helpful. The handsome and generous young Byzantine prince, Alexandre, obtains permission from his father the emperor to visit Arthur in Britain. On a trip with Arthur's court to Brittany, Alexandre and Soredamor, the lovely maiden-in-waiting to Guenevere, see each other and fall in love; neither dares speak. Meanwhile Arthur is betrayed by Angrés, to whom he had confided the kingdom of England during his absence. Alexandre distinguishes himself in the battles of reconquest and marries Soredamor. She gives birth to Cligés. The parents take their son and remove to Greece, where Alexandre expects to claim the throne now occupied by his brother Alis. The two agree to let Alis continue his reign but only on condition he not marry, in order that, eventually, Cligés might inherit the throne. Alexandre and Soredamor die. Urged on by his barons, Alis decides to break his vow and marry Fénice, the charming daughter of the emperor of Germany. When they meet, Cligés and Fénice fall in love with each other. Fénice confesses her love to Thessala, her sorceress nurse, who prepares a drink that will make Alis mistakenly believe he has enjoyed his wife's favors on their wedding night. Cligés behaves heroically, saving Fénice from a kidnap attempt. Deeply in love, he does not quite dare declare his passion, except somewhat obliquely when he takes leave of Fénice in order to visit Arthur's court. In Britain he triumphs over most of Arthur's knights—he even equals Gauvain—but he cannot forget Fénice. He returns to Greece and proclaims his love. Fénice reciprocates but refuses to live in adultery. She will instead feign death and will be buried in a specially designed (and very luxurious) tomb, where she and Cligés can be together. After duping three *fisiciens* from Salerno, Fénice is entombed and fifteen months of joy ensue. However they are eventually found out and obliged to escape to Britain, where they raise a great army. But the news of Alis' death arrives and the two lovers

158

are married and crowned. Subsequently, the romance concludes, Greek emperors have found it expedient to keep careful watch on their spouses.

The success of *Cligés* as romance depends on the degree of superiority we are consciously willing to confer upon the fashioning as opposed to the materials; "form" and "content" are contrasted. In itself the plot is absurd. Poeticized in the romance—that is, so long as we understand explicitly that we are meant to be conscious at all times that we are coping with a romance-type plot—then and only then does it give off its flavor of ironic persiflage and delicate humor. (The procedure reminds one of *Candide*.) Chrétien exploits here the resonances of literary convention. Thus, though many have said that *Cligés* is a kind of anti-*Tristan*—indeed Fénice herself declares that she is unable to "acorder / A la vie qu'Isolz mena" (3110f.)—it is not a simple "answer," or alternative, to the Tristan legend; *Cligés* depends on *Tristan* and the way this dependence functions constitutes its response: it transforms more thoroughly into gratuitous romance forms key elements of the Tristan story and its implications, in a sense trivializing it by stressing that *Tristan* too is a romance. After all, Fénice is hardly Yseut's moral superior. Similarly, as opposed to *Érec et Énide*, *Cligés* does not depict an Arthurian magic or mythology. There is no mysterious and wonderful Celtic Joie de la Cort to amplify or deepen the romance's dimensions. However, just as in *Érec,* Arthur's court constitutes here the courtly place *par excellence*; King Arthur is the greatest king of all and, interestingly, Queen Guenevere plays the go-between who facilitates the marriage of Alexandre and Soredamor, a bit as she had done in bringing Érec and Énide together. The Arthurian world "imitates" itself here within the framework of Chrétien's *œuvre*; it functions as its romanesque model had functioned. Guenevere does what she had done in *Érec et Énide* and the fact that she does so is integrated into the economy of *Cligés*. Indeed this may be one of the reasons explaining Chrétien's cataloging his works at the start of *Cligés*. His very literary experience—the sum total of his work—is poeticized. At any rate, instead of occupying an ambiguous position at once in the romance and as an extension of the romance, the Arthurian world merely serves the romance in *Cligés*.

Technical virtuosity becomes a matter of poetic economy in the case of *Cligés*. In the first part of the romance Arthur's court, Alexandre's acts of prowess, and the love of Alexandre and Soredamor are purely literary motifs that are once again combined in order to make literature. The higher degree, or greater quantity, of literary consciousness displayed and utilized in *Cligés* has, in fact, important qualitative repercussions. Alexandre goes off in search of adventure. All knights in romances do just that. (So will Alonso Quijano one day.) We recall that Alexandre's military effectiveness at Arthur's court is characterized by liberal use of ruse—and, incidentally, like his namesake, our hero is known for his generosity—and this too is typical of romance. In a very Greek fashion he and his companions disguise themselves in order to get into Angrés' castle. One is reminded, quite maliciously, of Troy; also, Tristan was famous for his trickery. Alexandre falls in love and proud Soredamor reciprocates his passion. This love occurs in a décor as romanesque as possible: a boat, at sea, exactly like Tristan and Yseut. Critics have pointed out that the play on *amer* (love), *la mer* (sea), and the sickness of love (confused by Guenevere with seasickness and consequently misconstrued), a kind of *annominatio* (540ff.), throws back to the Tristan story (see Bédier's reconstruction of Thomas, I, *SATF*, [Paris, 1902], 146). But our lovers remain chaste; in this they oppose, quite symmetrically, Tristan and his beloved.

Various kinds of symmetry characterize the first part of *Cligés*; these underscore the text's artifice. In her first love monologue (469ff.) Soredamor describes what she feels according to Ovidian convention: love enters through the eyes which, in this manner, "betray" the heart. The images are antithetical, centered on the concept of madness (*folie*):

160

"Doloir? Par foi, donc sui je fole,
Quant par lui voel ce qui m'afole.
Volantez don me vaigne enuis
Doi je bien oster, se je puis.
Se je puis? Fole, qu'ai je dit?" (503ff.)

In his parallel monologue Alexandre takes up the same image:

"Por fol, fet il, me puis tenir.
Por fol? voiremant sui ge fos,
Quant ce que je pans dire n'os" (618ff.).

Brought to the fore precisely within the rhetorical context of love casuistry and displayed almost ostentatiously, these parallelisms help proclaim the particularly romance character of *Cligés*. Chrétien uses romance convention as epitomized, say, in texts from the *matière antique* like *Énéas*, *Alexandre*, and *Troie*; this use implicitly proclaims the filiation of *Cligés* to that tradition. Both Alexandre and Soredamor are troubled; the chaste pride of the girl balances the hero's timidity. They are "worthy" of each other. But before their penchant for one another may be satisfied, Angrés must be defeated, and the false news of Alexandre's death must be circulated and disproved. We know that all this will lead to marriage (as, indeed, was the case of *Érec et Énide*), but—and I insist once again—we are supposed to focus on the manner in which the story unfolds. Nothing is more romance-like than the long monologues in which, with so perfect a conventionality that the effect is almost one of parody, the minds and hearts of the protagonists are explored in order to reveal a possible discrepancy. Thus Soredamor's great monologue (889-1038), coming after the narrator's depiction of her troubled *corage* (865ff.), illustrates brilliantly the romancer's technical competence. Her situation is entirely conventional: she is the young-maiden-in-love. Her rhetoric, as though to illustrate the *tançons* disturbing her, is based entirely on antithesis and

161

oppositions. In this fashion a kind of dialectic or dispute is formed, and this allows Soredamor to sound out more deeply her soul:

"Mes volantiers, se je savoie,
Plus sage et plus bel le feroie.
Par foi, donc ne le hé je mie.
Et sui je por itant s'amie?
Nenil, ne qu'a un autre sui.
Et por coi pans je donc a lui,
Se plus d'un altre ne m'agree?" (905ff.)

Similarly, the etymological figure in which Soredamor—and the romance—can fully indulge prompts the maiden, who, like many of her counterparts in OF romances of the *translatio studii* type (cf. *RPh*, XXVI [August 1972]) is highly intelligent, even a bit learned, to recognize her love by equating it with the realization of her own identity:

"Por neant n'ai ge pas cest non [Soredamor]
Que Soredamors sui clamee.
Amer doi, si doi estre amee,
Si le vuel par mon non prover" (953ff.).

She continues charmingly and very literarily in this "technical" and bookish image:

"Et autant dit Soredamors
Come sororee d'amors.
Doreüre d'or n'est si fine
Come ceste qui m'anlumine" (971ff.).

Confronted with this kind of romance love—and let us not confuse it with *amour courtois*—scholars have been tempted to call it cold and calculated, an *amour de tête*. Certainly the expressive artifice is calculated and very knowingly put together, but the context of this intellectuality remains very much the romance, not the character. Maidens like Soredamor, Fénice, or Lavinie (*Énéas*) do not fall in love in a reasonable, intellectual way. However, they do attempt to

162

assimilate this new passion into their understanding and, like Soredamor here, they often are depicted in their self-analysis as proceeding step by step, quite explicitly, from an initial amorous confusion to a conscious stock-taking and, finally, to an active decision. We are interested in this process and in the means by which it is revealed. Because of our technical concern some readers have been led to deny passion its rightful role even though, quite clearly, Soredamor and her lover suffer the same sweet pangs of passionate love as do Tristan and the blond Yseut. What *Cligés* is hinting at, however, is that the legend of Tristan and Yseut should also be seen as a romance, that the love of Tristan and Yseut is a story, like that of Alexandre and Soredamor, of, especially, Cligés and Fénice. This is the nature (and, we observed, the relevance) of *Cligés* as a critical commentary upon *Tristan,* a commentary quite different from that offered by *Érec et Énide.*

The fashion in which the adventures of Alexandre and his love for Soredamor are recounted strips this material of all "history" and even of "historical illusion." If everything here is more perfectly gratuitous, it follows quite logically that the second step, the "main story" of their son Cligés, must be at least as *romanesque,* if not more so. We recall Alexandre's return to Byzantium and his rather surprising agreement with the usurping Alis. (This agreement is essential, though, to avoid transforming the second part of the romance into a somber, and banal, *Vengeance Cligés.*) Note that as soon as the boy is installed at his uncle's court (like Tristan in Mark's palace), his parents conveniently die. Love, ruses, but chastity and honor, as well as a number of technical devices: orphan nephew dearly loved by a doting uncle, important play of reality and appearances—all this is clearly established in *Cligés* before the emperor's departure for Germany.

It has been said that the "German" part of *Cligés* constitutes a development of certain political and matrimonial projects that Frederick Barbarossa attempted unsuccessfully to bring off in league with the Greek emperor towards 1170-

163

1174. This is quite plausible. Chrétien might easily have felt free to combine here allusions to certain real happenings with the literary, very *Tristan*-like, and dramatic motif of the matrimonial embassy. By working historical events into the texture of the romance in a manner analogous to his utilization of the *Tristan* data, Chrétien contributes at once to the piquancy of his tale and to the trivialization—the game—it is called upon to bring off; the romance is all the more ironically "true-to-life." At the same time, of course, Chrétien furthers his plot: Cligés and Fénice meet; they may act out their drama within the contexts which were set up by the romance and, of course, largely determined by the story of Alexandre and Soredamor. Like Cligés' parents (and like Tristan and Yseut), Cligés and Fénice are deeply in love, but unlike Alexandre and Soredamor (however, like Tristan and Yseut), marriage is impossible because Alis (like Mark) stands in the way. This *impasse* suffices to provoke the introduction of Thessala's potion of chastity; the potion is structurally "justified." Fénice's body will belong *in reality* only to the man who possesses her heart, though, *in appearance*, she is a loyal and devoted wife. Meanwhile, Cligés dedicates his feats of prowess (in Germany as well as at Arthur's court) to his beloved. Possibly to avoid excessive seriousness at this juncture, the poet-narrator plays increasingly with his material; he intervenes with witty and explicitly literary commentary, turning his romance even from this angle into an ostensibly self-conscious object. Thus, during the tournament at Arthur's court, where Cligés so handsomely distinguishes himself, he refuses to enumerate the knights present (as Wace had done in the Arthurian *Fêtes de cour* scene from *Brut* [10,236ff.] and, indeed, as Chrétien himself, in imitation of Wace, had done in his description of the courtly *fastes* in *Érec et Énide*):

> Devers Galinguefort revint
> Li plus de la chevalerie.
> Cuidiez vos or que je vos die

Por feire demorer mon conte:
"Cil roi i furent, et cil conte,
Et cil, et cil, et cil i furent?" (4586ff.)

The play of reality and appearances may be considered simultaneously a theme and a motif in *Cligés*. Since, virtually by definition, such play constitutes a properly novelistic *theme*, it is used in *Cligés* as a motif, gratuitously, for its own sake, and, if I may be permitted the seeming paradox, in this way it turns out to be once again an authentic theme— refracted, so to speak, through the romance's various technical contexts. (It is analogous to the similarly contrived theme-motif pattern of, say, "optimism" in *Candide* or "honor" in *Orlando Furioso*.) As we observed, Alexandre loves Soredamor and is loved in return by her. We know this because the novelistic mechanism allows us to penetrate beyond mere appearance into the intimate being of the character (though only insofar as, and in the ways, this being concerns the romance: plot, thematic structure, etc.). However, love produces visible effects; according to the Ovidian convention embraced by most twelfth-century romancers, the lover pales or blushes, his breathing is troubled. Guenevere observes this *malaise* in our young heroes, but, in a delicious play on the theme of appearances vs. reality, she confuses the symptoms of love with those of seasickness! Appearances, we see, do indeed deceive! Yet, conversely, this is also a comment upon the authentic nature of passionate love. Whereas in the more properly novelistic *Érec et Énide* Chrétien attempted to establish a kind of correlation between reality and appearances— after all, Érec's idleness, resulting from his love and the voluptuous delights he enjoys with the apparently Dido-like Énide, does constitute a danger signal—in the first part of *Cligés* everything is centered on the fictional techniques to be used in getting Alexandre and Soredamor together; the problem will be compounded in the case of Cligés and Fénice.

By continuing to follow in this manner the development of

165

the reality-appearances motif in *Cligés*, we stand a better chance of grasping this fiction's special kind of intensity. Let us look at a few key texts.

First, Fénice's complaint. Cligés has just left for Arthur's court, but in taking leave of Fénice (to whom he has not yet revealed his love, nor she to him), he declares:

> "Mes droiz est qu'a vos congié praigne
> Com a celi cui ge sui toz" (4282f.).

She analyzes this statement in a very romance-like way, a bit scholastically:

> A li seule opose et respont,
> Et fet tele oposition (4364f.).

Herself in love, she is very impressed by Cligés' half avowal of devotion:

> "Cligés par quele entancion
> 'Je sui toz vostres' me deïst,
> S'Amors dire ne li feïst?
> De quoi le puis je justisier?" (4366ff.)

Motif and theme seem to combine here, for, in her monologue, Fénice attributes Cligés' words and tears to a variety of different causes. The transition is a masterpiece:

> "Par foi, donc m'a cil maubaillie
> Qui mon cuer a en sa baillie,
> Ne m'aimme pas, ce sai je bien,
> Qui me desrobe et tost le mien.
> Jel sai? Por coi ploroit il dons?
> Por coi? Ne fu mien an pardons,
> Asez i ot reison de quoi.
> N'en doi neant prandre sor moi,
> Car de gent qu'an aimme et conoisse
> Se part an a molt grant angoisse.
> Quant il leissa sa conoissance,

166

Si en ot enui et pesance,
Et s'il plora, ne m'an mervoil.
Mes qui li dona cest consoil,
Qu'an Bretaigne alast demorer,
Ne me poïst mialz acorer.
Acorez est qui son cuer pert.
Mal doit avoir qui le suen pert,
Mes je ne le desservi onques
Ha, dolante, por coi m'a donques
Cligés morte sanz nul forfet?" (4419ff.)

Fénice goes on from her memory of Cligés to rather more general considerations, and then returns to her own situation. She knows her own suffering, but what do Cligés' tears *really* mean? What is hidden behind these signs? She is caught up in her own romance.

Our second example is perhaps the capital text in the entire story: Fénice's avowal to Cligés of her love and of her maidenly reality (despite her outwardly apparent status as a married lady). Everything has built up to this confrontation. The "reality" is of course close to that of Tristan and Yseut; indeed it departs from the prototype in a direction leading to parody. Fénice's diction reinforces this impression:

"Qu'ainz vostre oncles n'ot en moi part,
Car moi ne plot, ne lui ne lut.
Onques ancor ne me conut,
Si com Adanz conut sa fame.
A tort sui apelee dame,
Mes bien sai, qui dame m'apele
Ne set que je soie pucele" (5176ff.).

We cannot take seriously Fénice's declaration of moral purpose, except insofar as it renders possible at last the union of the storybook couple of whom we have become fond, the "natural" *dénouement* of the romance. Her conduct is legitimate only in a romance world; note the play on the preten-

167

sion to exemplary value claimed by so many romances of the *translatio studii* type:

> "Vostre est mes cuers, vostre est mes cors,
> Ne ja nus par mon essanplaire
> N'aprendra vilenie a faire" (5190ff.).

And:

> "Se je vos aim, et vos m'amez,
> Ja n'en seroiz Tristanz clamez,
> Ne je n'an serai ja Yseuz" (5199ff.).

Chrétien is careful once again to reinforce the romance quality of all this by having Cligés quote learnedly from the legend of Troy when he proposes flight to Arthur's court as a solution to their dilemma (5239ff.), and by having Fénice, in reply, first quote from *Tristan* and then Saint Paul! The romance context intensifies and becomes even more pure; the play of realities and appearances turns out to be still more perfectly gratuitous. Thus, Saint Paul's doctrines concerning chastity are invoked to justify Fénice's playing dead!

The solution proposed by Fénice is unadulterated romance; the philtre, the feigned death, the refuge for the lovers. (One recalls that other *locus amœnus*, the isolated cave, where Tristan and Yseut dwelt in peace, the powerful topic of lovers against the world. The total artifice of the refuge-tomb in which Cligés and Fénice spend fifteen months of bliss—there is running hot water!—contrasts with the rustic simplicity of Tristan's cave; nevertheless Cligés seems here to see through this simplicity, down to the essential artificiality of the topos.) In any case the romance is ready to take off.

Reality and appearances, truth and lies, indeed, right and wrong—all these remain subject to the needs of the romance (and to its conditioning), especially starting with Fénice's confession of love. She pretends to be ill:

> L'empererriz, sanz mal qu'ele ait,
> Se plaint et malade se fait,

Et l'emperes qui la croit
De duel feire ne se recroit
Et mires querre li envoie,
Mes el ne vialt que nus la voie,
Ne les leisse a li adeser.
Ce puet l'empereor peser
Qu'ele dit que ja n'i avra
Mire fors un qui li savra
Legieremant doner santé,
Quant lui vendra a volanté.
Cil la fera morir ou vivre,
An celui se met a delivre
Et de santé, et de sa vie.
De Deu cuident que ele die,
Mes molt a male entancion,
Qu'ele n'antant s'a Cligés non:
C'est ses Dex qui la puet garir.
Et qui la puet feir morir (5627ff.).

These very sophisticated lines are important: They confirm
the light tone, the gentle irony that pervades the latter part of
the romance. As though he were elaborating a symmetrical
counterpart, a happy ending, to contrast with the pathetic and
sad story of Tristan, Chrétien gives free rein to lightness and
humor. A kind of *fabliau* quality is exploited, not only in the
witty *double-entendres* we have just read but also in certain
comic episodes, e.g., when Thessala obtains a urine specimen
from a dying woman in order to deceive Fénice's doctors:

Li mire vindrent an la sale,
L'orine voient pesme et male,
Si dit chascuns ce que lui sanble,
Tant qu'a ce s'acordent ansanble
Que ja mes ne respassera,
Ne ja none ne passera,
Et se tant vit, dont au plus tart
An prandra Dex l'ame a sa part.
Ce ont a consoil murmuré.

169

> Lors a dit et conjuré
> L'enpereres que voir an dïent (5677ff.).

Reality and appearances, truth and fiction!

Then there is Fénice's death, with all the lamenting. The funeral scene is doubly a *scene* since, first of all, it occurs in a romance and, secondly, it is put on, or staged, even within the fiction. Chrétien plays along with his public and everyone has a good time. It is pleasant to appreciate gratuitously, not with sadness but rather with gleeful irony, funereal eloquence (5718ff.). The scene is artfully constructed, reminding one of the burial of Esclados-le-Roux in *Yvain*.

The episode of the three physicians from Salerno adds to the narrative accumulation of this descriptive fresco. This episode is a kind of amplification upon the event of Fénice's "death." Through their sadism the doctors—pure villains like their equally "correct" and righteous counterparts, the jealous courtiers and mean dwarfs in *Tristan*—prove to be detestable and richly deserve the punishment inflicted upon them by the outraged town ladies. (Does Chrétien subvert to his comic purposes here the "psychology" of the love tribunals of his time?) This new *fabliau* helps him round out his narrative with yet another variation on the motif of reality and appearances. Besides, we all know that Thessala will find a balm to restore Fénice to her former health and beauty.

The poet-narrator's irony becomes, to say the least, ambivalent and ambiguous when the romance seems to carry over to the real world, that is, when the reader is tempted to make the transfer in his celebration of Cligés' joy. The text guards against such a transfer by seemingly encouraging it. The narrator utilizes a typical hyperbole to evoke the lovers' pleasure and its possible moral counterpart:

> Certes, de rien ne s'avilla
> Amors, quant il les mist ansanble;
> Car a l'un et a l'autre sanble,
> Quant li uns l'autre acole et beise,

170

Que de lor joie et de lor eise
Soit toz li mondes amandez;
Ne ja plus ne m'an demandez (6252ff.).

But by playing with the perspective—"it seems *to them* when they kiss and embrace each other that, because of *their* joy and happiness, the entire world is better off"—Chrétien stresses that they are living a romance, perhaps, in fact, that to a degree all such lovers live a romance and that love, so conceived, is "romantic." This ought not to be taken seriously, that is, outside the romance context. Once again the nature of this text as fiction shapes what it says and, concomitantly, provides an insight into the purposes Chrétien assigns to this kind of fiction: *Cligés* is largely a romance given over to telling us what romances are and what they can do.

Chrétien's technical mastery in *Cligés* is brilliant; moreover, it is intended to be brilliant. He pulls out all the stops. A catalogue of devices used by him in this romance would adequately fill a handbook of rhetoric. Furthermore, the ostensibly bookish frame of reference—*Tristan, Énéas, Statius, Troie,* and Wace—within which plot and characterization are achieved both accentuates and utilizes the high degree of literary consciousness built into the fiction. No wonder, then, that *Cligés* deserves to be seen as the prototype of a kind of sparkling, humorously ironic, and delicately contrived fiction so much in favor toward the close of the twelfth century and at the start of the thirteenth. One thinks of *Floire et Blanchefleur, Amadas et Idoine, Blancandrin, Aucassin et Nicolete,* and others. The character of Soredamor has been viewed by at least one critic, A. Micha, as the "type de l'orgueilleuse d'amour" and described as the model for characters in some of the above-mentioned texts as well as in *Ipomédon* and *Le Bel Inconnu.* Certainly, *Cligés* shares with *Amadas et Idoine* a similarly "literary" and "ironic" tone in respect to the Tristan myths from which they derive and against which they react *as romances. Cligés* is never "profound"; that is its main point, of course, and, one is tempted to add, its profundity. Rather than having "méconnu la vérité humaine et tragique du *Tristan*" (Frappier, 121), Chrétien does quite the opposite: he recognizes and isolates in *Cligés* the gratuitous romance hidden in the legend. He has hardly committed what Frappier called "un gauchissement du sujet véritable"; on the contrary, by providing it with an authentic romance form he has deepened the subject's meaning and, coincidentally, he has done much to widen the possibilities open to narrative fiction. Not only—as we shall see—do the later romances profit from the kind of technical mastery Chrétien explores and perfects in *Cligés*, but—and perhaps more significant for the subsequent development of the European narrative—*Cligés* stands at the head of a tradition that counts Ariosto, Cervantes, Voltaire, and Sterne among its more recent representatives.

The specifically literary artistry deployed in *Cligés* tends to undercut, then, the *matière* (here both that of Greece and the "vain" Breton matter); indeed the very concept of "content" is rendered problematic. However, such undercutting allows the romance to develop in conformity with its own purposes, gratuitously, as we saw, and with the literary resonances we observed. In *Cligés* Chrétien de Troyes is less the poetic philologist than his *confrères* of the *Alexandre* or *Thèbes* tradition—less even than Wace, whom, however, Chrétien resembles the closest—but he goes one step further: he clearly identifies his work in general with their spirit. This identification is what is surely meant by Chrétien's reference in his Prologue to the *translatio studii* and to the pairing of *clergie* and *chevalerie*. He is consistent in his reshaping, or celebration, of chivalric "ideals" according to the rhetoric and structures of romance fiction. Instead of serving a "history" he serves a literary tradition, a tradition that allows him to see through certain moral claims or propositions at the same time he can exploit in amusing ways a fine gamut of tales. This is, I think, the interpretation that ought to be given to Chrétien's rephrasing in the Prologue to *Cligés* of the familiar topos we had noticed in Wace (*Rou*) and elsewhere:

Par les livres que nos avons
Les fez des anciens savons
Et del siegle qui fu jadis (25ff.).

In short, it does not seem to me to be out of place or anachronistic to apply the label "anti-novel" to *Cligés*, especially since in tone, plot, and characterization it cultivates a flatness quite unlike (and even opposed to), say, *Érec et Énide* (a far more novelistic response to *Tristan*, we recall) or *Yvain* and *Perceval*. Yet, as we all know, opposites tend to attract, or influence, one another. The preoccupation with technique that so characterizes *Cligés* will hardly be shaken off in subsequent texts. If anything Chrétien states even more explicitly in his later prologues—implicitly in *Yvain*, quite explicitly in *Lancelot* and *Perceval*—the importance of his craftsmanship. With *Cligés* Chrétien has proved his master's skill in the narrative; perhaps, even, he has gained a certain independence from the same bookish tradition he poeticized in *Cligés*. Full control must imply a degree of detachment. He has certainly demonstrated his independence, his irony, with respect to the values and social myths indulged in by his patrons. Finally, he has formulated an unmistakable narrative point of view, a kind of narrative "I," that, to be sure, capitalizes upon the literary self-consciousness of the genre within which he has chosen to work, but also exploits the possibilities open to such self-consciousness. With *Cligés* and its technical focus Chrétien achieves a deepening, a thickening, I should say, in his narrative art. He will know how to incorporate these new complexities into his more authentically novelistic compositions.

THE CONSTRUCTION OF EPISODES AND SCENES

A more adequate understanding of Chrétien's conscious workmanship as well as a deeper appreciation of the varieties of his fictional art may be achieved by our looking closely at a number of key scenes, or episodes, in the later romances.

Such an examination ought to help us get a clearer sense of the position of *Yvain* within the overall context of Chrétien's *œuvre*.

I shall refer most specifically to three scenes. The first of these may be entitled "The Immodest Damsel," from *Le Chevalier de la charrette* (Roques, 931-1280, as well as, perhaps to a lesser degree, 1281-2010; Foerster [1899], 941-1292, 1293-2022). The second, from *Yvain*, includes the hero's seeing Laudine for the first time and falling in love with her, as well as her grief at her husband's demise (Roques, 1055-1592; Foerster [1887], 1055-1588); we might label this scene "Yvain's Lovesickness." The third episode is from the *Conte du graal* and may be called "The Three Drops of Blood on the Snow" (Roach, 4144-4602; Hilka [1932], 4141-4602.)

Of these three episodes the first, "The Immodest Damsel," is at once the most compact and the most diffuse. Let me summarize briefly what happens. The scene takes place shortly after Lancelot's separation from Gauvain and his successful combat with the Knight of the Ford (whose life he spares upon the entreaty of the knight's lady). Lancelot meets a maiden who promises him shelter (and help in his search for Guenevere?), providing he consents to spend the night in bed with her. Though—as the narrator informs us—most men would have given "five hundred thanks for this present," not so Lancelot, for whom the maid's offer constitutes yet another *don contraignant*. Yet he must accept the bargain. The two repair directly to the maid's castle, where, after suitable ablutions and change of dress, they sup. While the maid prepares for bed, Lancelot waits outside in the courtyard. Puzzled at hearing nothing, Lancelot reenters the building. He starts to explore the castle when he hears a woman crying out for help. Rushing upstairs, he sees the maiden, half-naked, lying under the embrace of a man obviously about to force her. Two knights guard the door; four servants, armed with axes and resembling robots in their behavior, protect their master. After a wonderful battle in which, among other feats, Lancelot ar-

ranges for one of the axemen to behead inadvertently the
would-be rapist, he shouts that he will take on all comers. At
this point the maiden swears that Lancelot will undergo no
more danger anywhere she might be; she sends away the
knights and the servants. (Did she arrange this whole scene in
the first place? One does not know, but the suggestion is
there, and it underscores the scene's function as a test for
Lancelot.) Next, Lancelot must keep his word. A bed is
prepared; the two of them, fully dressed, lie down. But Lance-
lot cannot touch her; he keeps his distance. The damsel finally
understands and removes to another room, where, in proper
medieval style, she "se couche tote nue," declaring to herself:

> Des lores que je conui primes
> chevalier, un seul n'an conui
> que je prisasse, fors cestui,
> la tierce part d'un angevin;
> car si con ge pans et devin,
> il vialt a si grant chose antendre
> qu'ainz chevaliers n'osa enprendre
> si perilleuse ne si grief (1270ff.).

Both sleep soundly until morning. The "compact" portion of
the episode is over. What follows is more diffuse.

At the light of day Lancelot and the maid rise and set out
together. He promises to defend her according to "the customs
of the kingdom of Logres," but refuses to engage her in
conversation. He is lost in meditation upon his love. Next to a
fountain, on a perron, they find a beautiful ivory comb in
which a half-handful of hairs remain. The damsel asks for
the comb and Lancelot gives it to her. Yet Lancelot cannot
restrain himself from staring at the golden hairs in the comb
(1392f.). Only after much pleading on his part does the
pucele inform him that the comb was Guenevere's, at which
point he almost faints with emotion. After removing the
hairs one by one and taking care not to break a single one,
he gives the empty comb to the damsel. Then, the narrator
tells us, "il les comance a aorer" (1462). There ensues a de-

175

scription of Lancelot's adoration, a charmingly and delicately ironic series of hyperboles during which the hairs are compared to relics, to precious jewels, and to all the riches of Lendit fair. What need does Lancelot have of Saint Martin and Saint James now that "an ces chevox tant se fie" (1476f.)? Both the connection and the separation of the maid and Lancelot are underscored in these lines:

> La pucele molt tost remonte,
> a tot le peigne qu'ele an porte;
> et cil se delite et deporte
> es chevox qu'il a en son saing (1496ff.).

They continue on their way, the damsel in the lead, over a narrow path. They see an armed knight and the maid informs an unconcerned Lancelot of this knight's passion for her. The knight greets the maid amorously; she hardly answers. He then declares that he will carry her off; she retorts that Lancelot will defend her, and, indeed, he is bound to do so. A duel is arranged. The two men seek an open field wherein to fight. They find a kind of *locus amœnus* where a crowd of knights and ladies are amusing themselves, some playing chess and dice games, others dancing. When these beautiful people see Lancelot arrive a cry is heard:

> "Veez le chevalier, veez,
> qui fu menez sor la charrete.
> N'i ait mes nul qui s'antremete
> de joër, tant con il i ert" (1666ff.).

The father of the *pucele*'s would-be lover arrives. This reasonable man, fearing for his son's safety, forbids him to go through with the combat. Father and son agree to follow Lancelot in order to see whether they might not discover grounds for challenging him another time. Meanwhile the crowd murmurs:

> les genz, qui par le pré estoient,
> si dïent tuit: "Avez veü?

Cil qui sor la charrete fu
a hui conquise tel enor
que l'amie au fil mon seignor
en mainne, sel siudra mes sire.
Por verité, poomes dire
que aucun bien cuide qu'il ait
an lui, quant il mener li lait.
Et cent dahez ait qui meshui
lessera a joer por lui.
Ralons joer" (1816ff.).

Lancelot and the damsel move on. They arrive at a her-
mitage, where a monk leads Lancelot to a marvelous ceme-
tery whose stones are engraved with the names of those who
will one day rest there: Gauvain, Leonés, Yvain. The list is
impressive. The hermit explains that the most beautiful tomb
of all is reserved for the knight who will lift up the stone slab
closing it, and, according to the inscription, he who will do
so will free the men and women from the prison from which
no clerk nor gentleman has ever as yet escaped. Lancelot lifts
the stone but refuses stubbornly to identify himself to the
monk beyond informing him that he is a knight, "del rëaume
de Logres nez" (1930). The monk tells the whole story to
the *pucele*, beseeching her to reveal to him the knight's name,
but, of course, she does not know it either. She gallops off in
order to catch up with Lancelot, who had already set out.
Meanwhile, the old man and his son reach the hermitage;
the monk tells them what has happened. The father has no
trouble convincing his son that he was fortunate in not having
fought Lancelot and that they would commit "grant folie"
were they to continue following Lancelot and the *pucele*. The
monk assures them that Lancelot will rescue the queen
(1972).

After entreating him in vain to tell her his name, the maid
requests Lancelot to give her leave. He does so willingly, in
fact with a smile. She goes her own way and never reappears
in the poem.

Now then, in their "Outline of the 'Charrete,' " T. P. Cross and W. A. Nitze (*Lancelot and Guenevere* [University of Chicago, 1930], 7ff.) divide the material I have just summarized into four sections entitled, respectively, "Arrival at the Second Castle," "The Temptation," "The Golden Comb," and "The Raising of the Tomb." (Let me note at this point that Cross and Nitze find *Lancelot* often "uninspired," that it "is by no means [Chrétien's] best composition, as all who have the fortitude to read through our first chapter [i.e., the summary] will realize" [2]. One suspects that they have little patience with such episodic proliferation.) Mario Roques breaks the same material down into five numbered paragraphs (out of the total of thirty-nine making up the entire romance; see the "Introduction" to his *CFMA* edition, xiif.). Obviously there is no sure-fire way to isolate the minimal episodic, or scenic, unit. Indeed, in a sense, we could have begun earlier in the tale since the *pucele* is the fourth (and last) in a series of damsels: the series itself, as such, should be taken into consideration. But, then, by the same token, one ought to tie this material to a later boon (*covant*) Lancelot is forced to swear to the lady of the house in which, on Meleaganz' behalf, he is held prisoner. Before she releases him on parole to fight at the Noauz tournament in the queen's presence, Lancelot must promise that she will "have his love" upon his return (5476ff.). It is more convenient, however, to view the above-mentioned series as operating upon the scene I have isolated, and the second boon as a reflection of the motif introduced in the episode of the Immodest Damsel. Finally, I have determined the length of the episode—perhaps arbitrarily—on the basis of Lancelot's accompanying the *pucele* throughout all the events recounted. In my judgment this brings the different elements of plot together far more than other factors tend to tear them apart, hence, as we noticed, the curious compactness of the first part of the scene and the contrasting (but nevertheless connected) diffuseness of the sections starting with the pair's awakening

(1281ff.). This type of organization epitomizes romance structure; a kind of polyphony occurs here.

We are concerned mainly with who and what Lancelot is, with, so to speak, the implications of his identity. This concern is at once substantial and formal. The question of the hero's name comes up repeatedly as does that of his reputation. Does not the immodest damsel herself, upon retiring alone to her bed, declare that he is the finest knight of all? And in counterpoint to the damsel's impetuous suitor as well as to the knights and ladies of the meadow who despise him because he rode in the infamous cart, we have the old knight's premonitions of Lancelot's true value—premonitions confirmed by the episode at the hermitage, where, of course, the monk predicts that Lancelot will rescue (*rescorre*, Foerster) or aid (*secorre*, Roques) the queen. Finally, the *pucele* and Lancelot part company when he refuses to divulge his name. (Indeed, we recall, it is Guenevere herself who finally identifies Lancelot, almost *en passant*, to her enquiring serving maid [3660]; this identification occurs close to the midpoint of the romance.) Let me state now, then, that the scene in question establishes Lancelot's worth, and, more important perhaps, that it does so within a context that at once permits and copes with all kinds of charges of ridiculous conduct. Such conduct is "handled by" the romance in an exemplary fashion; indeed it is suggested, even, that Lancelot's ridiculous behavior may well be indispensable to his worth. That idea is toyed with here.

These matters are alluded to and are developed within a general framework of mystery. Whether Chrétien's audience knew or did not know Lancelot's name is irrelevant. The romance obliges them to suspend that knowledge in their grasp of its events as they transpire. This is all very curious. The very matter of *knowing* seems to be narrationally exploited in the scene. Why does Lancelot accept the damsel's hospitality? He knows that she is part of his adventure, therefore part of the revelation making up the continuity of his quest; she must be endured for what she knows (in this sense), for the knowledge his experience with her will impart to him. In other words, Lancelot accepts her hard conditions (despite their ridiculous overtones) because, precisely, the romance must go on. Did she plan the rape scene? The question so put is beside the point. The scene as such is part of the romance and, so defined, it had to take place in order to illustrate, in a romance-like manner, the damsel's judgment of Lancelot's worth. There is no novelistic motivation here at all; hence one need not wonder why the damsel did not send her violators away earlier. Analogously, when the *pucele* does in fact know something (as in the case of Guenevere's comb), the needs of the romance authorize this knowledge and her imparting it to Lancelot. By the same token, the old man and his rash son—incidentally, a reverberation of the Bademagu-Meleaganz pair—bring on, over a length of time, the half-gratuitous, half-justified judgment of the hermit: Lancelot will rescue the queen. He knows this because, in romances, hermits have the function of knowing (and saying!) and because the mystery surrounding everything authorizes, indeed legitimizes, his knowing. The romance plays upon omniscience and mystery. As spectators, we too are meant to know and to marvel; this we do, alternately, throughout the scene.

Bearing this general context in mind, we may approach the dynamics of the episodes making up the Immodest Damsel continuity. I mentioned the fact that the scene opens upon Lancelot's fourth confrontation with a lady (or maid). Lancelot is viewed in his Adventure with Woman, all the more so in that the image of Guenevere, which, of course, partakes of this Adventure at the same time that the Adventure partakes of his love for Guenevere, accompanies him constantly. Each one of the women he meets serves to render Lancelot's character and his history more profound and dense. Concretely, his encounter with the immodest damsel—ridiculous and amusing as it is—prepares us for the comb episode (during which, in counterdistinction to the enraptured Lancelot, the maid laughs). Chrétien causes the narrative to move along concomitantly with the development of his protagonist. (I say "development," but, in fact, "revelation" would be more accurate. Lancelot does not "develop" at all; in this sense he resembles Cligés, even Roland, more than he resembles Yvain or Perceval.)

The comb is a metonymic construct, representing Guenevere through a process of contiguity, just as the *pucele* opposed Guenevere by being, like her, a woman. (Again the play: the *pucele* knows whose comb it is and laughingly identifies it.) What a wonderful idea, and how suggestive, to give the comb to the maid, but to retain and cherish the more concrete metonymy preserved in the true presence of Guenevere's golden hairs! The amusing religious imagery at this point in the story is hardly fortuitous. To the peals of the maid's laughter Lancelot performs a certain number of gestures that the narrator, more than just a little ironically, describes in glowingly pious terms. This is yet one more example of how this romance manages to have its cake and eat it too. Lancelot's worth is established, yet an ironic and amused perspective is both authorized and exploited. The spectator finds himself at once within and outside the substance of the romance at the same time that he participates fully in the story's telling.

Despite the plethora of events making up the Immodest Damsel scene, we see its coherence, first, in what might be called its technical virtuosity and, secondly, in the peculiar economy with which the major themes and motifs of the romance are treated. Everything has a gratuitous, "external" air, but, in point of fact, nothing is superfluous. Furthermore, unlike *Cligés*, the tone is essentially serious; the typically romance construct does not ostensibly undercut itself.

The coherence one observes in the Immodest Damsel scene suggests a wider, even ideological coherence upon which the entire *Lancelot* romance seemingly rests, or depends—a dependence analogous to that of *Cligés* upon the world of Tristan and Yseut. The text functions *as though* it were illustrating, either ironically or openly, a doctrine like, say, Gaston Paris' *amour courtois* (cf., *Romania*, XII [1883]), an ideal of civilization or behavior carried to the point of system. Lancelot's comportment thus "obeys the rules" of the "system," or so it would appear; his conduct with the *pucele* reflects this obedience. However, the rules are given nowhere; they are merely implications of the events of the romance and may be viewed usefully by the reader as functionally more or less implicit in these events. We invent them, or Gaston Paris did for us, more or less accurately, but ascribing them wrongly to a systematic *praxis* outside the romance structure. In other words, they constitute one of the means by which the fiction operates. It is consequently implied, then, that the "system" stands behind the piecemeal revelation of Lancelot's worth throughout his adventure. No lesson is intended, unless the undeniable sympathy and admiration we all feel for Lancelot—our liking him—is a "lesson." Nevertheless, and despite the various ironies and games, the fiction remains serious; the persiflage is constantly under control and Lancelot's heroic stature remains entirely intact. The comic night he spends with the immodest damsel justifies the ineffable pleasure of his night with Guenevere (4607ff.).

This is all pretty heady stuff, and one is not surprised that the author of *Cligés*, in setting out to do *Lancelot*, should have stressed his role as a serving—like Lancelot himself—and conscientious workman. In this connection and because Chrétien—at the bidding of Marie de Champagne?—must construct his fiction within the context of an *apparently* systematic code of values and beliefs, let me say that the scene we have just examined may nevertheless be fruitfully viewed as a kind of narrative meditation on the novelistic problem *par excellence*: the play and the depiction of the play of appearances and realities. We saw how, technically speaking, Lancelot's identity and the meaning of that identity were at issue. We are entirely justified in understanding the scene as representing, e.g., the problem of real vs. apparent honor (fame, self-esteem, recognition by others, reputation), and its sense as lying precisely in the fact of such a problematical representation. In this fashion the typically romance magic and mystery, as well as the mixture of the ridiculous and the sublime, are placed at the service of a novelistic purpose. Chrétien is not "illustrating" any doctrine of *amour courtois*; his romance instead utilizes the implications of such a doctrine (at which, incidentally, it only hints). This it does in order to concern itself, as a fiction, with other kinds of values. *Lancelot* is a romance, then, that remains, like *Cligés,* faithful to romance constructs. Unlike *Cligés,* however, it utilizes the constraints built into these constructs as tools with which to penetrate the assumptions on which romance values are based.

The scene I have called "Yvain's Lovesickness" depends on the ostensible subversion of what is told in the fiction to the how of the telling. In reading *Yvain* we must be conscious of this subversion, and, as we observed earlier, the "implied prologue" tells us so, whereas in *Lancelot* our attitudes remain quite different. Thus, we concluded, in *Yvain,* our loyalties are drawn directly into participation within the narration itself: its unraveling.

"Yvain's Lovesickness" is less eventful than the "Immodest Damsel." Fewer things take place. We recall what happens. Yvain has been placed under Lunete's protection; she has given him a magic ring (1026) thanks to which he remains invisible to those of Esclados' servants who wish to capture their master's killer. Considerable activity transpires. The servants look everywhere (1055-1145), in all *angles,* throughout the room. Meanwhile, during their search:

vint une des plus beles dames
c'onques veïst riens terrïene.
De si bele crestïene
ne fu onques plez ne parole (1146ff.).

It is Laudine who "de duel feire estoit si fole" she almost takes her own life. Nothing can comfort her, since she sees

183

her dead husband borne before her in his funeral bier. While she rips at her clothing and tears her hair, a procession takes place:

> L'eve beneoite, et les croiz,
> et li cierge, aloient avant
> avoec les dames d'un covant,
> et li texte, et li ancenssier,
> et li clerc, qui sont despanssier
> de feire la haute despansse
> a cui la cheitive ame pansse (1166ff.).

Yvain hears the lamentations. But as the procession moves into the middle of the hall, the dead man's wounds begin to bleed again—proof that the knight who killed him is still nearby. The servants redouble their efforts to locate Yvain. Laudine pronounces a long and touching monologue (1206-1242) in which she accuses her husband's murderer of being a *fantosme*, for "se tu fusses mortex / n'osasses mon seignor atendre," and which, of course, effectively contributes to our —and her future—appreciation of Yvain's real worth, since he is mortal. A brief *narratio* ensures; the weary servants give up their search and take the body away for burial, while the *nonains* and the *provoire*, their service ended, leave the chapel.

None of this interests Lunete; she goes to Yvain, who asks whether there might not be a little window through which he could see the funeral. But the narrator intervenes:

> Mes il n'avoit antancïon
> n'au cors, n'a la processïon,
> qu'il volsist qu'il fussent tuit ars,
> si li eüst costé cent mars.
> Cent mars? Voire, plus de cent mile.
> Mes por la dame de la vile,
> que il voloit veoir, le dist (1275ff.).

Yvain watches and listens to Laudine's moving prayer on behalf of her dead husband; she is apparently alone. As she continues tearing at herself in grief, Yvain—with whose sympathetically impetuous character we have by now become familiar—can barely restrain himself from rushing out to grasp and hold back her hands. (His native impetuosity and what one might call a narrational event combine to inform us on the progress of his love.) Lunete persuades him not to act foolishly, giving him sound advice concerning his future conduct. She leaves Yvain because her absence at the funeral would be noticed. (One observes the motivated conduct.)

One of the most interesting passages in the entire work follows. The narrator relates what goes on in Yvain's mind. Yvain regrets that he will have no token of his victory over Esclados to silence the taunting and malicious Kay: "Mal ranpones a sejor / li sont el cors batanz et fresches" (1359). But the very next line takes up a different kind of disturbance, at once partaking of strong emotion and serenely calming:

Mes de son çucre et de ses bresches
li radolcist novele amors
qui par sa terre a fet un cors (1360ff.).

The antitheses are strengthened: "son cuer a o soi s'anemie, / a'aimme la rien qui plus le het" (1364f.). And we return to the dialectic of the earlier contrast between Yvain and Laudine; she has well avenged her lord's death, even though she does not yet realize her success. The Ovidian development is charmingly carried out, with another delicate allusion to sweetness:

s'Amors vangiee ne l'eüst
qui si dolcemant le requiert
que par les ialz el cuer le fiert (1370ff.).

(A third reference to sweetness is made a few lines later in an analysis of love:

Celui sanble qui an la cendre
et an la poudre espant son basme
et het enor, et ainme blasme,

> et destranpre suie de miel,
> et mesle çucre avoeques fiel [1402ff.].

These allusions help tighten the scene and its organization.)
As is usual in this kind of framework (cf., the monologues in
Cligés), the images progress dialectically, through antitheses:

> et cist cos a plus grant duree
> que cos de lance ne d'espee:
> cos d'espee garist et sainne
> molt tost, des que mires i painne;
> et la plaie d'Amors anpire
> quant ele est plus pres de son mire (1373ff.).

The narrator's dependence upon such convention makes
for a diction that borders on gratuitous preciosity. The reader
wonders how certain difficulties will be vanquished. But
Chrétien attaches vv. 1379-1592 securely to the previous
narrative at the same time that he transforms this section of
the scene into a remarkable lyrico-dramatic "deepening" of
the elements of plot previously introduced and structured. To
be sure, then, the figure of Cupid, or Love, is employed, as
is the traditional *amis:anemis* dichotomy, in order to main-
tain the proper rhetorical framework. We ought not to neglect
the great talent with which Chrétien brings off certain ex-
pressive conceits, as in this delightful depiction of Laudine's
beauty (and God's workmanship):

> Oïl voir, bien le puis jurer [Yvain's inner monologue],
> onques mes si desmesurer
> ne se pot an biauté Nature,
> que trespassee i a mesure,
> ou ele, espoir, n'i ovra onques.
> Comant poïst ce estre donques?
> Don fust si grant biauté venue?
> Ja la fist Dex, de sa main nue,
> por Nature feire muser (1495ff.).

One should also mention the Cornelian overtones occurring
just after Yvain witnesses Laudine's departure (1520ff.);

staying and leaving are both equally impossible, "qu'Amors et Honte le retient" (1535). These marks of poetic craftsmanship must be seen as entirely integrated into the fabric of the scene. Yvain's passionate character is explicitly rendered, and the equally passionate nature of Laudine is suggested, all the more strongly, perhaps, for being a bit more mysterious and remote. The couple they will form is already quite authentic. Yvain's dilemma (as well as its motivation: his impetuousness, his love of adventure, his sincerity) is fully expressed and Lunete's role is clarified (1552ff.); the somewhat passive role assigned to Laudine is also outlined and narrationally exploited.

Perhaps most interesting of all, however, is the fashion in which both the elements of plot and their structuring are developed. Several novelistic modulations are brought to bear. Thus, we recall, at the beginning Yvain is "alone," i.e., invisible to the servants who are looking for him. This solitude finds a counterpart in Laudine's impassioned grief. She too is "alone." Yvain senses her presence and is already half in love before Lunete shows him the window through which he will finally see her (as we have seen her, thanks to the narrator [1146ff.]). Meanwhile his presence is known to Laudine because her husband's wounds bleed anew; she even addresses him. The scene continues: The funeral goes on—things happen, the world does not stop—while both Yvain and Laudine stand, as it were, transfixed, immobile. (We remember that Lunete has to leave Yvain so that her presence at the funeral will not be missed. Every so often we have a reminder like this of the passage of time and events.) In a sense the Couple is contrasted with Others, though ironically, since, from the perspective of the plot, Laudine is not yet aware of her role in the Couple. Nevertheless the configuration remains intact since she is viewed here as a widow and she expressly states her loyal affection for her dead husband. Lunete moves as a kind of go-between from the Couple to the Others, and back again.

The second half of the scene, when Yvain finally suc-

cumbs to his love and becomes aware of it, raises the level
of passion. Both he and Laudine are even more alone, each
more entirely wrapped up in his thoughts and feelings. She
is the creature of his passion, but, curiously, in the love he
articulates (to himself and *via* the narrator) for her, she takes
on genuine consistency. His suffering at her tearing her hair
and limbs renders *her* more vivid, more present; this con-
stitutes a novelistic exploitation of the depiction of conven-
tional behavior. Laudine is worthy of inspiring Yvain's pas-
sionate concern; she will be still more worthy a person when
Yvain, a better man than Esclados, actually becomes her hus-
band. (Analogously, the shock and the insult of Yvain's fail-
ure to return after more than a year elapses will be all the
more strongly felt.)

It may be stated that in a real way the scene becomes
"conscious" of all these matters, and that, in so doing, it
prepares us for Lunete's tactical intervention (1593ff.). Noth-
ing is gratuitous. The depth of consciousness attained may
be described as greater than the sum of all isolable elements;
the narrator certainly does not delegate his knowledge. He
functions in juxtaposition and in conjunction with the char-
acters, the events, and appropriate prevailing beliefs or con-
ventions. Of course we know all along that Yvain will fall in
love, that this love is at the core of his adventure, and we
realize that certain modes have to be observed, but the way
everything is worked out remains decidedly fresh and novel.
The Object of Passion that Yvain and Laudine become for
one another depends almost entirely on the putting together
of the scene.

With this much said it would be well, I think, to look even
more closely at a few technical aspects of the scene. Let us
examine first what might be called the "relief" provided by
characterization and then what, precisely, is added to the
scene by characterization. With respect to the scene itself it
may be said that certain previously acquired details act as
"data," as givens, whereas, in other instances, the scene

constructs givens that will be exploited at later points in the romance.

One of the givens is Yvain's impetuous character, his brio; I am almost tempted to call it his romantic nature. We are already aware of this trait, since it underlies his initial decision to avenge Calogrenant before Arthur leaves for the magic fountain; we also remember his decision to follow Esclados into the castle. Nevertheless Yvain is not foolhardy. He resolved the quarrel Kay had tried to provoke; Lunete recognizes his worth (he had once treated her with respect and deference at Arthur's court [1001ff.], and she remarks that he is no coward [998ff.]); finally, he succeeded where Calogrenant had failed, without being the evil spirit or devil that Esclados' servants and widow unjustly accuse him of being. Furthermore—and see the first installment of a brilliant series of articles devoted to *sire* and *messire* by Lucien Foulet in *Romania*, LXXI (1950), 16ff., esp. 20f.—Yvain, along with that perfect knight and friend Gauvain, is designated as *messire*, a very honorific term previously used to indicate saints and that Chrétien did much to secularize. Lucien Foulet counted some one hundred and forty-five mentions of Yvain out of which one hundred and thirty-one included the title *messire*. (Gauvain is named thirty-five times in the romance, only once, however, without the title; this designation is inherently his since, in both *Érec* and *Cligés*, he is the only knight to which it is applied.) To be sure, in *Yvain* Kay is also referred to as *messire* some ten times—out of twenty-four—but these allusions are at once reflections of the play involving Gauvain and Yvain (with whom he is contrasted) and ironic commentary (given his important position at court). Despite his importance as *seneschal*, Kay is what Gauvain and Yvain, in tandem, are not; meanwhile, of course, Yvain and Gauvain are simultaneously paired off together (against Kay) and contrasted with one another. Equally worthy, they differ nonetheless, and the difference lies, I think, in the romantic generosity implied in Yvain's

189

impetuousness. The contrast serves to ascribe a positive value to Yvain's brio. Yvain's love is quite different from the pleasant flirtation Gauvain (the sun) indulges in with Lunete (whose name is divulged at this point) at the time of Arthur's arrival (2395ff.). By the same token, Yvain's romanticism will lead him to forget his promise to return home to Laudine. His forgetfulness occurs during his adventures with the gentlemanly and worldly knight Gauvain. Neither the pairing nor the opposition could possibly be clearer.

The same type of unity-in-opposition obtains, then, in Yvain's own character: impetuosity and worth, along with kindness and consideration, as well as good sense, are opposed to forgetfulness and even madness. One might venture to say that impetuosity and worth constitute the two poles of character around (and between) which the action of the romance revolves. In a sense—and if I may be pardoned a reference to certain psychological theories of Erik Erikson— Chrétien would seem to be exploiting poetically the dynamics inherent in a typical young man, like Yvain, utilizing the driving force of an adolescent neurosis in order to heal his sickness and to advance to the more peaceful stage of mature manhood. (The term "peace" is entirely appropriate. As the narrator points out just before Yvain's final reconciliation with Laudine, he will have "peace": "Mes sire Yvains ot et antant / que ses afeires si bien prant / qu'il avra sa pes et s'acorde" [6767ff.]). The scene we have been studying both uses and explores the meanings of Yvain's passionate spirit.

The use and elaboration of Yvain's passion (or impetuosity) may be studied on a number of levels. Take, for example, the dichotomy to which we referred previously in passing: degrees and meanings of "folly" involving both Yvain and Laudine. Note Laudine's *folie*: "mes de duel feire estoit si *fole*" (1150), at her very entrance on stage. Also, some fifty-five lines later: "et crioit come fors del san." This is passionate madness, a kind of metaphoric *folie* (though, of course, very much alive in amorous diction). In counterdistinction we witness, with Yvain, a desire to behave like a madman (which in fact he will later become, but for other reasons); he has a hard time keeping back from rushing out to protect Laudine from herself (1304), but Lunete urges "qu'il se gart de folie feire" (1308). The die is cast. Lunete knows whom she is dealing with, and she says so:

"Gardez, se vos pansez folie,
que por ce ne la feites mie.
Li sages son fol pansé cuevre
et met, s'il puet, le san a oevre.
Or vos gardez bien come sages
que n'i lessiez la teste an gages,
qu'il n'en panroient reançon:
soiez por vos an cusançon,
et de mon consoil vos soveigne;
s'estez an pes tant que je veigne. . ." (1327ff.).

In part thanks to this play on *folly* we learn (or are reinforced in our knowledge): (1) The intensity of Yvain's passion for Laudine; (2) the fact that he can, through willpower, control himself when it is necessary (he is no mere comic *outrecuidant*); (3) Lunete's finesse. The term *folie* returns some hundred and fifty lines later during Yvain's lengthy inner monologue; he stares at Laudine (he has just seen her heartbreaking tears, her lovely eyes, her sad features): "Dex! Por coi fet si grant folie / et por coi ne se blece mains?" Himself in the grips of passion, Yvain recognizes his lady's suffering; the narrator intervenes:

n'ainz mes ne cuit qu'il avenist
que nus hom qui prison tenist,
tel com mes sire Yvains la tient,
que de la teste perdre crient,
amast an si fole meniere . . . (1513ff.).

All this constitutes a *way* of indicating that Yvain's love is entire, but that it is a function of his impetuousness, his very direct manner of behavior, and his capacity for love. At the same time a kind of counterpoint is played off on the *folie* of Laudine's grief as well as on Yvain's worth. We observe, then, in practice how the narrative takes up a "given" in order to develop it.

To continue discussing characterization, we might note that Lunete's audacious cleverness and good sense constitute both a given in our episode and an amplification. The first time one sees her—when she welcomes Yvain in the castle— one *knows* that her intelligence is far from ordinary. But her characterization is completed, thanks to her being contrasted with Yvain's wildness and her mistress's passion; Lunete is the only inhabitant of the castle who makes a point of not bewailing Esclados' demise. When she counsels wisdom to Yvain, we are sure of her competence and, more important, of her design:

> "S'or vos contenez a mon sens,
> si con je vos lo contenir,
> granz biens vos an porra venir" (1314ff.).

She brings off what Yvain and Laudine really want; she is an agent of their destiny (as well as of the story's plot). At the same time, their destiny is what Lunete has been in a sense planning for them. Furthermore, one notices, within the situations in which she acts, a very remarkable development of her person in this first part of the romance; there is something magic about her, though, to be sure, this magic never gets out of hand. If Lunete is initially defined—or "clarified"—in her opposition to the person of Yvain, her development is even more thorough in her later confrontation with Laudine. Finally, she blossoms forth in her own right at Gauvain's arrival: the sun and the moon, she and Gauvain are paired in counterpoint to Laudine and Yvain.

If Lunete may be viewed as partly a narrative given and partly an elaboration with respect to the scene we are studying, I should be tempted to consider Laudine as virtually a pure narrational development. We get to know her in terms of the events within the episode that, in her case, illustrate her worth, as well as in terms of the love she inspires in Yvain. As we observed, a kind of passivity and mystery are at issue. These qualities are strengthened by the fact that in his telling of the funeral procession, Chrétien substitutes for the "natural" order of events an "artificial" or "impressionist" order, a new descriptive disposition. We recall that at the very beginning of the scene Yvain has just eaten and Lunete has recommended that he be quiet because Esclados' men will soon come to avenge their dead lord. Lunete retires and Esclados' servants arrive immediately. Then, starting with v. 1144, we see:

> Que qu'il aloient[10] reverchant
> desoz liz, et desoz eschames,
> vint une des plus beles dames
> c'onques veïst riens terriene.
> De si tres bele crestïene
> ne fu onques plez ne parole.

We learn subsequently what this lovely lady is doing: "mes de duel feire estoit si fole / qu'a po qu'ele ne s'ocioit / a la foiee" (1150ff.). But it is only at v. 1161 that we discover why she is behaving the way she does; note, incidentally, the accomplished play of versification, paranomasia, and *annominatio* in these lines:

> ne riens ne la puet *con*FORTer,
> que son seignor en voit PORTer
> devant li, en la biere, MORT
> don ja ne cuide avoir *con*FORT.

First her beauty, next her ladylike condition, then her impassioned grief, and finally her identity as Esclados' wife. Yet her description precedes that of the funeral procession— despite its being made quite clear, at v. 1163, that *devant li* the body was being carried and that the procession was made

---

[10] Note Chrétien's innovative use of *que que* in the sense of the far more unwieldy *endementres que* "pendant que"; cf. Frappier, *op.cit.*, 237.

up of "holy water," "crosses," "tapers," which "aloient avant." Of all these elements in the procession Laudine is chosen or singled out; nevertheless, she remains a part of the procession. This is a way of telling us that her beauty imposes her upon us, that, thanks to her numerous qualities, she detaches herself from her surroundings. However, the order is hardly gratuitous, since it is the narrative itself, by the various juxtapositions it includes and through which it operates, that reveals these matters. Moreover, in the description what the narrator says and what Yvain senses (through a combination of hearing, desiring, and, perhaps, destiny) coincide perfectly; this is why Yvain declares, as we saw, that he wishes to see the procession (1271ff.) and why the narrator intervenes to inform us that neither the corpse nor the procession really concerned him, that Yvain wished only to see the lady (1275ff.). As a character, then, Laudine is subordinated simultaneously to the needs of the narrative and to the fulfilment of Yvain's adventure. (I do not claim by this that her rank is in any way inferior or even secondary; I mean simply that, except insofar as she is a "lady," her character is not a narrational given, that she is rather a development stemming out from the *récit*. Laudine undergoes a process of creation, of elaboration, concomitant to the progression of the episode.)

All this variety in the techniques of characterization is very subtle indeed. It contributes greatly to the "thickness" and novelistic texturing of the narrative.

What I have been remarking upon so far fits in perfectly with the high degree of "literariness" present throughout the scene. By "literariness" here I mean essentially the traditional elements of literary artifice that contribute so heavily to the kind of artistic self-consciousness we explored in an earlier section of our study of Chrétien, especially devices resembling those examined by Edmond Faral. Setting aside the learned dosage of *descriptio* and *narratio*, which we have already admired a great deal, let us glance at the use to which Chrétien puts a number of these literary devices, in particular the most characteristically Ovidian procedures taught in the schools and disseminated in earlier romances. (I stress the term "use"; in *Yvain* Chrétien depends far less on these devices than in a more intricately technical composition like *Cligés*, but he employs them all the same, with considerable flair.)

Obviously the most striking convention of all is Chrétien's variation upon the Ovidian amorous *coup de foudre*. Thus, Yvain implicitly follows the narrator's advice in Book I of the *Ars amatoria* when he agrees to rely on Lunete's good offices: "Sed prius ancillam captandæ nosse puellæ cura sit" (351f.). But note Chrétien's charming departure from convention: Yvain trusts Lunete and gains her good favor *before* he meets Laudine, hence before he falls in love. He is destined to fall in love; or rather, perhaps, the text underscores that this love is a matter of destiny, just as Yvain's impetuous and dangerous following of Esclados into the castle forces him to rely on Lunete's kindness. One views Chrétien's active incorporation of the tradition into his fiction. Also, as Frappier has pointed out, some verses from *Ars amatoria*, III, 429ff., seem to have provided the argument for our scene:

> Quid minus Andromedæ fuerat sperare reuinctæ
> Quam lacrimas ulli posse placere suas?
> Funere sæpe uiri uir quæritur; ire solutis
> Crinibus et fletus non tenuisse decet.

"The last thing that Andromeda, tied down to her rock, might have expected was it not that her tears would attract someone? Often at the burial of one man another may be found; it therefore becomes a lady to keep her hair in disarray and not to hold back her tears." Again in utilizing his source Chrétien has turned the tables. Yvain, not Laudine, falls in love first, but, of course, Laudine must accept him and, after all, her "adventure" is also secured. Nevertheless, to the twelfth-century connoisseur the literary irony must have been delightful!

195

By utilizing in these ways the advice provided in Ovid's *Ars amatoria* and by developing the entire *coup de foudre* motif, Chrétien accomplishes far more than merely exploiting a source. As he had done in *Cligés*, he renders the tradition operative and serviceable. He does not seem to wish to restrict his fictional purview, to proclaim, as he did in *Cligés*, that his work is an artfully constructed romance. Thus Yvain undergoes love-at-first-sight, but the *coup de foudre* takes place, so to speak, intermittently. Chrétien does not proceed in the classically medieval Ovidian manner, according to which the lover sees the lady, falls in love, suffers a certain number of characteristic ills, and engages in a long self-analytic monologue. Instead, he inserts this manner (with which, one must assume, his public was familiar) into contexts that subvert it and that, in so doing, help create an illusion of reality.

For example, we observed previously the ambiguity in what one might call the *sight* of the lady; the narrative presents Laudine whom, simultaneously, Yvain hears (or senses) without yet seeing her but desiring to see her. The two perspectives are confused. Given the convention, however, Yvain's desire to see the lady with his own eyes may be interpreted as a desire on his part to fall in love. The convention thus fulfills a mediating function for both Yvain and the reader; it is thoroughly poeticized. The intermittent character of Yvain's love-at-first-sight derives from the fact that the telling of his falling in love is spread throughout an episode containing a number of other occurrences. Though the *coup de foudre* is sudden and genuine, it is, so to speak, cut by the introduction of Laudine, the servants' search for their master's murderer, the activity surrounding Esclados' funeral, etc. Such film-like cutting into narrative stages serves, I think, to underscore the "natural" or true-to-life, observed authenticity of the event; this stress seems all the more to be the case when one recalls the coincidence of the *coup de foudre* tradition with the native impetuosity of Yvain's temperament. (Of course, this impetuosity fits in well with the medieval view of youthful personality too.) Yvain is already in love, because, starting with v. 1275, his desire to see Laudine places him in the position of one who wishes to receive, through his eyes, the arrows that will pierce his heart.

This mixture of Love's activity, Yvain's staring, and Laudine's grief is taken up a second time and, as we observed, it is recast in vv. 1343 to 1544. We are treated to the traditional monologue with its expected antitheses: "toz jorz amerai m'anemie" (1454). Chrétien puts literary tradition to good use; he at once subverts and epitomizes the convention by incorporating it as he does into the economy of his fiction. Just as, in general, Chrétien very openly subverts what is told in *Yvain* to the hows of the telling, so does he transform formal convention (subject-matter and procedural techniques) within the structure of his narrative. This strikes me, of course, as quite novelistic and as unlike both *Cligés* and *Lancelot*. Furthermore, Chrétien's detachment from the traditions within which he works would seem to justify our labeling them as essentially formal in nature, even when subject-matter is involved.

Similar conclusions may be drawn from the depiction of Laudine's mourning. Her grief constitutes the narrational counterpart to Yvain's love within the circumstances of the scene. Analogous "suffering" characterizes both passions. Moreover, the *planctus* is an old, familiar genre; we remember the various, classically oriented complaints in *Alexis* as well as Charles' lament over Roland's lifeless body, and Aude's suggestion of a lament. We ought also to call to mind the lengthy descriptions of anguished distress in texts like *Énéas* (e.g., Dido, at Eneas' departure). All that is very literary, and Chrétien very ostentatiously hitches his romance to that tradition. We also recall certain ramifications developed in *Yvain*, i.e., the clever play on Ovid's verses celebrating the seductiveness of mourning, which we quoted above. Once again we are dealing with a poetic transformation of a novelistic type. Laudine's grief does not constitute a quasi-

197

independent tableau; the romance is no mere frame. On the contrary, the fiction incorporates the tradition, making it very much its own substance.

Our sampling indicates that Chrétien has built a whole system of conventional literary values into the fabric of his romance. He utilizes a veritable gamut of learned devices. Some of those most conspicuously present in our scene include: (1) topoi, such as the one identified by Curtius as the "unutterable topos" (*Unsagbarkeit*):

> Mes sire Yvains oï les criz
> et le duel, qui ja n'iert descriz,
> ne nus ne le porroit descrivre,
> ne tex ne fu escriz an livre (1173ff.).

(2) verbal play; we have already noticed the sound games on *ort* and its combinations in vv. 1161ff., but, starting with v. 1244, another kind of play occurs, involving, in rhyme position, prefixes and stems: *de*-BAT:*con*-BAT, *con*-FRONT: *re*-FRONT; and later we observe very pretty rhetorical plays on *cheval*:*chevalier*, *conpaignie*:*amie*:*conpainz*:*sainz* (1291-1298); (3) proverbs, e.g., "Li sages son fol pansé cuevre / et met, s'il puet, le san a oevre" (1329f.); (4) a certain school-like preciosity: God has created Laudine without resorting to Nature's help; (5) a similarly clerkish anti-feminism, as in this delightful reference to the flightiness of women: "D'or en droit ai ge dit que sages, / que fame a plus de cent corages" (1439f.); we recall that it is Yvain himself who speaks these lines, using this old saw not to deprecate Laudine but rather in order to revive his own flagging spirits and hopes concerning her. These examples suffice, I think, to show the variety of literary devices put to use by Chrétien in the scene we are studying. The list is by no means exhaustive, however.

What does Chrétien achieve with this display of virtuosity? First, of course, he manages to add color to the narrative, making it more varied. A certain depth and breadth are achieved, and these contribute much to the story's "entirety."

Concomitantly, I believe, the various plays on novelistic and literary values are destined to strengthen our loyalty with respect to the fiction. We see once again that the way of telling is more important than the matter, or that what is meant derives from the proper fusion of matter and its putting together (*conjointure*). Meanwhile, the detached, ironic tone is maintained. In a very profound sense, here literature plays on history (or the events) at the same time the events play on literature. Traditional literary procedures are incorporated into the *récit*; consequently they serve the deployment, the unfolding of the romance. *Yvain* is no mere pretext allowing Chrétien to display his literary erudition, nor, as is the case with most *romans antiques* and even with *Cligés*, does this erudition constitute here, in and of itself, a poetic value. The story "deforms" while it utilizes the devices we have described; the traditional techniques of romance composition are, so to speak, attenuated by their novelistic context (e.g., Yvain's anti-feminine prejudice; the impressionist depiction of Laudine's mourning during the funeral procession, etc.).

A few remarks should be made concerning the integration of "Yvain's Lovesickness" into the romance as a whole. I shall limit my commentary to a few significant points.

The immediate implications of the scene are not hard to formulate. Thanks to Lunete's intercession, Yvain succeeds in meeting Laudine and in being accepted by her. Up to now his ardent and impetuous temperament has served him as well as his undeniable merit—or *prouesse*—has done. A danger remains, however, to which we pay real heed only when future developments become known to us. Yvain lets himself be too easily carried away by his enthusiastic temperament. Deprived of Lunete's counsels of moderation, Yvain would have spoiled everything. He recovers his calm only when Lunete reassures him that all will be well. As we noted earlier, those aspects of his personality which justify his passion for Laudine serve also to authorize his behavior at not returning to her after a year's adventures. (Unlike *Lancelot*, *Yvain* relies on a very high level of what might be called psychological motiva-

199

tion.) We remember as well the words used by Laudine's messenger when she denounces him at Arthur's court: *larron, ipocrite, traïtor* (2738)—words corresponding to the invectives pronounced earlier by Laudine when she accused her husband's murderer. Moreover, Yvain stands here charged once again with murder: "Mes sire Yvains la dame a morte / qu'ele cuidoit qu'il li gardast son cuer . . ." (2744ff.). This is all metaphorical, of course, but the undeniable parallelisms help strengthen the links connecting our scene with this one.

We all know what happens next. Yvain turns mad; his unhappiness and sorrow possess him:

> Lors se li monte uns torbeillons
> el chief, si grant que il forsane;
> si se dessire et se depane
> et fuit par chans et par arees (2806ff.).

(This conduct obviously parallels Laudine's passionate mourning.) Chrétien uses literally the imagery of madness; Yvain is, so to speak, absolutely carried away. If we may say that fire is used to fight fire, then we may conclude that Yvain's madness is a kind of purgatory, a purge designed to cure him of similar excess in the future. Yvain's madness proves that his character, as drawn up, is logically and consequentially conceived. He is now the victim of his dominant passion. Chrétien thus focuses in turn upon various facets of the same crystal; each helps illuminate the whole. Note that the dichotomy impetuosity:personal merit still remains in force, even at this juncture. In the depths of his madness Yvain performs charitably, as a good person should, responding to the hermit's charity (2841). His way of hunting and eating the raw flesh of the game he downs illustrates the madness, but his tacit agreement with the hermit proves his worthiness. The hermit offers him bread; it is so bad that the flour is worth less than twenty *sous* the measure (*setier*). Yvain gives the hermit of the meat he has hunted as well as the skins from the animals, and with the profit from selling these the hermit improves his daily fare. Thus, in a charming way, Chrétien manages to maintain the dichotomy and, in so doing, he recalls our episode at the same time he guarantees a way out for Yvain. By accomplishing feats of charity—i.e., by giving himself body and soul over to good works—Yvain will overcome all obstacles, and his personal merit will win out.

From the time of his cure onward—and again, it seems to me, the analogy with Erik Erikson's theories concerning emotional and moral growth is striking—Yvain will have learned how to hold his impetuousness in check. His courage becomes manifest, and after the Count Alier episode, he defends the lion. This crucial, indeed exemplary, episode occurs between vv. 3337 and 3478, occupying the center of gravity of the romance; the text comprises 6808 lines in the *CFMA* edition of Roques, or 6818 lines in Foerster's edition. It is important to bear in mind that Yvain is known as the *chevalier au lion* and that Chrétien himself gave this title to the romance (6804); the point made, namely, that Yvain acquires here a new identity is significant. Although, even in the lion episode, Yvain does no more than put to use qualities with which he has been endowed from the very beginning, the text nevertheless seems to tell us that there is here a far more authentic existential relationship between what one is and what one does—the person "constructs" himself far more—in *Yvain* than, say, in *Lancelot* or in any epic poem like *Roland*. At the beginning Yvain is "possible"; throughout his adventure he becomes what he is. In this sense *Yvain* may be viewed as an early *Bildungsroman*, like *Érec* and even more like *Perceval*.

The rest of the romance illustrates Yvain's progress, which is both moral and, if I may be allowed the term, vital; he "ages" somewhat. But by the time of the lion episode the essential trick has been turned: Yvain has passed from one *age* to another. The second half of the romance constitutes the celebration of an authentic mode of chivalric life. And, in my opinion, the tone of ironic detachment that so permeates the scenes we have studied contributes much to that celebra-

201

tion. Chrétien succeeds once again—but more thoroughly here than anywhere else—in establishing a fictional world, a system, a *pays de roman* (to borrow Descartes' phrase), that does not aim primarily at being the stylization of certain ethical and historical values. This fictional world possesses its own coherence as fiction; the values to which I have referred are here used as components of that fiction. Similarly, the "peace" to which Yvain aspires and which, at the end, he achieves cannot be reduced to a set of formulas, or even images. Were one to try to reduce this "peace" to familiar images of domestic bliss, say, or to maxims concerning moderation, duty, etc., the whole romance would be trivialized, and that is precisely what Chrétien has so brilliantly avoided. "Peace" depends entirely on the fictional system, on structures of the type I have tried to analyze. If *Lancelot* represents (along with *Cligés*, but with less persiflage) the perfect romance— and my argument in these pages has been that *Lancelot* indeed turns out to be the archetypal "serious" romance—then *Yvain* comes closest to being Chrétien's purest novel. In *Yvain* more entirely than in any other of Chrétien's narratives, romance conventions and procedures are set in a novelistic framework. To be sure, *Érec et Énide* shares many traits with *Yvain*, but in that marvelous exemplary tale the dimension of irony, structurally so central to *Yvain*, is far less evident. In comparison to *Yvain* the fiction of *Érec et Énide* seems a kind of lyric chronicle.

I well recognize that all these terms are in and of themselves devoid of precise meaning. Yet, when the texts we have analyzed are pertinently related to one another and when they are seen in terms of certain narrative and poetic traditions, these generic distinctions begin to make sense. I hope too that our distinctions permit a more finely honed appreciation of the scope of Chrétien's genius as well as of a more concrete sense of its experimental nature. Chrétien never repeated himself.

We cannot complete our study of Chrétien's construction of episodes and scenes without paying some attention to the

Conte du graal. This work, we remember, is dated later than *Yvain.* In some respects it is technically further advanced than the latter—it is more complex in a number of ways—but in other respects it is more conservative. Like *Lancelot, Perceval* is quintessentially a romance; however, like *Yvain,* it puts to good use a number of *Bildungsroman* devices: Perceval "grows up," and this process is depicted often with novelistic means. But, it seems to me, these novelistic procedures are subordinated to romance values of a new kind. What Jehan Bodel defined as the "wise," or "knowledgeable," character of the *matere de Rome* (and in this instance I understand by "matter" a body of narrative possessing formal as well as substantival definition) is transfigured, though it remains, like the texts making up the *matere de Rome,* romance in nature. What *Perceval* is all about—and this is also the case of *Lancelot*—is simultaneously a function of the story as it unfolds in the narrative and something mysterious deriving from outside the story to which the narrative alludes. Curiously enough, *Perceval* and *Cligés* (to a much lesser extent, *Lancelot* and *Érec et Énide*) will exert the main influences on subsequent narrative in the thirteenth century. The various *Continuations* and the whole Grail cycle (in part as these play off against the modes of *Lancelot*) testify to the vitality of the *Conte du graal,* whereas humorous and ironic fictions (*Aucassin et Nicolete, Cassidorus,* etc.) constitute the "vain" and "pleasant" progeny of *Cligés. Perceval* helps to explain why the novel, as opposed to romance, did not make much progress on its own—except in details of technique—during the thirteenth century.

These latter considerations need not detain us further at this point. But, before looking into the scene of the Three Drops of Blood on the Snow, I should like to clarify a number of preliminary points. First, we must note that in his Prologue to the *Conte du graal* (to which we referred earlier in this study) Chrétien establishes a number of explicit and implicit links with the spirit and the form of the learned and wise *matere de Rome.* The idea of the *translatio studii* is alluded to and poetically incorporated into the fiction. We remember the traditional topos of the exordium employed at the very beginning: "Ki petit semme petit quelt" (1). This very literary proverb (cf., Faral, *Les Arts poétiques*, 58) is followed by the equally poetic claim of the narrator that he is "sowing his romance" in a most fertile field, on behalf of the noblest man "qui soit en *l'empire de Rome*," Count Philip of Flanders. Even the somewhat unusual reference to Rome—and this word rhymes here with *preudome*—helps strengthen the connection with the world of romance as this world was established by Wace, Benoît, the *Alexandre* and *Énéas* poets, and illustrated by Chrétien himself.

But a new twist, an important modulation, occurs at this point in the handling of the *translatio* motif. To be sure, the traditional panegyric addressed to the noble patron follows its usual course, as had Chrétien's praise of the Countess Marie at the start of *Lancelot*. However, in the case of *Perceval* the eulogy not only reaffirms the poem's connection to the *matere de Rome* tradition; at the same time it marks its distance from that tradition. In a common enough *rapprochement* Philip is compared to Alexander the Great, the very prototype of the ancient hero much admired in romance. But he is then described as superior to Alexander ("Mais je proverai que li quens / valt mix . . ." [16f.]), a less ordinary statement, authorized, however, by the hyperbolic diction frequent in panegyric. The true modulation exploits what we have just observed, becoming explicit when the narrator specifies in detail Philip's distinction: (1) Alexander and Philip are opposed, since the one indulged in vices and in evil from which the other has refrained; (2) the count loves "droite justise / Et loiauté et sainte eglise" (25f.); (3) he is authentically generous—and we recall that Alexander was the very symbol of noble *largesse* in the medieval tradition— because he gives according to the Gospel, "sanz ypocrisie et sanz gille," not letting the left hand know "les biens quant les [fera] ta destre" (32). (This remark leads to a development of the opposition *senestre*, "vainglory," vs. *destre*, "charity,"—an obvious reprise and explanation of Alexander vs. Philip—which is subsequently followed by a discussion of charity and its godliness.); (4) "Good Count Philip" is authentically charitable in his gifts, not like Alexander "cui ne chalut / De carité ne de nul bien" (58f.). Only after these initial remarks does Chrétien return to stress his own handiwork in rhyming "le meillor conte / Qui soit contez a cort roial" (63f.), the *Contes del graal*, derived, apparently, from a book entrusted to him by the count.

All this is highly interesting. At the same time that Chrétien insists upon what his new fiction and the *matière antique* have in common, he underscores differences. "Wisdom" and "knowledge" prevail, along with his own incomparable craftsmanship, but it is clear that Chrétien also intends to exploit his own Christian modernity. The style of the *matere de Rome*—or of Chrétien's literary consciousness, as this is integrated into the texture of the romance—serves as an ostensible framework for Christian values and Arthurian subject. He means his text to be taken seriously, but in a different way from the seriousness of *Lancelot*. The very notion of gloss is incorporated into the givens of the romance; witness the explanations of *senestre* and *destre* provided in the Prologue. I repeat, however, that the general ambiance of a romance of the *translatio studii* type is preserved; it constitutes a conditioning for the unfolding of *Perceval*. The formal play is most impressive. Values one associates with the *matere de Rome* are preserved, but they are tuned into another, more transcendental key.

Perceval, we said, "grows up." In so doing he experiences a number of adventures that further his maturing and that, concomitantly, serve to illustrate the grandeur of his destiny. Though the romance remains unfinished, we have no doubt that Perceval will eventually discover the meaning of the grail procession and its attendant mysteries. Thanks to Perceval's opposition to *messire* Gauvain—Perceval, Lucien Foulet tells us, is never referred to as *messire* (*op.cit.*, LXXI, 21)—his inherent merit is properly underscored as well as his complexity. His very innocence and foolishness turn out eventually to be sources of strength. His night with Blanchefleur shows him to be at least potentially the equal, and perhaps the superior, of Lancelot and Yvain. Yet Perceval is something the other heroes are not; his destiny remains very much his own. In some respects, however, he reminds one of Énéas; his quest will be meaningful to all mankind.

The four hundred and fifty-odd lines comprising the Blood Drops on the Snow take place shortly before the halfway point of the romance as it has come down to us in its unfinished state. The scene follows immediately upon Perceval's defeat of the Orgueilleux de la Lande, the knight whose lady Perceval had foolishly ill-used earlier in the romance and who consequently had mistreated her himself in revenge; upon hearing the story from the vanquished knight himself, Arthur decides to seek out the unknown Perceval. (The scene preceding this one had been that of Perceval's visit to the Grail Castle and his subsequent meeting with his cousin to whom he reveals his name and from whom he learns of his mother's death.) The Blood Drops episode comes before two scenes involving Gauvain; these are followed by Perceval's Repentance, i.e., his meeting with the hermit and his communion on Easter Sunday.

The Blood Drops on the Snow scene is thus very strategically located at the very center of Perceval's maturity. It is true that he reacted inadequately to the events at the Grail Castle, but, once he understands them, these events provide him at last with a secure direction and purpose. A sense of his authentic attachments in the world is developed: his sister, righting the wrong done to the lady of the Orgueilleux de la Lande, his relationship to Arthur and the Round Table (e.g., the *pucele* whom Kay has insulted and whom he has sworn to avenge). Finally, what he is will be weighed against Gauvain, the perfect but somehow less worthy knight. He acquires a sense of sin, of the burden of his own past and destiny. All this furnishes a proper context to the episode of the Blood Drops, and the nature of the mediation governing Perceval's life is transformed thereby. Here are the principal events of the episode.

The king and his court set out to find Perceval; Arthur has sworn an oath to spend no longer than two days in one spot until Perceval is located. This lends urgency to the search. All the ladies accompany their menfolk in order, as the narrator informs us, to do them honor. The troop camps out the night on a field next to a wood. Despite the lateness of the season— the beginning of the poem makes it clear that it is springtime and Easter is close at hand—it snows. Seeking adventure, Perceval arises early and, riding along, arrives at the snowy and icy field where Arthur is camping. Before reaching the tents, he hears a flight of loudly honking wild geese. Dazed by the snow's glitter, the geese attempt to escape a falcon; one of the geese is struck down, but not killed, by the falcon. Perceval rushes up to the spot where it had fallen. By the time he gets there the goose has recovered and flown off again. Nevertheless, from its wound three drops of blood fall upon the white snow:

> La jante fu navree el col,
> si sainna trois goutes de sanc
> Qui espandirent sor le blanc (4186ff.).

The narrator comments: "Si sa[m]bla natural color." Seeing these drops of blood, Perceval leans against his lance and stands transfixed, hypnotized by the sight:

> Que li sanz et la nois ensamble
> La fresche color li resamble
> Qui ert en la face s'amie,
> Si pense tant que il s'oblie (4199ff.).

(This relationship is restated once again in the following ten verses.)

Perceval spends the whole morning alone, "musing." Meanwhile squires from Arthur's court see him; they go back to report, but Arthur is still asleep. They tell what they saw to Sagremor, a knight "qui par son desroi / Estoit Des-reez ["unruly, wild"] apelez." Sagremor imprudently decides to fetch Perceval; he wakes up the king and obtains permission to do so. He is brusque, indeed, quite impolite, with Perceval, who, without a word, unhorses him and sends him packing. Kay (not *messire Kex* here [4274]), who never could restrain himself "de felonie dire," mocks Sagremor before the king. Arthur chides him for the *gab* and sends him off to Perceval. History repeats itself. Still silent, Perceval defeats Kay, breaking his right arm "like a dry twig" and dislocating his collar-bone. Kay faints with pain, and when the Bretons see his horse return without him, they sally forth to look for him. Upon discovering him lying in a swoon, all cry out in sadness. But "Perchevax sor les trois goutes / Se rapuie desor sa lance" (4328f.); he pays them no heed. Arthur intervenes to say that Kay's wounds are not serious; he turns him over to the care of a doctor and "dous puceles de s'escole," who will soon cure him.

At this point Arthur's nephew, *messire* Gauvain, explains that no "chevaliers autre ne doit / Oster, si com cist dui ont fait, / De son penser" (4354ff.), that the unknown knight is probably reflecting upon some grievous loss or thinking of his absent lady. Gauvain offers to go and speak with Perceval. Kay says a few nasty words designed, one is sure, to contrast with Gauvain's moderate tone. "Ha! *sire* Ke," Gauvain replies, will you avenge your anger and your "mautalent a moi"? Arthur sends Gauvain off, but only after recommending full arms and much prudence.

As Gauvain approaches Perceval—and we are reminded that Gauvain is the veritable knightly archetype, Perceval's "ideal" ever since the beginning of the romance—the sun has evaporated (*remetre*) two of the blood drops, "Et la tierce aloit remetant" (4429). Therefore Perceval no longer "thinks so intently" on them. Gauvain is suave and polite; "je sui messages le roi," he tells Perceval, whom he gently invites to accompany him to Arthur's tent. Perceval explains that two others had tried to force him to do likewise, "as though I were a prisoner," but:

> ". . . j'estoie si pensis
> D'un penser qui molt me plaisoit
> Que cil qui partir m'en faisoit
> N'aloit mie querant son preu;
> Que chi endroit en icel leu
> Avoit trois goutes de fres sanc
> Qui enluminoient le blanc:
> En l'esgarder m'estoit avis
> Que la fresche color del vis
> M'amie la bele veïsse,
> Ne ja partir me m'en queïsse" (4446ff.).

Gauvain approves wholeheartedly: "Cist pensers n'estoit pas vilains, / Ainz estoit molt cortois et dols" (4459f.). Perceval asks whether Kay is at court, and Gauvain tells him of Kay's wound. Perceval replies with satisfaction to this news, since now the laughing *pucele* whom Kay had slapped because she had praised Perceval (1039ff.) was properly avenged, as he had promised she would be (1199ff.). This revelation proves to Gauvain that the knight before him is precisely the one Arthur has been seeking; he asks Perceval his name. Perceval tells him and, in turn, is overjoyed to learn that his interlocutor is the peerless Gauvain. The two become friends (4501) and disarm. Perceval is outfitted in fine clothing and, after a few more unpleasant words from Kay, Perceval is presented at court. Here is Arthur's welcome:

> "Ha! Perchevax, biax dols amis,
> Des qu'en ma cort vos estes mis
> Jamais n'en partirez mon wel.
> Molt ai eu de vos grant doel,
> Quant je vos vi premierement,
> Que je ne soi l'amendement
> Que Diex vos avoit destiné.

Si fu il molt bien deviné,
Si que toute ma cors le sot,
Par la pucele et par le sot
Que Kex le seneschaus feri;
Et vos avez bien averi
Lor devinal de tout en tout.
De che n'est or nus en redout
Que de vostre chevalerie
N'aie vraie novele oïe" (4563ff.).

The queen follows upon these words, in the company of the newly avenged *pucele qui rist*; Perceval, in perfect courtly style, salutes Guenevere:

". . . Diex doinst joie et honor
A la plus bele, a la meillor,
De totes les dames qui soient,
Tesmoinz toz icels qui le voient
Et toz ciaus qui veüe l'ont" (4587ff.).

The queen replies, and Perceval kisses the *pucele*, much as Gauvain would have done, offering her his service:

"Bele, s'il vos estoit mestiers,
Je seroie li chevaliers
Qui ja ne vos faldroit d'aïe" (4599ff.).

The ladies have done honor to Perceval.

Perceval's confrontation with Gauvain is central to the Blood Drops episode; this new friendship, as *articulated* in the scene, both partakes of and contrasts with the hypnotic, *unarticulated* trance that is focused upon Perceval's love recollection of Blanchefleur, his "amie." Also, Gauvain's appreciation and understanding of Perceval are meant to justify him as well as to distinguish Perceval. If the passage is read as a chapter in the story of Perceval's exemplary awakening to charity—and, we saw, charity is unequivocally stressed as a theme within the *matere de Rome*-type Prologue —then, on the one hand, Gauvain's behavior proves to be more charitable than that of Sagremor and Kay and, on the other hand, it is less profound than the deep meditation in which Perceval indulges. The concept of charity is more clearly defined, or perhaps more adequately delineated and nuanced in this fictional presentation; Gauvain is included, of course, but he is also—that is, simultaneously—superseded. Ironically and touchingly, it is precisely when Perceval has gone beyond what is represented by Gauvain (who in turn is the incarnation of the knighthood about which the young *nice* dreams at the beginning of the romance) that he finally meets up with his ideal and can behave, at last, in a truly courteous fashion. Gauvain's approval of Perceval's behavior—when he declares that his "pensers n'estoit pas vilains," but rather "cortois et dols"—does not adequately cope with the depth of Perceval's experience; Gauvain responds to Perceval's speech (4446ff.); but, in a sense, he misconstrues its implications. (After all, Gauvain belongs to a series made up also of Sagremor and Kay.) Conversely, Gauvain's approval is inevitable; it follows the givens of the romance. Arthur enunciates this inevitability when, in his warm welcome to Perceval (as well as in his search of this remarkable knight in the first place), he speaks of the *amendement* (a term unfortunately not glossed by Roach) which "Diex vos avoit destiné" (4568f.); Perceval has well fulfilled the prophecies of both the laughing maiden and the fool.

In a fashion recalling the Immodest Damsel episode from *Lancelot*, this scene deals with the problem of identity. Who Perceval is and what is his destiny concern us here as did the perfection and meaning of Lancelot's knighthood in the episode analyzed earlier. Similarly, the Blood Drops scene reflects the kind of *prise de conscience*, or process of growth, we observed in *Yvain*—the trance leads to an authentic self-understanding, a bit as Yvain's madness had. However, Perceval resembles more closely Lancelot in that the significance of his being is depicted essentially in what others think of him. Arthur's confirmation of his worth is tantamount to proving Perceval's exemplary status—all the more so in that Arthur had a premonition of Perceval's merit by insisting so irrevocably on seeking him out.

Perceval thinks of his *amie*, then, as he watches the blood drops on the snow. What he thinks is not specified, nor is such specification necessary. We are meant to note the intensity of his concentration and the fact that he is engrossed in another person, a woman—presumably Blanchefleur—whom he loves. (Note, however, that Blanchefleur is implied here, not directly named.) The "vermels sor le blanc assis" constitutes a sign, through resemblance, of "la face s'amie," and this is highly personal, as the narrator takes pains to indicate:

> En l'esgarder que il faisoit,
> *Li ert avis, tant li plaisoit,*
> Qu'il veïst la color novele
> De la face s'amie bele (4207ff.).

The red/white motif is common in OF love imagery; Chrétien exploits the usualness of the image, even, I think, its somewhat abstract, partly allegorical character. (In verse imitated from the *Song of Solomon*, the beloved—Christ—is often depicted as *blans et roges*; see, e.g., "Poème dévot," K. Bartsch and L. Wiese, *Chrestomathie de l'ancien français*$_{12}$, Pièce 16.) Perceval's love is sensual, to be sure; the concrete nature of the image itself—blood drops on the snow—and its provenance strengthen the fleshly character of the sight at the same time that this sensuality is made to coexist within, or is subsumed inside, the image's spiritualized framework; *penser* and its various congeners indicate mental concentration. Also, we recall, Chrétien was careful not to overplay the sexual aspect of the night Perceval—who "ne savoit nule rien / D'amor" (1941f.)—and Blanchefleur spend in each other's embrace (1947ff.); indeed the extent to which the two may justifiably be called lovers was deliberately left ambiguous in the text, and this, of course, has fomented no end of scholarly controversy. Perceval's trance clearly does not signify a kind of stupor or purely sexual reverie. On the contrary, it represents the first time that he has been able to feel total concern for another human being, the first time, plunged in thought, he "forgets himself" ("Si pense tant que il s'oblie" [4202]), and lives, in the words of Chrétien's Prologue, "en carité" (48). The drops of blood on the snow exercise a magnetic power upon him, a charm that weakens as they disappear.

The significance of this magnetic force may be gauged in part when one realizes that the red/white motif expresses a number of reverberations important throughout the romance. The connections are for the most part implicit, but they are nonetheless highly effective. The manner in which the Blood Drops scene is integrated into the romance determines the meaning of Perceval's experience. One thinks of the Celtic traditions from which Chrétien surely borrowed and which constitute a dimension within the romance. More important still is the bleeding lance—"le lance blanche et le fer blanc" (3197)—of the Grail Procession, which the individualized drops of blood on the snow surely recall. White and red are contrasted at the very start of the poem, when the dazed Perceval glimpses for the very first time "le blanc et le vermeil" (131) of the outfits worn by knights whom he naïvely takes for angels. Similarly, the description of the dwelling of the Tent Maiden (641ff.) stresses "white" (i.e., the bright gold of orfrois) and vermilion alongside certain light effects that remind one of the Blood Drops scene: "Avoit trois goutes de fres sanc / Qui enluminoient le blanc." Perceval's decision to take over a suit of vermilion armor from an early adversary strengthens the association of red and beauty pointed out by Grace Armstrong Savage.[11] (Mrs. Savage goes on to suggest very acutely more widely ranging resonances that derive from the red/white contrast. Corporeal/spiritual, life/sterility, as well as sensual/purity work themselves into the fabric of the romance. Thus, both sensuality and purity are implied in Perceval's encounter with Blanchefleur, for ex-

[11] I refer to Mrs. Savage's "The Scene of the Blood Drops on the Snow: A Crucial Narrative Moment in the Conte du graal," KRQ (in press).

ample, and, to continue along these lines, Perceval's deep reflection before the blood drops corresponds to his silence at the Fisher King's castle and to his apparent lack of curiosity when faced with the mysteries of Beaurepaire.)

These correspondences and their implications contribute considerably to the body of the romance—to its ironies and to its humor as well as to its "wise" truths. I do not believe, however, that they were meant to be explicated away, in allegorical or in other systematic terms of this kind. The structure of the romance not only permits, it utilizes certain contradictions; a number of complexities are thereby exemplified and, as we all know, complexities frequently add to the richness of narratives. Writings that adhere to the *matere de Rome* were known for their subtlety and intricacy.

Associations of the type we have been observing constitute authentically poetic constructs; they partake of the texturing of the romance at the same time as they contribute to this texturing. The *kind* of associations we are called upon to make suggests, for example, that the Gauvain vs. Perceval construct in the narrative reflects, or, perhaps, develops, the Alexander vs. Count Philip construct of the Prologue. Alexander is outshone by Philip—which is not at all to deny Alexander merit—in a fashion that shares a number of features present in Perceval's superiority over Gauvain. Philip is "generous"—more genuinely than Alexander himself—and, despite appearances to the contrary, Perceval is more authentically *courtois* than Gauvain, the very paragon of courtly behavior. The romance utilizes this confrontation *to hint at* vaingloriousness in the ideal represented by Gauvain without, of course, coming right out in accusing that knight. All would be lost were the narrator to accuse Gauvain of vaingloriousness; it would make no sense. Meanwhile it was possible to describe Alexander unfavorably because the description takes place within the context of an opposition central to a formalized panegyric.

There is little need to dwell further on the peculiar intensity and compactness of the Blood Drops episode. Each event

214

and every allusion are well linked to multiple counterparts in the narrative; this linkage generates in and of itself various meanings and values. Thus Kay is punished—but not too seriously—and Perceval's vow is kept at the same time that the scene plays out its course. The episode is inextricably and deeply rooted within the economy of the fiction. On a yet higher formal level, though, it makes sense to view the Blood Drops scene as an illustration of the kind of poetic integration through structural principle that typifies the whole of the *Conte du graal.* I mean more precisely that sort of relationships, or associations, to which I referred in the preceding paragraphs, as well as the attendant complexities pertaining to them.

Obviously the scene deals with the theme of appearance and reality, their juxtaposition and differentiation, and, in this, it develops one of the major themes of the entire romance. What is, is not always what it seems to be; furthermore, the sense of Perceval's pensive musing involves at least partly his own active reviewing the red/white image in terms of its important personal meanings to him. He registers these values at the same time we do, though, of course, not in the same way. His partaking of the various associations parallels our grasp of the *principle* of such association and its relevance.

The technique is one of unfolding; things occur in sequence, but a deliberately constructed revelation is at issue (as is the case with *Lancelot*). To this unfolding is joined a kind of growth or accretion. Events reveal themselves along with their meanings, either implictly or, in the person of the various explicators, quite explicitly. The fact that frequently what is Perceval's is not at all ours—the two perspectives are meant, usually, to be quite distinct, despite our sympathy for him— contributes to the "implicit accretions."

Perceval's distinction is rendered from the start in the very first scene. We have been prepared by the Prologue to beware of appearances; Philip's true generosity, though not always so visible, is far more authentic than Alexander's ostentation. Perceval is *nice*; his excessive and laughable in-

215

nocence is established concomitantly with his valor. As with Yvain's impetuosity and kindliness, these two traits of innocence and chivalric merit constitute characterological poles around which Perceval's growing up will be depicted. Obviously, many humorous situations develop—too many to be itemized. Most of the time Perceval hardly respects the outer forms of courtly behavior. To be sure, this is not his fault, but, I insist, the romance makes a great deal out of the proposition that despite Perceval's loutishness, and, by extension, *within* or *alongside* his loutishness—i.e., his distinction, too, his lack of formal *courtoisie*—he contains the ultimate in *courtoisie* and more. (No more perfectly nuanced example of courtly conduct may be found anywhere than Perceval's offer of service to the *pucele qui rist* at the close of the Blood Drops scene. Remember that this offer is narrationally tied directly to his musing upon the three drops of blood and the *face s'amie*.)

When we laugh at, or deplore, Perceval's silly conduct, say, with the Tent Maiden, or his gorging himself at table, our distancing ourselves from this conduct carries along with it, implied within it, an acceptance of his considerable worth. In this way the substantial humor of Perceval's behavior is integrated into the romance. At times only a suspicion of humor remains, though structurally it is allowed for. In the Blood Drops scene, for example, Perceval's musing partakes of the tragicomic (in that it is *analogous* to his silence at the Fisher King's castle), as does his almost mechanically matter-of-fact dispatching of Sagremor (a perfect comic "victim") and the irascible Kay. Conversely, the "seriousness" of his musing plays off in counterpart to his earlier silences and sins of omission; his silence is now a presence, not a mere absence. Meanwhile—to remain within our structural principle, but simply to expand its scope somewhat—much of Gauvain's subsequent conduct in the romance, where he invariably does what one would expect, is far more genuinely comic than what Perceval has done; the opposition is perfected.

I might add a note at this point in connection with Gauvain, namely, that despite the presence of this incomparable knight, Perceval is willing to interrupt his meditation only because the drops of blood have virtually disappeared in the sunlight. (It is of course true that Gauvain is legendarily related to the sun; see *Yvain*, 2405ff.)

Much more could and should be said. We have barely scratched the surface. The *Conte du graal* combines Celtic material with a "modern," or "Christian," viewpoint (as interpreted within the *translatio studii* framework), and the combination is brought off according to the learned techniques and high literary purposes one associates with the *matere de Rome*: antiquity is superseded, in twelfth-century terms, but it is also realized at its fullest—and at a quite valid—potential here. This is a formidable accomplishment. Yet the truth and wisdom suggested by *Perceval*, rendered though they may be according to authentically narrative modes of juxtaposition, implication, and association, still belong to the world of romance. Technically, the revelation of Perceval is novelistically constructed (at least to an important degree), but Perceval himself is not conceived in novelistic terms. He is identifiable with his history and with his destiny (like Eneas); his effect upon Arthur suggests broad implications for all mankind, a possible salvation. The type of profundity represented by the highly secular fiction of *Yvain* is replaced by a new variety of profundity here. *Perceval* looks to the verse continuations and their allegorical suggestions, to the prose Grail romances, to the doctrine-laden *Roman de la rose*, even to that Christian romance *par excellence* of the *translatio studii*, the *Divine Comedy*.

Celebration

San (or *sen*, sometimes even *sens* in various manuscripts) represents, I think, what is accomplished by a romance when *matere*, poetic artistry, and audience (or *clientèle*) are conjoined. Chrétien's term corresponds fairly closely to our term "novelistic world." To be sure, in the Prologue to *Lancelot*,

Chrétien confesses that "matere et san li done et livre / la contesse" (26f.)—his patroness and "audience"—and that he contrasts matter and *san* with what he himself has provided, namely his *clerkly* service, paralleling the *chivalric* service of Lancelot for Guenevere: "sa painne et s'antancïon" (29). But I do not see any real contradiction here. How, indeed, may one legitimately divorce the writer's "handiwork" and "purposeful application" (cf. Foerster-Breuer, *Wörterbuch*, sv. *antancion* "purpose," "intention," "meaning-intent" [*Meinung*], "sense-purport" [*Sinn*]) and what his romance ostensibly treats, especially when one takes into account the poetic function attributed to Chrétien's prologues? Obviously, in complying with Marie's instruction, Chrétien wishes to assure his audience that he is doing the best job in his power. And, as we saw, *Lancelot* is constructed in such a way that it appears based upon a coherent and previously extant courtly ideology: It "generates" such an ideology. Or, in other terms, "doctrine" may be deduced, up to a point, from the goings-on, though, on the contrary, such doctrine is neither anterior nor exterior to the text's construction. Chrétien's "novelistic world" remains the bedrock upon which everything rests. It is what everything else points to, and, moreover, his ascribing *san* to the countess fits perfectly within the panegyric tone of the Prologue. The very attribution serves a number of functions. (See, in this connection, fn. 6.)

The "novelistic world" as such, then, is always of first importance in Chrétien's undertaking. The perspective is quite different from those we observed in *Alexis* and *Roland*, though I do not deny that in Chrétien's work an equally high level of truth, or value, is maintained. Over and over again we have observed the primacy of what we have called the "putting together" of the romance, Chrétien's conscious and intricate artistry: the elusiveness, the ambiguities, the precisely non-doctrinaire character of his constructs. However, this by itself would amount to little; or rather, in my opinion, a sense of this artistry must be completed—articulated in the reader's mind—by an understanding of the uses to which it is being put; these uses constitute, then, a functional part of the artistry in operation, *à l'œuvre*. And, I submit, an authentic celebration is at issue in each of Chrétien's works—a celebration reminding one, *mutatis mutandis*, of the mythic rituals occurring during a performance of the *Alexis* as well as of the historical affirmations contained in the *Roland*.

But to be sure that I am understood, let me repeat that I do not in the least way mean to suggest point-blank that, say, in *Lancelot* Chrétien celebrates "courtly love" *qua* doctrine, even though—and this we shall never know for certain— Countess Marie may in fact have wanted him to. (The audience is very much a part of the romance, but, as we observed, the courtly narrative poet, the *clerc*, was specifically quite distinct from his audience, and this distinction is a given of the narrative.) On the other hand, I do mean that the romance celebrates *chevalerie* and, I think, especially the process of *dépassement* to which the exercise of *chevalerie* ideally lends itself when given expression by *clergie*. In *Lancelot*, furthermore, as well as in other romances, Chrétien celebrates the Lady, and, of course, all Chrétien's works celebrate what, in *Cligés*, he calls *clergie*. Considering all the romances together, what a picture of the Lady one might derive from juxtaposing and comparing Énide, Guenevere, Soredamor, Fénice, Laudine, Lunete, Blanchefleur, and others! The creation is overwhelming in its nuance, its sophistication, and in its sympathy; and, of course, it is profoundly literary.

Drawing a moral from the romances is pointless because doing so either results in banal trivialities or leads to impossible and gratuitous allegorizing. The moral of *Cligés* is that Greek emperors must look closely after their wives! The lesson of *Érec et Énide* counterbalances that of *Yvain*. What could possibly be the moral of *Perceval*? Yet the play of literary constructs remains highly suggestive; each of the romances works in an important moral dimension. An active reading of *Yvain*—and, I stress, an *active* reading—does much to suggest that that romance celebrates a sophisticated ideal of civilization, or, as I once put it elsewhere, that in

Yvain one finds a deep appreciation of the wealth of detail in reality and a celebration of civilized man's attitude to reality. Similarly, *Érec* depicts with profundity the complexities of marriage—i.e., of genuine personal commitment to the Other as well as to Self—against the backdrop of the wedding of *clergie* and *chevalerie*. Does not in fact Érec, at his coronation (the symbol, obviously, of his triumph), wear a gown adorned with the allegorical figures of the quadrivium? *Perceval*, we saw, combines certain religious mysteries with the learned tradition of the *matere de Rome* and, of course, with the motif of chivalric *dépassement*. Alexander the Great and Count Philip reverberate upon Gauvain and Perceval in this daring development of the *translatio studii* motif. Yet all this, I repeat, is a function of the reading, of the putting together. Abstracting a moral or a systematic doctrine is tantamount to destroying the romance by ripping apart its very fabric.

Let me be still more explicit. I do not intend to affirm that Chrétien is cynical or that he is uninterested in truth. Nor is there any reason to assume he was some kind of free-thinker either; on the contrary, he was certainly a Christian well acquainted with the subtleties and values of his faith. I judge moreover that the depth of his truth—though different perhaps in kind and in shape from that of the *Alexis* or the *Roland*—merits well of the tradition they established and, indeed, belongs, along with these texts, to the OF narrative tradition; Chrétien profits from their impetus. He believes strongly in the authenticity of poetic discourse. Finally, the fictional undercutting so typical of all his art—an undercutting carried out with particular thoroughness in *Yvain*—gives the lie to those who strive to make Chrétien's novelistic world fit a systematic and exterior doctrinal scheme. As we saw above, only *Cligés* lends itself to "systematic" reading of this sort, and that is, of course, because it is predicated upon an "anti-stance" vis-à-vis the *Tristan* romance system; the very system itself, as such, is poeticized in Chrétien's wonderful technical *tour de force*. One pins Chrétien down only by doing violence to his novelistic world—the same violence (with the same results) that one would commit by attempting to systematize the "thought" of Flaubert or Cervantes.

With this much established, then, we may go on to see in a number of cases what Chrétien celebrates and how he does it. I have already mentioned *chevalerie* and *clergie*, as well as the Lady. All of these are combined, in differing ways, in the five great romances. However, we note, in both *Érec et Énide* and *Yvain* the celebration is modulated by being set within the context of an apparent opposition between chivalric honor and marriage. One can imagine the great appeal such a conflict must have exerted upon Chrétien's *tançon*-loving audience, especially in that the issue as such hardly admits of abstract or definitive solution. Obviously, both honor and marriage are to be highly valued, as are the depth of feeling and courage they reflect; each case—and this is profoundly literary—rests on its own merits.

Even more important, however, from our point of view is the fact that this motif is ideally suited to fictional treatment (as was, precisely, Dido's dilemma in *Énéas*). The only way a non-lyric celebration of matters so complex (and yet so down-to-earth) as chivalric honor and noble marriage could be successfully brought off is precisely in a dichotomous construct analogous to those informing our two romances; the *Roman d'Énéas* worked out the contrast in the two confrontations: Eneas-Dido, Eneas-Lavinie. The fictional confrontation itself allows for, even requires, that *situational* inquiry into the contrast of realities and appearances without which "honor" and "love" would remain mere abstractions. Érec and Énide as well as Yvain and Laudine achieve the same happiness and dignity as a couple at the end of their respective stories, despite the ostensible thematic opposition contrasting them: Yvain leaves Laudine; Érec stays too close to Énide. Both couples have worked out their scheme of values, and in this working out lies the celebration itself—all against the backdrop, of course, of the Arthurian marvel. (The celebration takes on a lyric tone, even in *Érec et Énide*; *Yvain*, meanwhile, is far more frankly novelistic.) In the reconciliation effected by our

221

protagonists "love" and "honor" are clarified and made relevant to the reader who has experienced the putting-together of the romance. The reader has been made to grasp relationships, patterns, and juxtapositions.

We ought not to neglect entirely the technical advantages of the theme too. Not only did Chrétien's public like the debate and, in all likelihood, follow its development with interest, but also in polarizing Man and Woman in this fashion Chrétien was able to utilize our taste for a love story. The drama is built right into the construct; our sympathy goes to the couple, as such. Given the double perspective of the two characters (set up against that of the romance as a whole and against that of the narrator), events in the romance are refracted through their effects upon each member of the couple —Érec and Énide, especially, during their search of adventures. The romance extends itself to encompass and to juxtapose what underlies Érec's need to test himself and Énide's touchingly genuine fidelity (a fidelity that goes beyond mere rules). Does all this not allow Chrétien to celebrate the humanity of his heroes and heroines? Similarly, as we observed, the progression of the situations in which Yvain finds himself provides in and of itself a framework for the depiction of this character in all his many facets as well as in terms of his underlying "unity" or personality. His foolhardiness, his passion, his madness, and his courage all partake of the same initial impulse; these, in turn, reflect upon his moderation, his kindness, and his charity. The sense of a real person—of an identity—results.

More might be said at this point concerning the play of appearances and realities, the greatest novelistic gambit of all. The opening lines to *Perceval* are explicit on this subject. Real charity is hidden, whereas ostentation is frequently but a mask for hypocrisy: "Carité, qui de sa bone oevre / Pas ne se vante, ançois se coevre" (43f.). Thus, in his celebration of chivalry, Chrétien employs throughout his works a number of contrasts that delimit with considerable finesse the contingencies of authentic (as opposed to merely apparent) chivalry. Obviously, the Perceval vs. Gauvain contrast comes most readily to mind, especially as it in turn is modulated within the Blood Drops scene by the presence of Sagremor and Kay. Gauvain is not so much condemned as, on the contrary, the *dépassement* that Perceval accomplishes is praised. And, as the end of the scene shows, Perceval learns to speak to Guenevere and the Laughing Maiden as courteously as any Gauvain. Appearance and reality are contrasted (i.e., Count Philip and Alexander), but the dichotomy is not black and white in all its manifestations.

Within Chrétien's entire *œuvre*, the figure of Gauvain most aptly illustrates what we might call this tempered play of realities and appearances so characteristic of his novelistic world. Gauvain is what he is, but, structurally speaking, what he means is a function of how he is narrationally used, of the juxtapositions to which he belongs.

Abstractly, Gauvain is the paragon of knighthood; he is Arthur's own dear nephew and he participates in the king's prestige. Not only is he marvelously *preux*, he is courtly, well-spoken, and handsome—a veritable sun-prince, just as his legend seems to suggest. Moreover, he is *messire* Gauvain, the chivalric standard by which all others might be measured. As we saw earlier, he is kind and considerate.

In *Érec et Énide*, we recall, Gauvain was the one to remind Arthur quite sensibly of the potential danger in his going through with the ceremonial Hunt of the White Stag; after all, each damsel is considered the most beautiful by her knight, and no knight will like to see his favorite passed over in favor of another proclaimed more beautiful. Similarly, it is he who, in circumstances reminding one of *Perceval*, succeeds in bringing Érec and Énide back to Arthur's court after the insolent Kay had ignominiously and discourteously failed (3909-4252). Gauvain's kind nature and humor are opposed to Kay's total lack of manners, but no specific contrast of Érec and Gauvain is intended. Nevertheless, the motif of *dépassement* is already clearly present in this romance.

Gauvain's role is still more securely established in *Cligés*.

223

Thus, the fact that he becomes Alexandre's friend (388ff.) contributes directly to our appreciation of the latter's great worth. His joust with Cligés himself, who, incognito, had defeated all the other challengers, ends in a draw (4869ff.), and this is enough to prove Cligés' merit: "N'encore ne savoit nus dire / Quiex ert miaudres, ne li quiex pire" (4901f.). Gauvain is a very positive character, then, and our assurance in his regard becomes fictionally exploitable. Obviously, Gauvain's character reflects also the knightly ideal so highly esteemed by Chrétien's public; he incarnates the social myth in which this society professed to believe.

With *Lancelot*, however, Chrétien analyzes this ideal. He does not change Gauvain one whit; he simply profits from Gauvain as an established construct (i.e., with all his customary traits) and he pits him against the character of Lancelot. The two are paired, and, though the closest of friends, they are polarized. Lancelot turns out to be a bit ridiculous, but, despite the ironies implicit in the fact that it is the Immodest Damsel who speaks just after Lancelot has refused her favors, we must agree with her that he is the finest knight of all. Besides, subsequent events prove her right. A certain irregularity is missing in Gauvain; he is perhaps too perfect, or, maybe his perfection is merely too external. There is no vital tension between what he is and what he appears to be that might justify, on his part, the effort toward *dépassement* that Chrétien seems to celebrate above all else in his knightly heroes.

The same development occurs in *Yvain*, where, once again, the protagonist is paired with Gauvain—to the point, even, of unknowingly duplicating the match we observed in *Cligés*. (Yvain and Gauvain fight to a draw in a judicial tournament.) Similarly, Gauvain's charming dalliance with Lunete parallels Yvain's love for Laudine, and, we remember, it was Gauvain who taunted Yvain so as to convince him to seek adventure elsewhere; were he to stay home with his wife, his reputation (appearances) would be tarnished. Here once more knightly courtliness is dramatically and narrationally analyzed in terms of the play of realities and appearances. For the first time, it seems to me, Gauvain is at least mildly condemned; he is just not quite up to the complexities of real life. The alternative he represents—at least for Yvain—is somewhat childish. Gauvain is a bit of a playboy. Again, however, the dramatic construction of the romance suggests all this; no specific statements on the part of either author or narrator are forthcoming.

I have already discussed the Perceval-Gauvain polarity. Let me add at this point merely that Gauvain's virtues remain highly positive up through the Blood Drops scene, except insofar as the Alexander-Philip construct at the beginning clues us into the sense of the Gauvain-Perceval polarity. (Also, Perceval's exaggerated worship of the knights he meets in the forest not only reflects his naïveté; it also comments ironically upon such hero-worship in general.) However, after Perceval's welcome at court, Gauvain's limitations are increasingly stressed. Not only are we sure that Perceval is the better knight, we learn as well that the sort of knightly paragon Gauvain represents is a less than entirely satisfactory ideal; something essential is lacking, a kind of manliness perhaps. Once again the depiction is characteristic of narrative fiction; one arrives at these conclusions through submitting to the narrative structures at work—the juxtapositions, the polarities, the feedback to a Gauvain whose legend (even when limited to the *corpus* of Chrétien's own work) accompanies him wherever he goes, etc. In an important respect the five romances constitute a meditation on Gauvain; they profit from being read in that sense. The ways all these matters work themselves out, then, contribute immeasurably to Chrétien's sophisticated commentary on the relationship of realities and appearances. We return, finally, to his celebration of authentic knighthood.

The celebration of nature, though difficult to isolate and to describe, also constitutes an integral part of Chrétien's novelistic world. Indeed, we remember, Chrétien personifies Nature in his description of Laudine (1497ff.), whom God made directly, without Nature's collaboration. Similar personification occurs in *Érec et Énide*; Énide is so "gente" because "tote i ot mise s'antante / Nature qui fete l'avoit" (412f.) In a delightful little digression Nature herself marvels at her own handiwork (414-423). In *Cligés* an analogously personified Nature appears some seven times; she fashioned Soredamor and Fénice. Of course, this is a rhetorical ornament typical of medieval description. Nevertheless, the ornament has an interesting and, I believe, for us a significant history.

The conceit derives from certain traditions concerning the ancient concept of Natura, the pagan Physis whom Curtius characterizes as "one of the last religious experiences of the late-pagan world" (see his "The Goddess Natura," ch. vi of *ELLMA*). Curtius examines the fortune of the Goddess Natura tradition in twelfth- and thirteenth-century Europe, linking it to the "Platonism of Chartres," which he goes on to describe most intriguingly as a "rather protean phenomenon" whose importance "for the history of literature" is greater than "Abélard and Bernard of Clairvaux" (*op.cit.*, 108). He deals explicitly with what he calls the "pagan Humanism" (112) of Bernard Silvestris (*De universitate Mundi*) for whom "universal history becomes a series of rhetorical exemplary figures" (110), as well as with Alan of Lille's *De planctu Naturæ* and *Anticlaudianus,* works that lead to the vernacular didacticism of Jean de Meun's *Romance of the Rose*, where, as Curtius puts it, "Nature is the mistress of Venus' forge" (125).

Once again I do not wish to imply that Chrétien's references to Nature as God's handmaiden signify, on his part, any intent to express a systematic "naturalism" of one kind or another. On the other hand, Chrétien's celebration of nature may be better understood by projecting it against the backdrop of what Curtius and others (e.g., Gilson and Faral) have studied in terms of twelfth-century thought and expression. Namely, the praise of Nature so common at the time (despite its varying modalities) as well as Chrétien's almost affectionate allusions to a personified Nature would indicate that Chrétien indeed felt sympathy for the palpable, the concrete, and the "natural." Without adhering to any doctrinal system, he could nonetheless benefit from what surely must have been at the time a newly rediscovered love of the Creation. Furthermore, as we shall shortly see in greater detail, the expressive shape his grasp of the natural world takes is closely patterned on the rhetorical and poetic conventions his age saw fit to borrow, elaborate upon, and exploit. The very personification of *Natura* is a case in point. Obviously, moreover, Chrétien's celebration of Nature in this personified sense reverberates upon his celebration of love. In most instances throughout Chrétien's work Nature's handiwork is a beautiful maid or lady, the object and inspiration of the knight's devotion.

Another of Curtius' remarks is worth quoting at this point. Speaking of thirteenth-century developments, Curtius notes that the "goddess Natura has become the servant of rank promiscuity, her management of the life of love is travestied into obscenity" (126). He asks, "How was this possible?" The answer: This transformation "corresponded with the libertinism of an epoch which had exchanged the heritage of antique beauty for the small coin of academic hair-splitting." The thirteenth-century's ambiguous partial rejection of literature and the implications of the *translatio studii* led to this corruption of the notion of Nature. The point is interesting, of course, because Chrétien worked exclusively within the literary mode; he was the purest and most complex vernacular poet of his age. His Nature is no bawd. She is rather a participant in an order of things that, though finally irreducible to abstract definition, provided a model for behavior and a coherent manner of apprehending reality.

Nature, then, is marvelously varied in Chrétien. A component of his novelistic world—part of the *san*—nature is also a matter of celebration within it. Thus, implicit in nature is a system of décor and background against which human events take place and from which they derive part of their meaning. These usually take the familiar forms of received convention. One thinks of the start of the *Perceval* narrative:

227

the lyric springtime, with its leafy trees and warbling birds who "en lor latin / Cantent doucement au matin / Et tote riens de joie aflamme" (71ff.). Regeneration, obviously, as well as newness, reflecting what Perceval himself will do and be, and juxtaposing him next to the sterility and barren quality of the Fisher King's castle. Creation is reborn, according to the natural processes that govern her rebirth. We also recall the artifice of nature—the anachronistic snow—of the Blood Drops scene, here in part adduced in order to prepare us all for the Good Friday episode and Perceval's meritorious communion on Easter Sunday (6512f.). A counterpoint of event and setting is established; it contributes much to the romance's economy and value. How beautifully and easily what is natural fits into the poem's transcendental scheme! This nature is not a matter of the poet's personal, or direct, experience—Chrétien is no Wordsworth—but its conventionality does not undercut its authenticity; the forms the depiction takes are quite genuine on their own terms, and, in working within the conventions, Chrétien expands the expressive range of his romance.

Nature includes a kind of Celtic *merveilleux*; the insertion of Celtic legendary marvels widens the scope of the narrative at the same time that it is poetically interesting for its own sake. In some instances it may serve as an element of plot, or even several of these functions concomitantly.

So common a figure as that of the Fairy Lady participates in the construction of many of Chrétien's heroines. Laudine— not to mention Lunete and the Dame de Norison—has much of the fairy about her; she inhabits a world of magic rings and storm-producing fountains. Guenevere too is closely related to the fairy seductress for whom so many brave knights commit acts of madness. Chrétien's fictions authorize the use he makes of such personages; they are fictions, clearly, that offer themselves to us as fictions and not as something else. Marvelous characters rub elbows with everyday people in a fashion recalling Chrétien's mixing down-to-earth events with magic goings-on. The only mystery about Fénice's loyal servant

Thessala is her sorceress' capacity, and we accept her talents along these lines because we accept the principle of the story. However, by the same token, this *merveilleux celtique* (along with its ancient counterpart) contributes much to our sense of these ladies' charm and wonder. An aura of the fabulous "naturally" adheres to them.

Similarly, splendid episodes like the extraordinary Joie de la Cort, from *Érec et Énide*, or magnificent constructs like the Magic Fountain in the Forest of Brocéliande impart a grandeur to the story that helps remove it from all extraneous, or useless, contact with the humdrum. A romance "system of nature" is adumbrated that allows this kind of narrative to celebrate the essential mystery of reality by, so to speak, rising above it. (Similar dimensions are present in the hagiographic and epic traditions too, we observed.) Of course, when handled ineptly, this "romanticism," or *pays de roman*, merely leads to gratuitous fancy. This is the essence of much anti-romance criticism, from the twelfth and thirteenth centuries down to Cervantes' Canon of Toledo and even Montaigne and Sir Francis Bacon.[12] (Indeed, even Wace's attitudes are not free from ambiguity on this count.) However, there is no danger of such ineptness in Chrétien. In each instance the marvelous fits perfectly into the context of the narrative and serves, not subordinates, the celebration of nature.

Fiction possesses its own system; the novelistic world obeys rules of its own and it establishes its own coherence. Everything we have observed so far concerning Chrétien de Troyes

---

[12] In the *Advancement of Learning*, Bacon strikes yet another blow in the war between fiction and truth: "For as for the natural magic whereof now there is mention in books, containing certain credulous and superstitious conceits and observations of sympathies and antipathies, and hidden proprieties, and some frivolous experiments, strange rather by disguisement than in themselves, it is as far differing in truth of nature from such a knowledge as we require, as the story of King Arthur of Britain, of Hugh of Bourdeaux, differs from Cæsar's Commentaries in truth of story. For it is manifest that Cæsar did greater things *de vero* than those imaginary heroes were feigned to do. But he did them not in that fabulous manner" (Bk II, viii:3).

confirms these statements. Myth as well as legend is inevitably restructured according to the demands and intentions of the *san*. Nature, therefore, is in and of itself open-ended in Chrétien's works; its particular iconography, or "furniture," drawn from Celtic sources, from the *matere de Rome*, from direct observation, as well as, above all, from the *fact* of literary tradition, freely combines the most disparate images. Magic fountains and mysterious cemeteries, the Ovidian *coup de foudre* and the textbook *locus amœnus*, Arthur's court and an almost epic code of honor—these are among the many effective ingredients of that immense variety Chrétien celebrates with such gusto and with such fervor. Whereas in the *Life of Saint Alexis* everything in the poem focuses, laser-like, upon the *imitatio Christi*, explaining its meaning and, indeed, serving its glory, whereas, analogously, in the *Song of Roland*, we experience intricately and intensely what it means to be Charles' loyal subject—the narrative is designed to render that experience possible—our necessary concentration upon Chrétien's fictional system itself, for its own sake, leads to the celebration of what I have tried to define.

It is this novelistic essence in Chrétien that permeates, within the nature he celebrates, symbols so potent and yet, in isolation, so unattainable as the grail. Within the frame of Chrétien's romance there is nothing "unnatural" about this mysterious object (nor about the bleeding lance either), just as, in *Cligés*, all of Thessala's amusing potions fully belong to the story. However, the very mystery of the grail must be set into the context of the tale's fictional operations: the décor of the Grail Castle, Perceval the *nice* overeating and not asking the proper questions (i.e., Perceval's own development), the Wasteland motif, etc. The grail mystery remains a mystery because Chrétien never finished his romance, and, up to the point where he presumably left off writing it, the mystery still remained necessary to the economy of his story. (Other continuators, we know, tried to solve the problem of the grail.) Meanwhile, the system of nature in *Perceval* did provide for such an object as the grail in all its grandeur and mystery—

the point where the marvelous touches most explicitly upon the authentically divine. (The very *touching* is novelistically controlled: the grail contains a communion wafer.)

At the risk of being unpleasantly circular, then, I shall conclude that ultimately what is celebrated is *san* itself, namely, the novelistic world seen as such in all its literary splendor. Each in its own way, the five great romances constitute hymns to the power and charm—I take this word in its literal, or Valéry-style, sense—of literary discourse. I have tried to suggest, however, that the celebration of Chrétien's novelistic world provides at the same time for the glorification not only of certain values but, more importantly, of the great diversity present in the reality both around and inside us. None of this contradicts Church teachings. On the contrary, it is very much to the credit of twelfth-century religious styles of thought and custom that, despite criticisms from certain quarters, the spiritual ambiance of the time was such as not to discourage Chrétien's work. After all, though, his novelistic coherence—a form of poetic order—points to other, perhaps more ineffable, kinds of order. So far from denying, even implicitly, the universal system that governs us, Chrétien's system, in its celebration, might even be viewed as hinting at it. At any rate, his marvelous fictions would lend themselves a half-century and more later to re-elaborations along these lines.

Jehan Bodel's "Song of the Saxons": Epic Binarism and Narrative Meaning

OBVIOUSLY, OF narrative hardly stops with Chrétien de Troyes; the thirteenth century is extraordinarily rich. But important changes take place. Some of these are so fundamental as to require, I believe, book-length treatment. This is neither the time nor the place to attempt even to outline thoughts on these matters. Consequently, I think we are justified in closing our study with Chrétien's "celebrations." Nevertheless, I should like at least to hint at the *kind* of developments that occur subsequently to Chrétien, in the hope that students might be tempted to look into these problems and, perhaps, shed some light on them. There is material here for fascinating dissertation research projects—unexplored material that cries out for serious and experimental analysis.

For these reasons, then, I offer here, virtually verbatim, remarks first delivered at a meeting of the Société de Rencesvals (American branch), during the Modern Language Association convention of 1970. This paper grew out of the type of study to which the main sections of the present volume were dedicated; it is related to what we have observed in the *Song of Roland* and in romance narrative. The fact that Jehan Bodel was a keen critic and a marvelous student of literature during a most crucial period of OF literary history might also serve to justify my reproducing these remarks here, despite their unpolished character.

Quotations from the poem are taken from the two-volume edition by F. Menzel and E. Stengel, *Jean Bodels* SAXENLIED (Marburg, 1906-1909).

Jehan Bodel's *Chanson des Saisnes* deserves minute study. I do not claim that this poem ranks quite so high as the

233

Oxford *Roland*, as *Yvain*, or as the *Romance of the Rose*; I do mean, however, that though it stands at some remove from these high points in the OF narrative canon, the distance is less great than most of us realize. And for our purposes, this subordinate position constitutes a decided advantage. As is also the case with, say, Chrétien's *Cligés*, Bodel's work embodies an extremely high degree of literary consciousness, a kind of artistic intensity and craftsmanship that are built right into the poem's form and that, indeed, are constituent to it. This enables us to grasp better certain poetic mechanisms in the *Song of the Saxons*. Such mechanisms and devices are closer to the surface, more obvious. Furthermore, *Saisnes* offers a marvelous vantage point from which to survey the development of romance narrative at a significant formative stage. First of all, it attempts to contain and, more important, both utilize and reconcile certain narrative structures that preceded it: the qualities of earlier epics as well as several characteristics we associate with romance. Secondly, it deals, in its own unique and very informative way with the crisis of narrative fiction that OF literature underwent toward the close of the twelfth century (a crisis concerning which, incidentally, we know far too little but which, in its focus upon problems of "truth" and "poetry," does much to provoke the rise of new forms during the thirteenth century and, moreover, to prove the vitality of imaginative literature in the vernacular). Furthermore, the problematics of narrative, as these are embodied in *Saisnes*, remind one most interestingly of Ariosto and, especially, of Tasso. Some kind of constant in the Western European narrative might well be at issue.

Pondering these matters has led me to venture a number of preliminary hypotheses which, though somewhat disjointed, may be of some value at this juncture. My interest is at least double: It extends from the poem itself—that is, understanding this fascinating work—to using the poem to get a more secure purchase on important continuities in the history of OF narrative. Let me insist, however, that these are working hypotheses; they remain very much subject to discussion and modification, as well as, of course, to further and more intensive development.

Charles Foulon—to whose exhaustive study of Jehan Bodel (*L'Œuvre de Jehan Bodel* [Paris, 1958]) we all owe a great deal—concludes that the *Song of the Saxons* is neither epic nor romance but instead a *roman épique*. He sees a generic blend, or fusion, rather than the "mixture" referred to by hastier critics. He is on the right track. *Saisnes* may not be construed usefully as a *chanson de geste* to which certain romance ingredients have been added, as a kind of spice, so to speak. Foulon concentrates on matters of tone, characterization, and plot line. He stresses quite correctly the close links between Jehan Bodel's poem and the *geste du roi* (along with other epic reminiscences recalling the *Doon de Mayence*-type poems and even the *Garin de Monglane* cycle). Needless to say, the famous Prologue to *Saisnes* is alone enough to justify one's insisting upon these links. The *geste du roi*—or, more properly, the *matere de France*—is the "truest," the narrator-poet reminds us; it must be contrasted with vain and pleasant Breton tales. "Truth" is meant to be constitutive in the *Song of the Saxons*. But then so are the poet's artistry and his concern for form. In *laisse* II we come across remarks worthy of a Wace, a Benoît de Sainte-Maure, or a Chrétien:

Seignor, ceste chançons ne muet pas de *fabliaus*,
Mais de chevalerie d'amours et de cembiaus.

Jehan Bodel is no *bastart jougleour*; for him "li chans et li dis est raisnables et biaus."

Indeed, the very generic question is itself structurally constitutive of the poem; unfortunately, Foulon does not sufficiently dwell on this fact. By proclaiming with particular emphasis its adherence to the *matere de France*, the *Song of the Saxons* is telling us what it purports to be and do. This proclamation is brought off in various ways. Of course Charles is the Charlemagne of epic tradition; Baudouin, in his relationship to Charles and through his role in the poem, is meant to recall Roland (as well as to prove the continuity

235

of French power despite the losses at Roncevaux). But far subtler hints are made too, as in *laisse* CXXXVI when Charles fights seven Saxon kings "de pute guise" on the banks of the Rune. One of these is named Burnof and he is "plus noir qe poiz remise" (3318), reminding us of *Roland* (Bédier, *laisse* CXIII) where Turpin confronts a Saracen, Abisme, who is "neirs cume peiz ki est demise" (even the rhyme-word fits!). A black Saxon king is, to say the least, improbable, whereas, on the other hand, a Christian warrior combatting a pagan so described belongs to epic convention. The Saxons are "Saracens," the "Saracens" of epic tradition, i.e., those who oppose Charles.

Much more fundamental, however, is the matter I refer to in the title of this paper: epic binarism.

The entire *Song of Roland* is organized *on all its levels* according to a system of binary oppositions that are explicitly charged with making that text function properly. Structurally, the individual *laisse* is opposed to the whole poem; each scene involves in turn one or more dichotomies. The dynamics of the poem depend exclusively on the operational mechanics of these dichotomies. Thus Roland is opposed to Olivier— the one is *preux*, the other is *sage*—but we must remember that at all times this particular opposition is brought off within the context of Roncevaux, where, of course, the Franks are pitted against the Saracens, i.e., within the context of a larger dichotomy with which it is supposed to contrast and function. Both Roland and Olivier are marvelously brave, we learn, and when the enemy is finally defeated, they are reconciled in fraternal charity; Olivier dies in his friend's arms. Similarly, Charles is opposed to Baligant, who becomes thereby "the" anti-Charles and all such status implies. More subtly, perhaps, Charles stands in opposition to his subjects: all-powerful, he is nevertheless essentially helpless without them. The skinny, dark-haired everyman—a kind of average Frenchman quite fully described in the portrait of Thierry— is opposed to the superb (and thereby ironically idealized) Pinabel. Even episodes are structured "against" one another.

236

The Aude episode, we recall, is interpolated into the scene of Ganelon's judgment at the very point when the Franks begin to falter in their resolve to judge the traitor. In her death scene she constitutes a pathetically modulated, metonymic extension of her dead *fiancé* as well as of her betrayed brother. Finally, the pagans are anti-Christians, i.e., given over to material things (money, land, women) while—thanks to this opposition—the poem clarifies Christian spirituality. (Indeed—and excuse the parenthetical remark—I have often thought that the whole Hurepois episode of *Saisnes* reflects this Christian anti-materialism. We recall that Charles decides to tax the Hurepois, who violently object, since they have been traditionally free from *chevage*. After many twists and turns of plot, including the grave threat of civil war—Christian disunity—Charles decides that the only tribute he requires is their help in the struggle against the common enemy. Here Jehan Bodel comments upon the vision of Christian empire that had been given shape by the structuring of the *Roland*.)

Time forbids summarizing further this principle of binarism that so pervasively underlies the economy of the Oxford *Roland*. But just as the figure of Bramimonde, the Saracen queen whom Charlemagne converts and brings back to Aix, authorizes the character Sébile in the *Song of the Saxons*, so does, in my opinion, the epic binarism of the *Roland* authorize —indeed compel—similar constructs in Jehan Bodel's work. The acceptance and development of these "authorizations" constitute the basic attachment of *Saisnes* to the *matere de France*. Jehan Bodel takes over—both utilizing and modifying—the conventions of epic binarism.

There is no need to go into great detail here. Christian vs. Saracen, Charles vs. Guiteclin; also Baudouin and the young Bérart de Montdidier, paired with one another and opposed simultaneously, their paramours, the sensual Sébile (Guiteclin's wife) and the innocent captive Christian maiden Hélissant (note the "mature" couple of Baudouin and Sébile contrasted with the idyllic young lovers Bérart and Hélissant).

There is much poetic nuance. Thus, Hélissant, though a Christian and originally promised by both Charles and her father to Bérart, is Sébile's captive. Yet, of course, Sébile will be converted to Christianity and will marry Baudouin, who was pointed out to her in the first place by the young Hélissant. Baudouin in turn "opposes" both Charlemagne and Guiteclin, along with, as I suggested, the youthful Bérart. (Nor ought we to forget Baudoin's opposition to Baudamas, Guiteclin's nephew, whom he kills in *laisse* CIV, much as Roland had defeated Marsile's nephew Aelroth.) Lastly, the very symbolism of the Rune river underscores what I have been saying. The two great armies face each other on either side of the river, which, quite appropriately, the two Christian knights frequently cross in order to meet with their ladies and also, on occasion, in order to fight. Indeed—and this shows also the extent to which certain binary constructs present in the *Roland* are self-consciously revived in the *Song of the Saxons*—the highly-strung Baudouin reproaches Charlemagne for not crossing the Rune (at least in MSS *TL*) and goes so far as to claim that Charles is but one man among many, a nobody without his knights (*laisse* CXXXIV).

When we remember the intense degree of literary consciousness displayed by *Saisnes*, especially in the Prologue, we are forced to the conclusion that, in Jehan Bodel's view, the binary structuring typical of epic composition could cope adequately with the kinds of accretion and new formulation he meant to include. That is, on the one hand, his poem would develop in given ways elements specifically authorized by the epic tradition: Sébile is in this fashion "authorized" by Bramimonde in the *Roland* and by Guiborc in the *Guillaume* cycle. On the other hand, the very generosity, or open-endedness, present in the kind of structuring that epitomizes *chansons de geste* permits the author of the *Song of the Saxons* to incorporate within his poem certain values, tastes, and meanings that one does not usually associate with epic texts. Jehan Bodel clearly intends to preserve—indeed further— the *matere de France* that he is at great pains to distinguish from the other *matières*. But he must do so by utilizing devices not needed by the earlier epic redactors.

My feeling is that, according to his understanding of the processes involved (and as we have recapitulated them briefly here), Jehan Bodel has written an authentic *chanson de geste,* despite superficial appearances to the contrary. (The only way we might dispute this claim implies a revision of our criteria, but more of this in a little while.) I am reminded of some of the later revisions of the OF *Alexis* tradition, e.g., the thirteenth-century *rédaction rimée*, which elaborates considerably on the wedding-night scene:

> Kant Alexis ot se femme veue,
> Ki tant par est cortoise et bien creue
> Et covoitose et blance en se car nue
> Et voit le cambre ki si est portendue,
> Dont li ramembre de se cheleste drue
> (ed. G. Paris and L. Pannier, 282).

The suggestion to the effect that in the early MSS *LPA* Alexis was carnally tempted by his lovely bride is here rendered explicit. However, the amplified *rédaction rimée* develops only what the *LPV* tradition authorizes, both structurally and thematically. It is still very much an "authentically vernacular" *Life of Saint Alexis*, though quite unlike the sober masterpiece of which we have all become so fond.

Jehan Bodel was especially audacious in his utilization of epic possibilities—the freedoms provided by the binary structuring that underlies the *chanson de geste* form—in order to include a whole thematics of love. I insist, however, that the love stories involve no mere gratuitous accretion, that, on the contrary, the poet boldly constructs an almost Virgilian thematic counterpoint of love and war, just as he outlines in *laisse* II: "de chevalerie d'amours et de cembiaus." (And, interestingly enough, this statement, as we saw, is inserted into a *laisse* that deals specifically with formal matters!) To put it another way—and to oversimplify somewhat—he subverts a frivolous romance-type situation in which, all too of-

ten, the hero's prowess and "truth" were—at least superficially
—but mere adjuncts to amorous activity and, indeed, sinful
behavior. (Sébile's adultery turns out to be a kind of *felix
culpa*.) "Love" and "battle," i.e., love and serving Charles'
empire, are terms of a whole described by Jehan Bodel as
chevalerie. The *Song of the Saxons* performs a kind of literary
rescue. What might be called *courtoisie* is given new meaning
in terms of the epic genre and scheme of values. Though, as
Jehan Bodel realizes, chivalric behavior cannot be praised for
its own sake—it is an adequate, perhaps even dangerous, myth
—it does not intrinsically negate the values expressed by the
best *chansons de geste*. Therefore such conduct may well lend
itself to depiction and, so to speak, to revamping in a poem
like *Saisnes*. Meanwhile, Jehan Bodel will entertain a sophisti-
cated—or at least a middle-brow—audience with an up-to-
date glorification of Charles and his France.

Unfortunately—or fortunately, as the case may be—we
cannot stop at this point, for Jehan Bodel's very considerable
achievement undermines the purity of his intentions, though
not necessarily his success. If we discount Charlemagne him-
self, as we must if we are to follow the model provided by the
Roland, then, it seems to me that, *narrationally speaking*, the
central character of the work has to be Sébile, not Baudouin
or Bérart. She, along with the legend itself, is our main point
of contact with what transpires. In a sense the *Song of the
Saxons* reshuffles the *Song of Roland* in such a way as to make
Bramimonde the central figure. That was the price Jehan had
to pay in order to pull off his formal *gageure*.

Some conclusions are now in order.

Apart from the sections not represented in all the extant
MSS—sections from which she is absent—Sébile has the
greatest continuity of all the characters in the poem; indeed,
she forms a kind of couple, finally, with Charlemagne, who
constructs the abbey to which she eventually retires. Her role
is by far the most interesting of all. What is more important
still is that she is certainly the most complex character in the
work. In the last analysis the reader must identify himself

largely—though not exclusively—with Sébile, whose situation is in many respects analogous to his own. Like Don Quixote or Emma Bovary, Sébile is simultaneously a spectator and an actor in the fiction. (Similarly, in an epic *chanson de geste*, the spectator acts out the *geste* by understanding it.) Sébile actually lives out the *geste Francor*, i.e., the legend, or story, of which she is so fond; the legend, we recall, is her history, and she makes every conscious effort to plan her history—her life —according to the models set up for her by the legend. Is this not in fact the sense of her eventual conversion? In any case, precisely because her own life is so mediated, she in turn mediates, as it were, situationally between the reader and the story's "truth," just as the legend mediates between her conduct and her existential possibilities; we are called upon to live out the history in a fashion analogous to that of Sébile: thanks to her relationship with Baudouin—a relationship involving familiarity with the *geste* as well as personal experience, and all this set in a most curious narrative temporality —we understand fully the relevance of that knight. In a very real way Sébile manages to accomplish what Emma Bovary tries and fails to do. One cannot overstress Sébile's self-consciousness. Already at the beginning she eggs Guiteclin on so that he will take the young Hélissant prisoner. She does this in order that the maid might soon recite to her the tales *de la geste Francor* (199). Then, of course, in *laisse* LXVII Sébile and her ladies observe the French knights; Hélissant identifies Baudouin as Charles' nephew, "Ses freres fu Rolanz li compainz Olivier" (1489), and Sébile promptly falls in love:

> Tant la destraint s'amors et deçoit et engraingne,
> Que son signor en het et sa loi en desdaingne (1502f.).

(The scene reminds one of the Dido episode in *Énéas*. But whereas Dido falls more deeply in love as she listens to Eneas' long and pathetic story, here, of course, Sébile is already familiar with the *geste Francor*. All she has to do is see and meet Baudouin; everything is set up for her.) Though subsequently the MSS tradition is less than unanimous—versions

241

differ considerably—in at least one tradition Sébile buries Guiteclin, who had been killed in battle, in honorable fashion; she is then baptized and able to marry Baudouin. She next assumes a role quite analogous to that of Guiborc in the *Guillaume* cycle, helping her husband overcome tremendous odds. When Baudouin is finally killed, Charles attempts to console Sébile. Quite characteristically, she declares in response:

> "S'or poïsse morir, com Aude o le vis fier
> Fist por Rolant le conte avoc por Olivier,
> Dont eüsse a mon chois trestout mon desirrier" (7542ff.).

Her situation, the generic implications of her story, and her view of herself coincide. The mediation is to all intents and purposes total. To my knowledge this is the first reasonably clearcut case in French literature of a fictional character consciously modeling his—or her—life on a fiction. (The case of Fénice in *Cligés* is analogous, however she is determined *not* to be Iseut; the romance itself tends to trivialize the *Tristan* legend by inventing a *Cligés* legend. The *Song of the Saxons* purports to do just the opposite.)

Of course all this is not one whit epic. But, I hasten to add, it is not romance either, and Jehan Bodel took some pains to tell us so. Rather, in my opinion, it is novelistic. I do not mean to contradict what I stated earlier and say that *Saisnes* is a novel. Not at all. However, I do claim that the poem makes considerable use of novelistic procedures—Sébile functions novelistically—in order, precisely, to revive more authentically the spirit of the old epic. The *Song of the Saxons* purports to be more than a mere literary entertainment (though it is that too). It claims to serve truth. But in the interests of efficacy the poet had to downplay the role of his narrator (who is barely *there*) and rely increasingly on an indirect mediation of his text in its representation of truth. Whereas the poet-narrator of the Oxford *Roland* officiates in a ritual designed to acquaint his public directly with the truth of its history and, above all, to affirm its faith in this truth,

Jehan Bodel had to cope with an intermediate literary tradition which was just as important as the *matière* itself. Quite simply, he is a late epic poet and is obliged to make the best of the means at his disposal. As we saw, he understood the mechanisms of epic structure—the binary nature of its constituent elements—and he knew how to exploit what these elements authorized. But coming after Wace and Chrétien de Troyes, as well as after St. Bernard of Clairvaux, he could not forget these—that is, functional literary history—and merely return to the pristine ways of the Oxford *Roland.* In order to accomplish his ends, then, and not "romanticize" the epic, he had to make it somewhat novelistic. Thanks to devices like the character of Sébile—our representative, so to speak, at Charles' court and the personage whose experience of the epic world most closely parallels our own—Jehan Bodel was able to handle the intermediate literary tradition by simply incorporating it into the form of his fiction. The additional fictional complexity is made to serve the stated cause. However, it is amusing and, I think, highly significant to note that as early as 1200 quintessentially novelistic procedures were used to provide the illusion of authenticity without which Jehan Bodel's epic truth and his narrative would have foundered on the rocks of anachronism, and that these procedures should suggest so intriguingly future developments in the novel.

Index Nominum

245

Index Rerum

252

INDEX

INDEX

256